Autism
Spectrum
Disorders

Autism
Spectrum
Disorders

A HANDBOOK FOR PARENTS
AND PROFESSIONALS

Volume 1: A–O

Edited by
Brenda Smith Myles, Terri Cooper Swanson,
Jeanne Holverstott, and Megan Moore Duncan

Westport, Connecticut
London

Library of Congress Cataloging-in-Publication Data

Autism spectrum disorders : a handbook for parents and professionals /
edited by Brenda Smith Myles, Terri Cooper Swanson, Jeanne Holverstott,
and Megan Moore Duncan

    p. cm.

  Includes bibliographical references and index.

  ISBN-13: 978–0–313–33632–4 (set : alk. paper)

  ISBN-13: 978–0–313–34632–3 (v. 1 : alk. paper)

  ISBN-13: 978–0–313–34634–7 (v. 2 : alk. paper)

  1. Autism in children—Handbooks, manuals, etc.

  [DNLM: 1. Autistic Disorder—Handbooks. 2. Child Development
Disorders, Pervasive—Handbooks. WM 34 A939 2007] I. Myles, Brenda
Smith. II. Swanson, Terri Cooper. III. Holverstott, Jeanne. IV. Duncan,
Megan Moore.

  RJ506.A9A92377 2007

  618.92′85882—dc22   2007030685

British Library Cataloguing in Publication Data is available.

Library of Congress Catalog Card Number: 2007030685

ISBN-13: 978–0–313–33632–4 (set)

       978–0–313–34632–3 (vol. 1)

       978–0–313–34634–7 (vol. 2)

First published in 2007

Praeger Publishers, 88 Post Road West, Westport, CT 06881

An imprint of Greenwood Publishing Group, Inc.

www.praeger.com

Printed in the United States of America

The paper used in this book complies with the
Permanent Paper Standard issued by the National
Information Standards Organization (Z39.48–1984).

10 9 8 7 6 5 4 3 2 1

Contents

List of Entries

Guide to Related Topics

ASD AND ABA TERMINOLOGY

ADVOCACY AND SELF-DISCLOSURE
Advocate
Discrimination
Emotional Support
Functional Skills
Life Skills Support
Person First Language
Self-Advocacy
Self-Determination

PROFESSIONALS
Behavior Analyst Certification Board (BACB)
Board Certified Associate Behavior Analyst
  (BCABA)
Board Certified Behavior Analyst (BCBA)
Certified Behavior Analyst

STRATEGIES
Analysis of Behavioral Function
Behavioral Rehearsal
Behavior Modification
Chaining
Contingency
Contingency Contracting
Differential Reinforcement
Discrete Trial Training (Brief Definition)
Discrete Trial Training (Extended Definition)
Error Correction
Escape Training
Extinction
Fading
Functional Protest Training
Graduated Guidance
Guided Compliance
Habit Rehearsal
Hand-over-Hand Assistance (HOH)

Massed Practice
No-No Prompt Procedures
Operant Conditioning
Overcorrection
Prompt Hierarchy
Prompting
Punishment
Respondent Conditioning
Response Cost
Response Latency
Shaping
Task Analysis
Time-out
Token Economy
Wait Training

TERMINOLOGY
Antecedent
Behavior
Behavioral Objective
Behavior Health Rehabilitation Services
  (BHR)
Behaviorism
Behavior Principles
Consequence
Contingency
Desensitization
Discriminative Stimulus
Establishing Operation
Functionally Equivalent Alternative Behavior
Functions of Behavior
Intraverbal
Learned Helplessness
Mand
Prompt Dependence
Reinforcer
Schedule of Reinforcement
Setting Events

Stimulus
Stimulus Control
Stimulus Overselectivity
Systematic Desensitization
Tact
Target Behavior
Trial

ASD AND EDUCATION

ADULT ISSUES
Adult Supports
Career Planning
Facility-Based Employment
Independent Employment
Integrated Employment
Masturbation
Postsecondary Education
Residential Supports
Supplemental Security Income (SSI)
Supported Employment
Vocational Rehabilitation
Vocational Rehabilitation Programming
Voting
Work Adjustment Period

CONTINUUM OF SERVICES
Correctional Facility
Homebound/Hospital Bound Program
Residential Facility
Resource Room
Self-Contained Classroom
Special Day School or Alternative School

DAILY LIVING
Activities of Daily Living
Daily Living Skills
Environmental Stressors
Functional Goals
Functional Limitations
Functional Outcomes
Functional Skills
Self-Help Skills

SCHOOL TERMINOLOGY
Accommodation
Adaptive Behavior
Annual Goal
Behavior Intervention Plan
Bullying
Cognitive Processes
Collaborative Team
Curriculum
Due Process

Early Intervention
Educational Placement
Eligibility
General Case Programming
Generalization
Impairment
Inclusion
Intelligence Tests
Learning Styles
Local Education Agency
Maladaptive Behavior
Multidisciplinary Team
Notice of Recommended Educational
    Placement (NOREP)
Transition Planning

SPECIAL EDUCATION LAW
Americans with Disabilities Act (ADA)
Due Process
Extended School Year (ESY)
Family Educational Rights and Privacy Act
    (FERPA)
Free and Appropriate Public Education
    (FAPE)
Individualized Education Program (IEP)
Individualized Family Service Plan (IFSP)
Individualized Health Care Plan (IHCP)
Individualized Transition Plan
Individual Plan for Employment (IPE)
Individuals with Disabilities Education Act
    (IDEA)
Least Restrictive Environment (LRE)
Mainstreaming
Mediation
Mutually Acceptable Written Agreement
No Child Left Behind Act 2001
    (PL 107-110)
Present Level of Educational Performance
    (PLEP)
Rehabilitation Act of 1973
Section 504 of the Rehabilitation Act of
    1973
Zero Reject

ASD AND MEDICINE

STRATEGIES
Antianxiety Medications
Antidepressant Medications
Antipsychotic Medications
Casein-free
Chelation
Detoxification
Elimination Diet and Food Sensitivities

Feingold Diet
Gluten-free
Hormone Replacement
Mood Stabilizing Medications
Nutritional Supplements
Yeast-free

TERMINOLOGY
Allergy
Amino Acids
Amygdala
Antibiotics
Bowel Problems
CAT Scan
Clinical Assessment (Educational)
Clinical Assessment (Medical)
Clinical Opinion
Clinical Practice Guidelines
Clinical Trial
Clostridium tetani
Co-morbid/Co-occurring
Constipation
Differential Diagnosis
Dimethylglycine (DMG)
Dopamine
Dysbiosis
Electroencephalogram
Encopresis
Enuresis
Epidemiology
Functional Magnetic Resonance Imaging
  (fMRI)
Fusiform Gyrus
Genotype
Hair Analysis
Head Circumference
Heavy Metals
Hippocampus
Immunoglobulin
Immunological Tests
Immunotherapy
Lactose Intolerance
Leaky Gut Syndrome
Limbic System
Magnetic Resonance Imaging (MRI)
Mercury
Metallothionein
Neuroimaging
Neurology
Neuromotor
Neuropsychology
Neurotoxic
Neurotransmitter
Peptide

Pharmacology
Phenotype
Placebo
Positron Emission Tomography (PET)
Prevalence
Psychobiology
Psychopharmacology
Psychosocial
Rumination Syndrome
Secretin
Serotonin
Stimulant Medications
Symptom
Syndrome
Toxicology
Treatment Effectiveness
Twin Studies

ASD AND RELATED DISORDERS
Asperger's Disorder
Autistic Disorder
*Diagnostic and Statistical Manual of Mental
  Disorders*–Fourth Edition–Text Revised
  (DSM-IV-TR)
High-Functioning Autism
International Statistical Classification of
  Diseases and Related Health Problems
  (ICD)
Pervasive Developmental Disorder–Not
  Otherwise Specified
Pervasive Developmental Disorder–Not
  Otherwise Specified Diagnostic Criteria
  (Diagnostic Criteria for 299.80, Including
  Atypical Autism)
Pervasive Developmental Disorders (PDD)

BEHAVIOR
Adaptive Behavior

ETIOLOGY
Diet
Environment
Genetic Factors/Heredity
Pesticides
Vaccinations (Thimerosal)
Viruses

RELATED DISORDERS
Angelman Syndrome
Anxiety Disorders
Attention Deficit Hyperactivity Disorders
  (ADHD)
Catatonia

Das-Naglieri Cognitive Assessment System (CAS)
Differential Ability Scales
Leiter International Performance Scale
Object Sorting Test
Social Faux Pas
Stanford-Binet Intelligence Scales–Fifth Edition
Test of Language Competence (TLC)
Trail-Making Test
Twenty Questions Task
Universal Nonverbal Intelligence Test (UNIT)
Wechsler Intelligence Scales for Children–Fourth Edition (WISC-IV)

Diagnostic Instruments
Asperger Syndrome Diagnostic Scale (ASDS)
Autism Diagnostic Observation Schedule (ADOS)
Childhood Autism Rating Scale (CARS)
Gilliam Asperger Disorder Scale (GADS)
Gilliam Autism Rating Scale (GARS)
Krug's Asperger's Disorder Index

Interview Instruments
Autism Diagnostic Interview–Revised (ADI-R)
Family Assessment Interview

Pre-Academic and Vocational Assessments
Adolescent and Adult Psychoeducational Profile
Psychoeducational Profile–Third Edition (PEP-3)

Screening Instruments
Ages and Stages Questionnaires: Social/Emotional
Asperger Syndrome Screening Questionnaire (ASSQ)
Autism Behavior Checklist (ABC)
Autism Screening Instrument for Educational Planning–Second Edition
Checklist for Autism in Toddlers (CHAT)
Childhood Asperger Syndrome Test (CAST)
Modified Checklist for Autism in Toddlers (M-CHAT)
Pervasive Developmental Disorder Screening Test-II (PDDST-II)
Red Flags
Screening Tool for Autism in Two-Year-Olds (STAT)
Social Communication Questionnaire (SCQ)

Sensory Assessments
Adolescent/Adult Sensory Profile
Analysis of Sensory Behavior Inventory–Revised Edition
Checklist for Occupational Therapy
Indicators of Sensory Processing Disorder
Infant/Toddler Sensory Profile
Sensory Integration and Praxis Test (SIPT)
Sensory Integration Inventory–Revised (SII-R)
Sensory Profile
Short Sensory Profile

Social Cognition Assessments
Comprehensive Assessment of Spoken Language
Test of Problem Solving–Adolescent (TOPS-A)
Test of Problem Solving–Elementary (TOPS-E)

Tests in Research Paradigms
Embedded Figures Test (EFT)
Object Integration Test
Prototype Formation
Tower of Hanoi (TOH)
Wisconsin Card Sorting Test (WCST)

BIOGRAPHIES
Asperger, Hans
Bettelheim, Bruno
Bleular, Eugen
Eisenberg, Leon
Kanner, Leo
Rimland, Bernard
Schopler, Eric

COMMUNICATION
Interventions
Communication Board

Professionals
Audiologist
Speech Language Pathologist

Terminology
Concrete Language
Dysphasia
Echoic/Verbal Behavior
Echolalia: Immediate, Delayed, Mitigated
Expressive Language
Figurative Language

TERMINOLOGY
Gross Motor Developmental Quotient
Locomotion
Motor Imitation
Praxis

PROGRAMS
American Sign Language (ASL)
Applied Behavior Analysis (ABA)
Assistive Technology
Assistive Technology Device
Assistive Technology Service
Auditory Integration Training
Augmentative and Alternative Communication
Cartooning
Circle of Friends
Cognitive Behavior Modification
Cognitive Learning Strategies
Comprehensive Autism Program Planning System (CAPS)
Developmental Individual-Difference Relation-Based Intervention (DIR)
Developmental Therapy
Discrete Trial Training (Brief Definition)
Discrete Trial Training (Extended Definition)
Facilitated Communication (FC)
Fast ForWord
Gentle Teaching (GT)
Incidental Teaching
Integrated Play Group Model (IPG)
Life Skills and Education for Students with Autism and Other Pervasive Behavioral Challenges (LEAP)
Milieu Teaching
Natural Language Paradigm
Options (Son-Rise Program)
Picture Exchange Communication System (PECS)
Pivotal Response Training
Play-Oriented Therapies
Positive Behavior Support (PBS)
Precision Teaching
SCERTS Model
Sensory Integration
Sibshops
Social Skills Training
Structured Teaching (TEACCH)
Total Communication
van Dijk Approach
Verbal Behavior
Ziggurat Model

SENSORY

INTERVENTIONS
Bolles Sensory Integration
Hug Machine
Sensorimotor Early Childhood Activities

PROFESSIONALS
Occupational Therapist
Physical Therapist

TERMINOLOGY
Apraxia
Brushing
Deep Pressure Proprioception Touch Technique
Fine Motor Skills
Gravitational Insecurity
Gross Motor Skills
Hyperresponsiveness
Hyporesponsiveness
Low/Poor Registration
Oral-Motor Skills
Oral Sensitivity
Overselectivity/Overfocused Attention
Proprioception
Self-Regulation
Sensation Avoiding
Sensation Seeking
Sensorimotor
Sensory History
Sensory Processing
Sensory Processing Dysfunction
Sensory Sensitivity
Sensory Stimuli
Sensory Threshold
Somatosensory
Tactile
Tactile Defensiveness
Touch Pressure
Touch Therapy
Vestibular
Visual-Motor
Wilbarger Protocol

STRATEGIES
Biofeedback
Double Interview
Embedded Skills
Four Steps of Communication
Good Grief!
Graphic Organizer
I LAUGH Model of Social Cognition

Irlen Lenses
Joint Action Routines
Lindamood-Bell
Neurofeedback
Patterning (Doman-Delacato Treatment)
Power Card Strategy
Priming
Situation-Options-Consequences-Choices-
    Strategies-Simulation (SOCCSS)
Social Autopsies
Social Behavior Mapping
Social Scripts
Social Stories
Social Thinking
Story*movies*
Surthrival
Video Modeling

Video Self-Modeling
Virtual Environment
Visual Strategies

THERAPIES

Animal Assisted Therapy/Assistance Dog
    Placements for Children with Autism
Art Therapy
Dance Therapy
Diet Therapy
Hippotherapy
Music Therapy
Occupational Therapy
Physical Therapy
Speech Therapy
Touch Therapy

A

ABSURDITIES

Absurdities refer to the verbal and pictorial components of the **Stanford-Binet Intelligence Scales** designed to test nonverbal knowledge.

JEANNE HOLVERSTOTT

ACCOMMODATION

Accommodations are changes made to the general education curriculum or instructional techniques that do not substantially change the requirements of the curriculum or standards, but assist the student in making adequate progress. The accommodations are determined by the **Individualized Education Program** (IEP) team and are documented on the IEP. Accommodations must be provided in all appropriate environments and subject areas.

KATHERINE E. COOK

ACTIVITIES OF DAILY LIVING

Activities of daily living refer to the ongoing behaviors that occur on a daily basis. Such behaviors include eating, cooking, bathing, social interactions (such as leisure activities, attending school or work, or assisting with chores), and other activities that one might routinely expect an individual to perform or participate in. For many school-aged students, the skills to perform daily activities and develop independence for adult life may be included in the student's **Individualized Education Program** (IEP) as goals and objectives.

ANDREA M. BABKIE

ADAPTIVE BEHAVIOR

Adaptive behavior refers to the manner in which a person copes with the demands of the environment. It includes responses to biological demands (e.g., hunger), as well as social demands such as community expectations (e.g., following rules, personal responsibility), interpersonal requirements (e.g., communication, socialization), and practical challenges of daily living (e.g., using money, preparing meals, toileting; Nihira, Leland, & Lambert, 1992).

Requesting help is an important adaptive skill.

A significant deficit in adaptive behavior is a key criterion in the diagnosis of **mental retardation** (APA, 2000). In adaptive behavior assessment, clinicians commonly use checklists and questionnaires that yield standardized scores comparing a person's level of adaptive functioning with age-matched samples (see **Vineland Adaptive Behavior Scales**). These instruments are also used to determine the individual's relative adaptive strengths and weaknesses, as well as to identify "next step" instructional goals. For example, if it is determined that a child is using a spoon at mealtime, consideration might be given to instruction in using a fork.

Level of adaptive functioning is determined by both the repertoire of adaptive skills an individual possesses and his or her ability to use those skills at the appropriate times. For example, in order to keep their hands clean, individuals must be able to carry out the multistep skill of hand washing (e.g., turning on the faucet, applying soap, and so on), use that skill when necessary (e.g., before lunch), and complete it appropriately (e.g., without taking "too much time" or requiring repeated prompting from others in a school or vocational setting).

Independent of overall level of cognitive functioning, persons with autism display significant deficits in the ability to apply the skills that they possess in adaptive ways. For example, they may have relatively large vocabularies but use spoken language almost exclusively to make requests rather than to interact with peers. Similarly, they may demonstrate a relative strength in reading or arithmetic, but not use the skill to participate in classroom activities (Carter et al., 1998). Self-care skills, such as dressing and toileting, are often areas of relative strength; however, because of the complex social and practical requirements of these tasks, specialized instruction is often necessary in these areas as well (VanMeter, Fein, Morris, Waterhouse, & Allen, 1997). Due to this "scattered" profile, careful adaptive behavior assessment is necessary.

Through systematic instruction, as well as specialized supports (e.g., picture-based prompts or directions), persons with autism may learn complex adaptive skills and eventually generalize those skills to relevant settings. For example, communication and social skills (e.g., problem solving, requesting help) may be taught through specialized curricula implemented with a combination of **structured and incidental teaching** (e.g., Frost & Bondy, 2002; McGinnis & Goldstein, 1997). Daily living skills, such as toileting and tooth brushing, may be taught using task analytic procedures that break activities down into small units of instruction (Baker & Brightman, 1997). Because the construct of adaptive behavior focuses upon participation in everyday activities, it is a key consideration in comprehensive curricula designed to promote independence and quality of life.

REFERENCES

American Psychiatric Association. (2000). *Diagnostic and statistical manual of mental disorders* (4th ed., text rev.). Washington, DC: Author.

Baker, B. L., & Brightman, A. J. (1997). *Steps to independence: Teaching everyday skills to children with special needs*. Baltimore: Brookes Publishing Co.

Carter, A. S., Volkmar, F. R., Sparrow, S. S., Wang, J., Lord, C., Dawson, G., et al. (1998). The Vineland Adaptive Behavior Scales: Supplementary norms for individuals with autism. *Journal of Autism and Developmental Disorders, 28,* 287–302.

Frost, L., & Bondy, A. (2002). *The picture exchange communication system training manual* (2nd ed.). Newark, DE: Pyramid Educational Products, Inc.

McGinnis, E., & Goldstein, A. P. (1997). *Skillstreaming the elementary school child* (2nd ed.). Champaign, IL: Research Press.

Nihira, K., Leland, H., & Lambert, N. (1992). *AAMR Adaptive Behavior Scale-Residential and Community: Examiner's manual*. Austin, TX: Pro-Ed.

VanMeter, L., Fein, D., Morris, R., Waterhouse, L., & Allen, D. (1997). Delay versus deviance in autistic social behavior. *Journal of Autism and Developmental Disorders, 27,* 557–569.

DANIEL W. MRUZEK

ADHD. *See* Attention Deficit Hyperactivity Disorders

ADOLESCENT/ADULT SENSORY PROFILE

The Adolescent/Adult Sensory Profile (Brown & Dunn, 2002) was designed to identify sensory processing patterns in individuals 11 years and older. An individual can self-evaluate by completing a Self-Questionnaire that addresses how an individual typically responds to various situations and experiences. It is used to identify patterns of sensory processing consistent with those described in Dunn's Model of Sensory Processing. The items on the profile address the areas of taste/smell, visual, touch, movement, auditory, and activity level.

REFERENCE

Brown, C., & Dunn, W. (2002). *Adolescent/Adult Sensory Profile manual*. San Antonio, TX: Harcourt Assessment.

LISA ROBBINS

ADOLESCENT AND ADULT PSYCHOEDUCATIONAL PROFILE

The Adolescent and Adult Psychoeducational Profile (AAPEP; Mesibov, Schopler, Schaffer, & Landrus, 1989) is an extension of the Psychoeducational Profile-Revised designed as an assessment instrument for the TEACCH program. The AAPEP is applicable to the needs and goals of adolescents and adults with autism spectrum disorder (ASD), and is used to provide an evaluation of current and potential skills that are necessary for successful, semi-independent functioning in the home and the community. It contains a Direct Observation Scale, a Home Scale, and a School/Work Scale, with each scale divided into six function areas: vocational skills, independent functioning, leisure skills, vocational behavior, functional communication, and interpersonal behavior.

REFERENCE

Mesibov, G., Schopler, E., Schaffer, B., & Landrus, R. (1989). *Adolescent and adult psychoeducational profile: Individualized assessment and treatment for autistic and developmentally disabled children.* Austin, TX: Pro-Ed.

JEANNE HOLVERSTOTT

ADULT SUPPORTS

Individuals with autism transitioning into adulthood continue to require habilitation to prepare for community-based day and vocational programs and the possibility for competitive employment, with or without supports. Individuals must be provided the opportunity to attain independence through a variety of services to include all realms of daily living across all environmental settings. Services consist of supports ranging from counseling, extended care, employment, family, financial, and health.

Counseling supports are provided through face-to-face, individual, group, or family therapy. Sessions are designed to promote problem-solving skills, to improve communication, and to address behavioral, emotional, and cognitive concerns. Crisis intervention is available in emergency situations when individuals experience specific and time-limited problems that threaten to disrupt their home, school, or community situations.

Extended care supports include recreation, habilitative, and social components. Recreational supports offer leisure and social activities to promote interactions with members of the community as well as developing hobbies one can participate in independently at home or in the community. Day habilitation services provide a non-residential setting, separate from the individual's home residence. Transition and adaptation skills are addressed according to skill levels and interests and assist in improving skill acquisition, retention, self-help, socialization, and motor manipulation. Further development of social skills, communication, safety awareness, and **daily living skills** is essential to increasing independence. Social components are integrated throughout both recreation and day habilitation services.

Employment supports include all aspects of transitioning into the workforce and continued vocational support. Individualized assistance includes vocational training, job coaching, travel training, technological aids, job placement, and employment maintenance. Services may include job training, on- or off-site, to enhance job duty performance, work behaviors, use of community resources, and transportation to and from the workplace. More information is available at the local **vocational rehabilitation** office.

Family supports include licensed residential programs, support groups, in-home services, **respite care**, parent advocacy and training, and service coordination. Services begin with a referral to a service provider. The service provider will then go through an intake process to identify needs and link to services after establishing eligibility. Coordinators then use a person-centered process to develop, implement, and maintain an **Individualized Family Service Plan** and to determine the level of support the individual and/or family needs. Parent support and education is provided through parent advocacy and training. In the event an individual becomes unable to be cared for in the home, residential services may be sought, including supervised group living, semi-independent group living, and other residential options.

Financial supports offer guidance and consultation about sources of funding, benefits, and entitlements. More information is available at the local Social Security Office.

Depending upon the individual's needs and insurance coverage, health care supports may consist of medical, dental, and other health-related services. More information can be obtained by contacting the individual insurance company.

See also self-determination.

STACEY L. BROOKENS

ADVOCATE

An advocate is an individual who speaks, writes, or acts on behalf of another, especially in a legal context. According to the **Americans with Disabilities Act** (ADA) of 1990 (PL 101-336), individuals with disabilities and their families may advocate for themselves or appoint another to do so.

REFERENCE
Americans with Disabilities Act, 42 U.S.C. §§ 12101-12213 (1990).

JEANNE HOLVERSTOTT

AGE APPROPRIATE

Age appropriate refers to the principles used for students with disabilities when a decision is required for placement, setting, and environment. Based on **chronological age**, not **mental age**, children with disabilities should be served in the same setting and environment with their nondisabled peers of the same or similar age.

KAI-CHIEN TIEN

AGES AND STAGES QUESTIONNAIRES: SOCIAL/EMOTIONAL

Ages and Stages Questionnaires: Social/Emotional (ASQ: SE; Squires & Potter, 2004) is a screening system used to evaluate social-emotional development at various stages (6, 12, 18, 24, 30, 36, 48, and 60 months). Completed in approximately 15 minutes by parents or caregivers at the eight designated intervals, the ASQ: SE screens the following behavioral areas: self-regulation, compliance, communication, adaptive functioning, autonomy, affect, and interaction with people.

REFERENCE
Squires, J., & Potter, L. (2004). *Ages and stages questionnaires.* Baltimore: Brookes Publishing Co.

JEANNE HOLVERSTOTT

ALLERGY

An allergy is an exaggerated reaction to a specific or multiple substances. This reaction is specific to the immune system. Symptoms to specific substances produce no ill effects or symptoms to the majority of individuals. Allergic reactions occur through exposure via the skin, respiratory system, or the stomach and intestinal system.

KATHERINE E. COOK

ALTERNATIVE ASSESSMENT

Alternative assessment measures are nontraditional approaches to obtaining information regarding a student's strengths and needs. The information gained from these measures directly relates to current and future curricular content. Examples of alternative assessments include the portfolio assessment, performance-based assessment, authentic assessment, **curriculum-based assessment**, and **criterion-referenced assessment**.

FURTHER INFORMATION

Overton, T. (2003). *Assessing learners with special needs: An applied approach.* Upper Saddle River, NJ: Merrill/Prentice Hall.

THERESA L. EARLES-VOLLRATH

AMERICAN SIGN LANGUAGE (ASL)

American Sign Language (ASL) is a special visual language that has existed for over 200 years. ASL relies on visual/manual properties and requires visual perception for decoding and encoding. The production of ASL involves movement in space and is formed using hands, body, and facial expressions. Individuals are able to communicate the meaning of a concept through a single sign or combination of signs. ASL has been compared and contrasted to many other languages and is reported as having a similar structure, however it varies greatly from the English language (which has auditory/spoken properties). A key difference from other languages is the way in which ASL is acquired. ASL is usually learned through a peer transmission process, rather than through the passing on of a language from generation to generation within families. The most fluent users of ASL are children who have deaf parents and children who have attended schools for the deaf or residential schools.

RASCHELLE THEOHARRIS

AMERICANS WITH DISABILITIES ACT (ADA)

The most comprehensive legislation that protects the rights of individuals with disabilities is the Americans with Disabilities Act (ADA). This legislation applies to both public and private sectors, including libraries, state and local governments, restaurants, hotels, theaters, transportation systems, and stores (Fleischer & Zames, 2001).

Prior to ADA, several laws served as the driving force in the creation of the Americans with Disabilities Act. The Civil Rights Act of 1964 prohibited discrimination based on race, color, sex, religion, and national origin in employment, public accommodations, and the provision of state and local government services. A decade later in 1973, the Federal Rehabilitation Act protected the civil and constitutional rights of people with disabilities. **Section 504 of the Federal Rehabilitation Act of 1973** prohibited against discrimination of people with disabilities involved in a program or activity receiving federal assistance. Both of these laws guaranteed that people with disabilities would not be discriminated against in certain areas of their life, such as in being served at lunch counters, bus stations, and as recipients of federal assistance. However, these laws did not protect people with disabilities who sought employment where the company did not receive federal funding or assistance.

The Americans with Disability Act provided this protection by regulating the rights of people with disabilities in the public and private sectors. ADA provided full citizenship, independent living, and economic self-sufficiency for people with disabilities, assuming equality of opportunity (Turnbull, Turnbull, Shank, & Leal, 1999) as well as the accommodations needed in public places for people with disabilities to use.

COMPONENTS OF THE AMERICANS WITH DISABILITIES ACT

As stated in Section 3 of the Americans with Disabilities Act, disability is defined as (a) a physical or mental impairment that substantially limits one or more of the major life activities of such individual; (b) a record of such an impairment; or (c) being regarded as having such an impairment (ADA, 1990). In addition, ADA also applies to those who have an association with an individual known to have a disability (such as a parent) as well as those who are coerced or subjected to retaliation for assisting people with disabilities.

ADA is divided into five titles. Title 1, or Employment, addresses business accommodations, such as restructuring jobs, altering the layout of workstations, or modifying equipment. Applying for a job, hiring, pay, and benefits are also covered under Title I. Title II, or Public Services, includes state and local government, public transportations systems, and other commuter authorities. The third title, or Public Accommodations, gives rules and regulations to all new construction and existing facilities to be accessible to all people with disabilities. This includes hotels, restaurants, grocery stores, and privately owned transportation systems. Title IV, or Telecommunications, regulates that all telecommunication companies offering telephone service must have telephone relay services for individuals with disabilities. The final title, or Miscellaneous, includes a provision prohibiting coercion or threatening people with disabilities from asserting their rights under ADA or retaliating against those that speak up for their rights.

REFERENCES

Americans with Disabilities Act, 42 U.S.C. §§ 12101-12213 (1990).

Fleischer, D. Z., & Zames, F. (2001). *The disability rights movement: From charity to confrontation* (pp. 88–109). Philadelphia: Temple University Press.

Turnbull, A., Turnbull, R., Shank, M., & Leal, D. (1999) *Exceptional lives: Special education in today's schools.* (2nd ed.) Upper Saddle River, NJ: Prentice Hall.

MELISSA L. TRAUTMAN

AMINO ACIDS

Amino acids are the building blocks of proteins. There are approximately 80 naturally occurring amino acids, of which 20 are necessary for human growth and health. The body is capable of producing some amino acids in the liver, but others must be obtained from food. Some food proteins contain all the necessary amino acids and are therefore considered to be complete proteins such as milk, cheese, eggs, and meat. Vegetables and grains are considered incomplete proteins.

BRUCE BASSITY

AMYGDALA

A brain structure located deep in the temporal lobes, the amygdala is involved in perceiving threats and producing a response to such threats. It receives input directly and quickly from sensory pathways as well as from other areas of the brain that filter the sensory input and put it into context so an appropriate response can be made. The amygdala is part of the **limbic system**.

BRUCE BASSITY

ANALYSIS OF BEHAVIORAL FUNCTION

Analysis of behavioral function is a process of determining the function of a challenging behavior. This is a data-driven process that often includes **direct observation** and the use of formal assessment measures designed to assess behavioral functions. These tools are used to form a hypothesis regarding the function of the behavior; this hypothesis is tested with the implementation of strategies designed to replace the undesirable behavior with appropriate behavior.

JEANNE HOLVERSTOTT

ANALYSIS OF SENSORY BEHAVIOR INVENTORY–REVISED EDITION

The Analysis of Sensory Behavior Inventory–Revised (ASBI-R; Morton & Wolford, 1994) is designed to collect information about an individual's behaviors as they are related to sensory stimuli. It assesses six sensory areas and is designed to evaluate both sensory-seeking and sensory-avoidance behaviors within each modality. The ASBI-R can be completed by anyone who is familiar with the individual and may be done individually or by a group. Results may be used to develop effective intervention strategies and accommodations.

REFERENCE

Morton, K. & Wolford, S. (1994). *Analysis of Sensory Behavior Inventory–Revised.* Arcadia, CA: Skills with Occupational Therapy.

LISA ROBBINS

ANECDOTAL REPORT

The anecdotal report is a technique used to describe behavior. An observer watches a person or group of people and writes down what they observe during a specified time period. This provides rich information about behavior and should also include a description of the setting, what others say and do, and time notations.

FURTHER INFORMATION

Alberto, P. A., & Troutman, A. C. (2003). *Applied behavior analysis for teachers* (6th ed). Upper Saddle River, NJ: Merrill/Prentice Hall.

PAUL G. LACAVA AND RASCHELLE THEOHARRIS

ANGELMAN SYNDROME

Angelman syndrome is a rare (approximately 1 in 25,000 births) genetic disorder that results in severe neurological problems. It is named after Dr. Harry Angelman, the pediatrician who discovered the common traits evident in three of his patients. He first named it "Happy Puppet" syndrome, based on several features characteristic to the three children. Over the years, the name was changed to the more respectful "Angelman syndrome."

Angelman syndrome is caused by one of several problems with gene material on chromosome 15. One of the most common is a deletion or "turning off" of some genes from the maternal chromosome 15. There may also be a mutation of this particular genetic material, or a double portion from the father's chromosome 15, or an imprinting defect, and in some cases, there is no apparent cause found on chromosome 15.

Common prenatal tests cannot bring these genetics problems to light. It is difficult to detect Angelman syndrome from birth to about three months of age. As these babies develop and grow, the identifiable characteristics become apparent. Since this is a syndrome, and there are varying problems on chromosome 15, not all features will be present in each child with Angelman syndrome. Some children may be more or less affected than others.

The most frequently cited characteristics include:

- Little or no spoken language, although receptive language may be somewhat better
- Unusually affectionate
- Very happy affect, including bursts of laughter and giggling
- Severe developmental delays (mental retardation)
- Disjointed, awkward gait and large muscle movements
- Some unusual features, including a distinct mouth, protruding tongue, and somewhat flattened head
- Seizures of all kinds
- Sleep problems such as insomnia
- Impulsive behaviors, extreme hyperactivity
- Dual diagnosis of autism
- Misdiagnosed as having cerebral palsy, autism, etc.
- Obsessions with water

There is no cure or remediation for Angelman syndrome, although use of best practices in a well-designed and implemented IEP via special education services can ensure a brighter future than was previously imagined possible. Use of **augmentative and alternative communication** systems such as the **Picture Exchange Communication System**, signing, and/or communication devices all can improve quality of life. Use of behavioral strategies that include **applied behavior analysis** and **positive behavior supports** can be used to teach new skills as well as help the individual learn to control disruptive behaviors. Making environmental changes that can help with impulsive behaviors and ensure personal safety can make it easier for the individual with Angelman syndrome to enjoy family, school, and community life.

Students with Angelman syndrome can be included in neighborhood schools with special education supports; some can participate in athletic and leisure activities shared by the rest of the family. Due to impulse problems that impact sleeping and safety issues as well as extreme cognitive delays, they most likely will require constant supervision and not be able to live unassisted.

Parents report some of their greatest challenges as being sleep deprived due to their child's insomnia, finding the proper medications for seizures, continual household chaos caused by the child's hyperactivity, and teaching toileting skills. Again, getting good behavioral and medical supports to help with some of the traits of Angelman syndrome can vastly improve the quality of home life for the entire family.

See also augmentative and alternative communication; Picture Exchange Communication System.

FURTHER INFORMATION

Angelman Syndrome Foundation; 3015 E. New York Street, Suite A2265; Aurora, IL 60504; Phone: 1-800-432-6435; Fax: 630-978-7408; E-mail: info@angelman.org.

ANN PILEWSKIE

ANIMAL ASSISTED THERAPY/ASSISTANCE DOG PLACEMENTS FOR CHILDREN WITH AUTISM

Intelligent selection of a canine partner is of central importance in creating a successful assistance dog placement for a child on the autism spectrum. The job description of a dog slated to work with a child with autism should be individually tailored to meet the unique needs of the child; the training of the dog, as well as the teaching of the child, should be positive, not corrections based, and should move in tandem with both the dog's and the child's natural development. Educated parental involvement, appropriate temperamental fit, and proper supervision of the child-dog team are all essential elements in creating an assistance dog placement that is safe as well as effective.

Creating assistance dog placements for children on the autism spectrum differs from creating placements between assistance dogs and physically challenged adults. Specific task training takes a back seat to being certain the assistance dogs selected are safe and social companions to the children on the autism spectrum that they will serve. The primary emphasis in selecting an assistance dog must be on achieving a correct temperamental fit between the child and the puppy, along with having the puppy's early socialization dovetail with his or her future role. Without specific exposure to the profile of a child with autism, a puppy has no clue as to how to interpret autistic behaviors and therefore may react unpredictably. Children with autism may throw loud tantrums or fail to grant the body space that we unconsciously and consistently grant each other. Dogs depend greatly on nonverbal communication, and are apt to be uncomfortable with a child's violation of their "personal space" or with a child's unusual sounds or movements; but with proper communication and appropriate early socialization, a puppy can easily learn to interpret a child's unusual behavior as positive events that are predictive of reward.

Considerable energy should also go into teaching the child to interact appropriately with his or her dog. As the quality of the relationship they share matters more than any other variable, the communication between the puppy and child must be properly facilitated. The same difficulties with communication that children with autism experience with people can exist with dogs as well, as dogs take their cues from humans regarding how relationships are structured. It is important for the caretakers of a child with autism to understand that their role is to ensure that the relationship between child and puppy is consistently gentle and mutually enjoyable.

The concept of "time out" with an assistance dog reliably holding a down-stay position to provide comfort and support can be a positive way for a child with autism to regain control over his emotions, as research has shown the mere presence of a trusted dog can have a calming effect on a child. Use of the assistance dog can be preventive, as a dog may be employed as part of a structured activity to reduce stress and avoid meltdowns. Assistance dogs can be used to help meet other therapeutic goals, such as those established in occupational or physical therapy, either directly, such as being brushed or fed by his or her child, or simply by providing motivation. (One little girl took a break to pet her North Star dog after every 10 repetitions of a particularly grueling exercise.)

Children with autism often have great difficulty in generalizing learned speech to new situations and people, due to their overly selective attention and tendency to respond to only a limited number of cues; using an assistance dog as a tool for teaching pragmatic language at home as well as in the community can be as simple as rehearsing stock responses to the fairly predictable questions people are likely to ask when they see a well-trained dog wearing a vest with a patch that reads "Please Ask to Pet Me." As children with autism tend to be dependent on verbal cues provided by others, this positive and predictable social response is a valuable tool to help develop speech within natural settings in the home as well as the outside community. It should also be noted that people who may have shied away from the responsibility of starting a conversation with a child with autism, as well as maintaining it, often relax and rise to the challenge when a dog is available to help structure the questions and comments.

Occasionally an assistance dog can also provide a safety role for a child with autism, either by being trained to deliver a warning bark when a child with autism wanders away or to shadow his or her charge (in which case a global positioning device and an easy-to-read name tag attached to the dog's collar may well help a nonverbal child to be safely returned home). A technique known as *blocking* is also being developed at North Star Foundation; this technique can only be employed if a child is small enough in comparison to the dog to be safely blocked when in flight. National Service Dogs (NSD) in Canada tethers assistance dogs to some children with autism who are prone to running off, but this method of keeping a child safe can only be employed if the child is small enough to be physically stopped by the weight of the assistance dog.

Unfortunately, some children are not good candidates for placements involving a dog, such as children who are aggressive. Some children with poor impulse control may still be appropriate candidates for an older, more stable dog with the necessary guidance and supervision, but in general children who tend to lash out physically are not good candidates for an assistance dog unless such tendencies are brought under strict control. For the right child on the autism spectrum, a properly selected and trained canine companion can be a valuable tool in helping to achieve social, emotional, educational, and safety goals.

FURTHER INFORMATION

Gross, P. D. (2006). The *golden bridge: A guide to assistance dogs for children challenged by autism or other developmental disabilities*. West Lafayette, IN: Purdue University Press.

McNicholas, J., & Collis, G. M. (1995). Relationships between young people with autism and their pets. Paper presented at the 7th International Conference on Human-Animal Interactions, Animals, Health and Quality of Life, September 6–9, 1995, Geneva, Switzerland. North Star Foundation: www.NorthStarDogs.com E-mail: northstarfoundation@charter.net.

Toeplitz, Z., Matczak, A., Piotrowska, A., & Zygier, A. (1995). *Impact of keeping pets at home upon the social development of children*. Paper presented at the 7th International Conference on

Human-Animal Interactions, Animals, Health and Quality of Life, September 6–9, 1995, Geneva, Switzerland.

PATTY DOBBS GROSS

ANNUAL GOAL

A required component of the **Individualized Education Program**, annual goals is a statement of desired educational attainment for an individual student that is written based on information from the **present level of educational performance**. Annual goals must be written in measurable terms, include the skill or behavior to be achieved and direction for the behavior. They are written for a 1-year period and must contain either short term **objectives** or benchmarks.

KATHERINE E. COOK

ANTECEDENT

The antecedent is the behavior that precedes a given situation or behavior. Since behavior cannot occur in isolation, what occurs in the environment before the behavior (the antecedent) and after the behavior (the consequence) is often key to addressing or changing the behavior. The antecedent may provide insight into the purpose or **function of behavior**. For this reason, most **functional behavior assessments** include the observation and recording of antecedents, such as on an **Antecedent-Behavior-Consequence (ABC) Analysis**.

KATIE BASSITY

ANTECEDENT-BEHAVIOR-CONSEQUENCE (ABC) ANALYSIS

Antecedent-Behavior-Consequence analysis was first described by Bijou, Peterson, and Ault (1968) as *anecdotal observation*, a process of analyzing the events that precede and follow a behavior. The conditions may be modified to change the behavior.

REFERENCE

Bijou, S. W., Peterson, R. F., & Ault, M. H. (1968). A method to integrate descriptive and experimental field studies at the level of data and empirical concept. *Journal of Applied Behavior Analysis, 1,* 175–191.

JEANNE HOLVERSTOTT

ANTIANXIETY MEDICATIONS

Antianxiety medications include various drug classes that are used depending on the severity of anxiety, length of treatment, and age. Drugs that have a mild sedative effect and are short acting such as hydroxyzine (Atarax) or diphenhydramine (Benadryl) are commonly used for short-term relief. Hypnotics like benzodiazepines (Valium family) are used along with some others for more significant agitation. A number of the newer selective serotonin reuptake inhibitors (SSRI) and antidepressants also have antianxiety properties and are specifically indicated for treatment of various kinds of anxiety.

See also antidepressant medications.

BRUCE BASSITY

ANTIBIOTICS

Antibiotics are medications used to treat infectious disease. This may involve treatment to eliminate microorganisms causing acute infection, or prevention or maintenance of a less acute or chronic infection. Antibiotics may be broad spectrum (effective against many different microorganisms), or narrow spectrum (specific for just a few microorganisms). Antibiotics may be used in oral, injectable, intravenous, or topical form.

BRUCE BASSITY

ANTIDEPRESSANT MEDICATIONS

A variety of medications are prescribed to alleviate the signs and symptoms of depression and some have additional uses as well. The most prescribed class of these is known as selective serotonin reuptake inhibitors (SSRI) such as paroxetine (Paxil), fluoxetine (Prozac), and sertraline (Zoloft). Older antidepressants that are less used include tricyclics (TCA) and monoamine oxidase inhibitors (MAOI). There are additional older and newer groups as well. Most antidepressants alter **neurotransmitter** activity, specifically **serotonin**, norepinephrine and **dopamine**.

BRUCE BASSITY

ANTIPSYCHOTIC MEDICATIONS

These medications are most commonly used for treating conditions such as **schizophrenia**, but some of the newer medications have broader uses. There are three categories: (a) typical, which are the oldest medications and include chlorpromazine (Thorazine), haloperidol (Haldol), and fluphenazine (Prolixin); (b) atypicals, which include clozapine (Clozaril), ziprasidone (Geodon), risperidone (Risperdal), quetiapine (Seroquel), and olanzapine (Zyprexa); and (c) others, which includes aripiprazole (Abilify). All of these medications can have potentially serious side effects, some of which can be irreversible. Careful monitoring is required by the healthcare provider.

BRUCE BASSITY

ANXIETY DISORDERS

Anxiety disorders include social phobia, obsessive compulsive disorder, posttraumatic stress disorder, and generalized anxiety disorders.

Social phobia (or social anxiety disorder) is characterized by marked and substantial distress or discomfort in social situations such as meeting new people, appearing for interviews, and speaking in public. For something to be considered a phobia, the *Diagnostic and Statistical Manual of Mental Disorders* (DSM-IV-TR; APA, 2000) states that for individuals under 18 years of age, the fear must persist for at least 6 months and be intense enough to interfere with normal activities. Children may not complain about their fears, but when placed in the feared situation may express their anxiety by crying, having tantrums, freezing, or clinging. Adolescents and adults are more likely to experience a panic attack—several minutes of terror where they feel they are about to have a heart attack, lose control or "go crazy" (Gelfland, Jensen, & Drew, 1997, p. 174). A diagnosis of social phobia should not be made in an individual with an autism spectrum disorder because degrees of anxiety are often present in this population. However, there may be occasions when the distress and symptoms are so severe that diagnosis and treatment beyond the autism spectrum disorders are warranted.

Obsessive compulsive disorder (OCD) is a condition where either obsessions (abnormal thoughts, impulses or images) or compulsions (repetitive acts that the individual feels they must complete) or both are present. DSM-IV-TR (APA, 2000) states that they must also meet the following: (a) are unrealistic and dysfunctional, (b) are experienced as unwelcome but irresistible, (c) are experienced as products of one's own mind and not external in origin, (d) are ritualistic and stereotyped, (e) are time-consuming, taking more than 1 hour each day, and disrupting other activities.

Typical obsessive themes by school-age children involve aggression, contamination, and maintaining order (Clarizio, 1991), and both children and adults are more likely to engage in rituals at home rather than in public. Obsessions and ritualistic behaviors are often seen in autism spectrum disorders but do not usually meet the specific criteria for OCD as previously outlined and would not warrant a separate diagnosis of OCD in the majority of cases.

Posttraumatic stress disorder (PTSD) is an anxiety disorder that develops following a traumatic experience such as witnessing a severe accident, assault, natural catastrophe, life-threatening illness, and sexual or physical abuse. PTSD can develop immediately following the event, but may appear months or years afterwards. Primary symptoms in children include agitated and disorganized behavior, re-enacting of the traumatic event or avoidance of anything associated with it, difficulty sleeping, irritability, attention problems, exaggerated startle responses, and hypervigilance. Children may also show physical symptoms such as stomach aches or headaches, regression, loss of toilet training, or clingy behaviors.

Generalized anxiety disorder (GAD) consists of uncontrollable, excessive anxiety and worry, occurring consistently for at least 6 months, and pervasive in that it covers several events or activities. Other characteristics required for the diagnosis include irritability, restlessness, fatigue, muscle tension, concentration difficulties, or sleep disturbance. According to Beidel, Christ, and Long (1991), the persistent disorder in childhood usually begins around 10 years of age and often co-occurs with depression.

While many difficulties with anxiety can be seen in children and adults with autism spectrum disorders, the differentiation here is due to the specificity of the anxiety difficulties. Usually, therefore, anxiety disorders are not given as co-morbid diagnoses to ASD except in circumstances where the impact of the anxiety difficulties has become so pervasive and interfering with normal functioning that additional diagnosis and anxiety treatment measures are appropriate. Treatments for anxiety disorders include psychotherapy and pharmacological treatments (Gelfland et al., 1997, pp. 170–192).

REFERENCES

American Psychiatric Association. (2000). *Diagnostic and statistical manual of mental disorders* (4th ed., text rev.). Washington, DC: Author.

Beidel, D. C., Christ, M. G., & Long, P. J. (1991). Somatic complaints in anxious children. *Journal of Abnormal Child Psychology*, 19, 659–670.

Clarizio, H. F. (1991). Obsessive-compulsive disorder: The secretive syndrome. *Psychology in the Schools*, 28, 106–115.

Gelfland, D. M., Jensen, W. R., & Drew, C. J. (1997). *Understanding child behaviour disorders* (3rd ed.). Orlando: Harcourt Brace.

FURTHER INFORMATION

Csoti, M. (2003). *School phobia, panic attacks and anxiety in children.* London: Jessica Kingsley Publishers.

March, J. S., & Mulle, K. (1998). *OCD in children and adults.* London: Guilford Press.

FIONA J. SCOTT

APPLIED BEHAVIOR ANALYSIS (ABA)

Applied Behavior Analysis (ABA) employs principles of learning theory to help people change behaviors and learn new skills (Cooper, Heron, & Heward, 1987). ABA is perhaps best known as an intervention for persons with autism spectrum disorders (ASD), but it is also used effectively for other populations, including children and adults with **attention deficit hyperactivity disorder**, conduct disorder, **schizophrenia**, and **developmental delays**. In addition, ABA is also used for teaching academic skills in both general and special education settings, for increasing productivity in the workplace, and for promoting healthy lifestyles.

As defined originally by Baer, Wolf, and Risley (1968), the term *applied* means that ABA focuses on socially relevant outcomes. For example, when ABA interventions for individuals with ASD were initially developed in the 1960s and 1970s, a primary goal was to enable these individuals to move out of institutional settings such as state hospitals (Lovaas, Koegel, Simmons, & Long, 1973), where most lived at that time. Later ABA interventions centered on increasing opportunities for **inclusion** in community settings such as general education classes in public schools (Lovaas, 1987) and improving relationships with peers and caregivers (Koegel & Koegel, 2005).

The term *behavioral* in ABA reflects an emphasis on measurable outcomes. According to Baer et al. (1968), any action that can be measured is a behavior. Thus, the defining features of ASD (problems with reciprocal social interaction, limited social communication, and intense repetitive behaviors or narrow interests) are all considered behaviors. In addition, associated features of ASD (characteristics such as delays in cognitive and self-help skills that are displayed by many but not all individuals with this diagnosis) are also viewed as behaviors.

Finally, the term *analysis* as used indicates that decisions about interventions derive from an examination of data. Thus, ABA investigators conduct studies in which they systematically start and stop interventions to determine whether they reliably change behavior. Such research has identified an array of interventions that can help individuals with ASD. When ABA practitioners implement these interventions for a particular individual, they collect objective data to evaluate whether the interventions are working.

ABA INTERVENTION STRATEGIES

ABA studies show that many effective intervention strategies involve *operant learning*. Operant learning occurs in all humans and many other organisms. It takes place when an antecedent event sets the occasion for a behavior, and a consequent event either increases or decreases the likelihood that the behavior will occur again. An antecedent event is a change within the individual or in the external environment that occurs just prior to the behavior of interest and that acts as a trigger for the behavior.

A consequent event is a change that immediately follows the behavior of interest. Consequent events that increase behavior are called *reinforcers*; consequent events that decrease behavior are said to result in **extinction**. For example, when a student with ASD sees an instructor (antecedent event), she may make eye contact and say, "Hi." If the consequence is a smile and praise from the instructor (a reinforcer), the student is likely to greet the instructor in the future. However, if the instructor walks by without acknowledging the greeting, the student may not greet the instructor on subsequent occasions as the behavior was not reinforced.

Two related forms of learning are modeling and rule-governed behavior. In modeling, the individual observes the antecedent-behavior-consequence relationship instead of experiencing it directly. Thus, a person with ASD might learn how to make greetings by observing two people greet each other. In *rule-governed behavior*, on the other hand, the individual is told about the antecedent-behavior-consequence relationship. For example, a person with ASD might learn about greetings by hearing an instructor explain, "When you greet others, it's important to make eye contact and say 'Hi' or 'Hello' to show you're interested."

To promote operant and related forms of learning, ABA practitioners often use **prompting**. Prompting involves systematically providing physical, gestural, or verbal guidance on performing a behavior in response to a cue. Prompts are gradually reduced and eventually eliminated as the individual masters the behavior. Other common procedures include *task analysis*, which consists of breaking down a complex skill into smaller steps; then **chaining**, in which steps are taught separately and subsequently linked together; and **shaping**, in which successive approximations of a behavior are taught. For example, eye contact may be shaped by reinforcing the individual first for casting fleeting glances in the general direction of the communicative partner, and then increasingly for better accuracy and sustained lengths of time. The shaping process may also be extended to more advanced skills, such as looking back and forth between another person and an object or activity of mutual interest (a skill called joint attention), modulating eye contact during conversations, and alternating gaze among several communication partners.

ABA FOR TEACHING NEW SKILLS

Many ABA strategies have been designed to promote learning in individuals with ASD of all ages and developmental levels. Some strategies are highly structured. For example, discrete trial teaching (DTT) simplifies instruction as much as possible by breaking down learning trials into their component parts and carefully planning how to implement each (Smith, 2001). The instructor begins each discrete trial with a brief instruction or cue (referred to as a **discriminative stimulus**), which may include a prompt. The person with ASD then gives a response. The instructor immediately gives a **consequence**—corrective feedback for an incorrect response or positive reinforcement such as praise or access to preferred objects for a correct response. After this exchange, which typically lasts only seconds, there is a brief pause (*intertrial interval*) before the next trial. During DTT, an instructor often minimizes distractions by working individually with a person with ASD in a setting away from other activity.

Other ABA strategies include **incidental teaching**, which makes use of a person's motivation for preferred items or activities to encourage communication or social initiations (Fenske, Krantz, & McClannahan, 2001). It is usually embedded into naturally occurring activities throughout the day such as work time, play centers, or snack. During these activities, the instructor generally withholds a preferred item, thereby creating an opportunity for the person with ASD to use language to request it. For example, if a child is putting together a favorite puzzle, the instructor may withhold a puzzle piece so that the child is apt to request it. The instructor may prompt the child by asking, "What do you want?" or simply waiting expectantly.

Additional ABA strategies involve providing instruction to groups rather than to one individual (Heflin & Alaimo, 2006), or having an individual work alone by following instructions presented in pictures, written words, or audio-taped recordings (McClannahan & Krantz, 1998). Having typically developing peers serve as models or tutors for the individual with autism is another commonly used approach (Strain & Schwartz, 2001). Across all strategies, the aim is to provide opportunities to learn new skills and to have positive interactions with instructors. Contemporary ABA programs blend these various strategies, rather than relying exclusively on any one approach, in an effort to individualize interventions and optimize outcomes.

ABA FOR CHALLENGING BEHAVIORS

Sometimes a goal of ABA treatment is to decrease or eliminate challenging behaviors while teaching more appropriate skills (Horner, Carr, Strain, Todd, & Reed, 2002). Through assessment methods such as interview and direct observation, ABA practitioners seek to identify the various functions that challenging behaviors serve. For example, some students are especially likely to display challenging behaviors when requests are made of them, indicating that the function of the behavior is to escape or avoid requests. Others exhibit challenging behaviors when they cannot immediately get something they requested, suggesting that the function is to gain access to preferred objects or activities.

After identifying a possible function, practitioners can develop individualized interventions. One aspect of the intervention is to reinforce behaviors that are alternatives to or incompatible with the challenging behavior. For example, if the challenging behavior is screaming and the function is getting attention from others, the student might be reinforced for raising his hand, or for a behavior such as pulling objects off shelves, the student might be reinforced for putting her hands in her pockets.

Along with reinforcing alternative behaviors, ABA practitioners may withhold reinforcement for the challenging behavior. For example, they may praise the student for raising his hand but not for screaming. Alternatively, they may respond to screaming by placing the student in time-out, where no reinforcement is available, for a time. Another intervention is **overcorrection**, in which the student restores the environment to a state better than it was before the challenging behavior occurred. For example, if a student throws a drink on the floor, she may be directed to clean up the spill and the surrounding area.

A **token economy** combines procedures for reinforcing appropriate behavior and withholding reinforcement for challenging behavior. In this system, a student can earn tokens for appropriate behavior and cash them in for a reinforcer such as additional time with a favorite peer. Conversely, he may lose a token for challenging behaviors such as aggression (a procedure called *response cost*). All of these strategies for reducing challenging behavior are most successful when implemented in conjunction with instruction and reinforcement for more appropriate behaviors.

MODELS FOR IMPLEMENTING ABA

Some ABA intervention models for persons with ASD are comprehensive, designed to address all areas of need. Others are directed toward a more circumscribed, specific set of goals. One comprehensive approach is early intensive behavioral intervention (EIBI). Applied with children under 5 years old, EIBI typically consists of 20–40 hours weekly of ABA treatment, much of it involving one-to-one instruction (Handleman & Harris, 2001). EIBI often occurs in the home or child-care setting, with active participation from parents and others in that setting, and may be employed for two to three years. Studies indicate that EIBI can yield significant gains such as increases in IQ and other standardized test scores, along with increased access to special education services (Smith, Groen, & Wynn, 2000). However, additional research is necessary to confirm these exciting findings.

Comprehensive ABA treatment programs for older children and adults with ASD take place in specialized classrooms or occupational settings (Handleman & Harris, 2006; Holmes, 1997). Such programs usually mix individual and group instruction throughout the day. The learner may spend a portion of the day engaged in one-to-one, individualized instruction to pre-teach or review skills to be addressed later in the day during group instruction and spend other portions of the day in typical academic group activities. Research shows that persons with ASD in these programs learn many new skills. Still, little information is available on long-term outcomes such as whether graduates of the programs succeed afterward in less specialized settings.

Specific skill models may involve working directly with persons with ASD in a particular area (e.g., social interaction) or training parents, peers, or personnel in educational or occupational settings to implement ABA interventions. Training typically includes instruction on characteristics of ASD, assistance with identifying skills to teach, guided practice in applying ABA methods, direction on how to collect data on the effects of intervention, and establishment of a system for communication and collaboration between the intervention setting and home. Many studies document that, with training, parents, peers, and educators can become proficient at implementing ABA interventions under supervision of a professional ABA practitioner.

CURRENT STATUS AND FUTURE DIRECTIONS

Though not a cure for ASD, ABA is an effective approach to teach many new skills and alleviate challenging behaviors. As a result, it has become an important intervention for persons with ASD. Research continues on how to enhance its effectiveness.

REFERENCES

Baer, D. M., Wolf, M. M., & Risley, T. R. (1968). Some current dimensions of applied behavior analysis. *Journal of Applied Behavior Analysis, 1,* 91–97.

Cooper, J. O., Heron, T. E., & Heward, W. L. (1987). *Applied behavior analysis.* Columbus, OH: Merrill/Prentice Hall.

Fenske, E. C., Krantz, P. J., & McClannahan, L. E. (2001). Incidental teaching: A not discrete trial teaching procedure. In C. Maurice, G. Green, & R. M. Foxx (Eds.), *Making a difference: Behavioral intervention for autism* (pp. 75–82). Austin, TX: Pro-Ed.

Handleman, J. S., & Harris, S. L. (2006). *School-age education programs for children with autism.* Austin, TX: Pro-Ed.

Handleman, J. S., & Harris, S. L. (Eds.). (2001). *Preschool programs for children with autism* (2nd ed.). Austin, TX: Pro-Ed.

Heflin, L. J., & Alaimo, D. F. (2006). *Students with autism spectrum disorders.* Upper Saddle River, NJ: Merrill/Prentice Hall.

Holmes, D. L. (1997). *Autism through the lifespan: The Eden model.* Bethesda, MD: Woodbine House.

Horner, R. H., Carr, E. G., Strain, P. S., Todd, A. W., & Reed, H. K. (2002). Problem behavior interventions for young children with autism: A research synthesis. *Journal of Autism and Developmental Disorders, 32,* 423–446.

Koegel, R. L., & Koegel, L. K. (2005). *Pivotal response treatments for autism: Communication, social & academic development.* Baltimore: Brookes Publishing Co.

Lovaas, O. I. (1987). Behavioral treatment and normal educational and intellectual functioning in young autistic children. *Journal of Consulting and Clinical Psychology, 55,* 3–9.

Lovaas, O. I., Koegel, R., Simmons, J. Q., & Long, J. S. (1973). Some generalization and follow-up measures on autistic children in behavior therapy. *Journal of Applied Behavior Analysis, 6,* 131–166.

McClannahan, L. E., & Krantz, P. J. (1998). *Activity schedules for children with autism: Teaching independent behavior.* Bethesda, MD: Woodbine House.

Smith, T. (2001). Discrete trial training in the treatment of autism. *Focus on Autism and Related Disorders, 16,* 86–92.

Smith, T., Groen, A., & Wynn, J. W. (2000). Randomized trial of intensive early intervention for children with pervasive developmental disorder. *American Journal on Mental Retardation, 104,* 269–285.

Strain, P. S., & Schwartz, I. (2001). ABA and the development of meaningful social relations for young children with autism. *Focus on Autism and Related Disorders, 16,* 120–128.

CHRISTINE R. PETERSON AND TRISTRAM SMITH

APRAXIA

Apraxia is the inability to plan, organize, and carry out a physical, motor action. Individuals with apraxia may have difficulty putting on their shoes, climbing on play equipment, or skipping.

KELLY M. PRESTIA

ART THERAPY

During the 1940s, psychiatrists became more interested in the artwork of their mentally ill patients. About the same time, educators became interested in their students' work as it showed differences in development (cognitive and emotional). As popularity grew, art therapy began being offered alongside traditional psychoanalytic therapy programs. It is through the creative process that art therapy has grown to be used in the assessment and treatment of individuals with various disorders as well as for promoting wellness.

Art therapy is a mental health profession that uses art and the creative process to improve the lives of the clients who are served. These clients range in ages (from children to older adults), and levels of wellness. Art therapy combines the areas of human development, visual arts, and counseling. It can be utilized with diagnoses such as depression, anxiety, mental illnesses, addiction, relationship issues, abuse and domestic violence, disability, loss, and medical illnesses.

In order to enter into the art therapy profession, completion of a master's degree in art therapy or with an emphasis on art therapy is required. The Art Therapy Credentials Board (ATCB) is the credentialing agency that defines the requirements for certification. In order to be considered a registered art therapist (ATR or ATR-BC) 1,000 hours of direct client contact must be accrued after graduation. The national organization for art therapists is the American Art Therapy Association, Inc. (AATA). This professional organization defines and regulates the educational, professional, and ethical standards for art therapists. A separate entity, the Art Therapy Credentials Board (ATCB) awards registration as an art therapist (ATR) and after passing a written examination confers the credentialing of a board-certified art therapist (ATR-BC). This credential must be maintained with continuing education hours (American Art Therapy Association, 2006).

Art therapists work in a variety of settings including hospitals, mental health facilities, residential treatment centers, shelters, schools, correctional facilities, nursing homes, private practice, and art studios. Art therapists may work independently or as part of a treatment team. In addition, treatment settings vary from individual sessions to group placements.

REFERENCE

American Art Therapy Association, Inc. (2006). Retrieved July 24, 2006 from www.arttherapy. org/about.html.

LYNN DUDEK

ASPERGER, HANS

Hans Asperger (February 18, 1906–October 21, 1980) was an Austrian pediatrician who published the seminal research on the disorder that is now called *Asperger syndrome*. In his original findings, he noted that four boys from his clinical practice exhibited distinctive characteristics that he labeled as *autistischen psychopathen*. Asperger identified the traits within this disability as: (a) social isolation and awkwardness, (b) self-stimulatory responses, (c) insistence on environmental sameness, (d) normal intellectual development, and (e) normal communication development.

See also Asperger's disorder.

FURTHER INFORMATION

Frith, U. (1991). *Autism and Asperger syndrome.* Cambridge: Cambridge University Press.

TERRI COOPER SWANSON

ASPERGER'S DISORDER

Like all autism spectrum disorders, Asperger's disorder (or Asperger syndrome) involves difficulties in three major areas: social interaction, communication, and behavior (Wing & Gould, 1979). While lower-functioning individuals with autism might show little desire for social interaction and spontaneous communication, those with Asperger's disorder are typically quite verbal, and often eager to share information. It is the unusual quality of their language, their poor social skills, and their unusual habits or behaviors that distinguishes them. Because the symptoms are more subtle than those of classic autism, most children with Asperger's disorder are not diagnosed until elementary school, or even much later (Attwood, 1998).

There is a certain amount of debate among experts today about what, exactly, constitutes Asperger's disorder. The **Diagnostic and Statistical Manual of Mental Disorders** (DSM-IV-TR; APA, 2000), which publishes the official criteria used by psychologists and psychiatrists in the United States, uses much of the same language to describe Asperger's disorder and Autistic disorder (e.g., at least two symptoms of "impairment in social interaction" and one symptom of restricted, repetitive interests or behaviors). However, to receive the Asperger's diagnosis, the individual may not have **mental retardation** and may not have had a significant delay in learning to talk. Given those criteria, many argue that Asperger's is not, in fact, a separate disorder in itself, but a form of **high functioning autism**.

Other experts argue, however, that Asperger's disorder has more distinct characteristics than those covered in the DSM-IV-TR criteria. Commonly mentioned ones include poor social skills, special interests, language peculiarities, sensory processing difficulties, gross and fine motor problems, and difficulties with self-help and organizational skills.

SOCIAL SKILLS

While small children with Asperger's disorder may initially show little interest in playing with other children, they are generally described as being very attached to parents and family members. Older children and adults with Asperger's generally *do* want to establish friendships and relationships—but they lack the knowledge to do so. Others may view them as quirky, shy, or, in some cases, even frightening. This is due to the fact that while most people automatically develop an understanding of social rules and nonverbal communication, people with Asperger's disorder do not. They need to be explicitly taught.

LANGUAGE

Children with Asperger's disorder are often described as sounding like "little professors" because of their often extraordinary vocabularies and their tendency to lecture. While their speech may be superficially perfect, they often tend to be overly literal in their use and interpretation of language. Metaphors and idioms (e.g., "beating a dead horse") might be baffling. Others' inexact use of language, such as Mom asking, "Would you mind getting that?" when she really means "Get that!" can cause frustration and anger. The pragmatics (social aspects) of speech—such as the ability to carry on back-and-forth conversations—often do not come naturally to people with Asperger's, and must be explicitly taught. One distinctive language feature of many individuals with Asperger's disorder is their love of perseverative scripting—telling the entire story line of, say, a cartoon, video game, or movie, over and over again, complete with exact dialogue and, sometimes, speech inflections and accents.

SPECIAL INTERESTS

Individuals with Asperger's disorder often have one or more all-encompassing special interests. These interests go far beyond those of a normal hobby, and can interfere with social skills, academics, and work. The amount of information on a particular topic that an individual with Asperger's may acquire can be quite staggering. Sometimes the area of interest may be typical for their age group—for example, baseball scores, video games, or cartoons—but the degree of interest sets the person with Asperger's apart. Other interests can be quite unusual, such as vacuum cleaners or train schedules. When the person reads or views the *same* material over and over again, this is a form of **perseveration**.

DESIRE FOR SAMENESS

While many people love surprises, individuals with Asperger's typically crave consistency. "Sameness" seems to provide comfort and security in a world with so many unwritten rules to decipher. Parents and teachers report that a change in routine—even a "fun" one like a party or school assembly—can often trigger a "meltdown" in a child with Asperger's disorder.

SENSORY AND MOTOR DIFFICULTIES

Many individuals with Asperger's disorder seem to be overly sensitive to light, sound, noise, smells, and/or touch. Clothing, especially tags and sock seams, may cause discomfort for them. Others seem to be *less* sensitive to sensory input than the average person, and not even notice, say, a scraped knee that would set another child crying. Some seek out unusual sensory activities, such as spinning. These are all examples of difficulties with *sensory integration dysfunction* (also known as **sensory processing dysfunction**). Many people with Asperger's also have difficulties with gross motor skills (e.g., running, jumping, riding a bicycle) and tend to be clumsy. Some also have difficulty with fine motor skills, such as handwriting.

SELF HELP AND ORGANIZATIONAL SKILLS

Contrary to the DSM-IV-TR (APA, 2000) criteria, clinicians today report that most individuals with Asperger's disorder have difficulties in self-help skills and adaptive behavior (Attwood, 2006). These difficulties extend logically from the other difficulties characteristic of individuals with Asperger's. For example, tying shoes and getting dressed require fine motor skills; shopping at the supermarket requires an ability to adapt to change (as groceries are often rearranged, or out of stock) and often some social interaction at the cash register. Going from class to class in middle school requires tolerating loud noise, being bumped into, and other students behaving in unpredictable ways. Many people with Asperger's disorder also have difficulties with **executive functions** (e.g., organizing and planning skills).

Not every person with Asperger's disorder manifests the same characteristics in number or degree. Therefore, it is important to keep in mind that Asperger's disorder is a spectrum disorder, ranging from relatively mild to quite severe. One person might be so impaired that he or she is unable to live independently, while another might be able to hold down a job—even be quite talented and successful at it—but still have significant difficulties in interpersonal relationships.

REFERENCES

American Psychiatric Association. (2000). *Diagnostic and statistical manual of mental disorders* (4th ed., text rev.). Washington, DC: Author.

Attwood, T. (1998). *Asperger's syndrome: A guide for parents and professionals.* London: Jessica Kingsley Publishers.

Attwood, T. Is there a difference between Asperger's syndrome and high-functioning autism? Retrieved August 25, 2006, from http://www.tonyattwood.com.au.

Wing, L. & Gould, J. (1979). Severe impairments of social interaction and associated abnormalities in children: Epidemiology and classification, *Journal of Autism and Developmental Disorders, 9,* 11–29.

FURTHER INFORMATION

Myles, B. S., & Simpson, R. L. (2002) Asperger syndrome: An overview of characteristics. *Focus on Autism and Other Developmental Disabilities, 17*(3), 132–137.

Myles, B. S., Barnhill, G. P., Hagiwara, T., Griswold, D. E., & Simpson, R. L. (2001). A synthesis of studies on the intellectual, academic, social/emotional and sensory characteristics of children and youth with Asperger syndrome. *Education and Training in Mental Retardation and Developmental Disabilities, 36*(3), 304–311.

Powers, M. D. (2002). *Asperger syndrome & your child: A parent's guide*. New York: Skylight Press.

LISA BARRETT MANN

ASPERGER SYNDROME DIAGNOSTIC SCALE (ASDS)

The Asperger Syndrome Diagnostic Scale (ASDS; Myles, Bock, & Simpson, 2000) is a norm-referenced measure that can help determine if a child or adolescent has Asperger syndrome. It is composed of 50 items, divided into five subscales: language, social, cognitive, sensory-motor, and maladaptive. Respondents indicate the presence or absence of certain characteristics in each area, and the resulting standard score shows the probability that the child or adolescent has s syndrome. Parents and teachers can complete the scale and share the results with their clinician.

The ASDS can be also used with confidence to document behavioral progress as a consequence of special intervention programs, target goals for change and intervention of the child's **Individualized Education Program**, and measure the characteristics of Asperger syndrome for research purposes.

See also Asperger's disorder; norm-referenced assessment.

REFERENCE

Myles, B. S., Bock, S. J., & Simpson, R. L. (2000). *Asperger Syndrome Diagnostic Scale*. Austin, TX: Pro-Ed.

SUSANA BERNAD-RIPOLL

ASPERGER SYNDROME SCREENING QUESTIONNAIRE (ASSQ)

The Asperger Syndrome Screening Questionnaire (ASSQ; Ehlers & Gillberg, 1993; Ehlers, Gillberg, & Wing 1999) was designed to screen for possible cases of Asperger syndrome or **high-functioning autism** in children. The ASSQ has cut-off scores for both parent and teacher ratings of the child's behavior, and there have been a range of studies published highlighting the **validity** of the instrument. For parent ratings, the true positive rate (those who score as having Asperger syndrome or high-functioning autism on the instrument and who really do have the condition) is 62 percent with a false positive rate (those who score as having AS or HFA but who do not have the condition) of 10 percent. For teacher ratings the true positive rate is 70 percent with a false positive rate of 9 percent.

See also Asperger's disorder.

REFERENCES

Ehlers, F., & Gillberg, C. (1993). The epidemiology of Asperger syndrome: A total population study. *Journal of Child Psychology and Psychiatry and Allied Disciplines, 34*, 1327–1350.

Ehlers, F., Gillberg, C., & Wing, L. (1999). A screening questionnaire for Asperger syndrome and other high functioning autism spectrum disorders in school age children. *Journal of Autism and Developmental Disorders, 29*, 129–142.

FIONA J. SCOTT

ASSESSMENT

Assessment is the overall process of gathering information, evaluating students, and making decisions based on what is learned. Assessment may involve many components including gathering background information, **direct observation**, formal and informal evaluation measures, report writing, team problem solving, interpretation of testing, decision making, and ongoing monitoring of student progress.

FURTHER INFORMATION

McMillan, J. H. (2004). *Educational research: Fundamentals for the consumer* (4th ed.). Boston: Allyn & Bacon.

PAUL G. LaCAVA

ASSESSMENT OF BASIC LANGUAGE AND LEARNING SKILLS (ABLLS)

The Assessment of Basic Language and Learning Skills (ABLLS; Partington & Sundberg, 1998) is an assessment tool, a curriculum, and a skills tracking system that can be used for students with language delays, autism, cognitive disabilities, and many other areas as well. The ABLLS is built around skills students use in everyday activities and by using task analyses for the different indicators. **Applied behavior analysis** is the theory around which the ABLLS is centered, incorporating verbal behavior strategies for teaching skills to students.

The introductory set for the ABLLS contains two books: The ABLLS protocol is used for each student to score how students perform on the skill sets and The ABLLS Scoring Instructions and IEP Development Guide. Once completed, the protocol becomes a curriculum tool individualized for the student.

There are four sections that make up the ABLLS protocol: (a) Basic Learner Skills, (b) Academic Skills, (c) Self-Help Skills, and (d) Motor Skills. Within each section skills are identified within 25 domain areas (e.g., visual performance, receptive language, motor imitation, play and leisure).

The ABLLS is not designed to provide age norms or to compare students to their peers. Typically developing students completing kindergarten or first grade should know the majority of the areas covered. Parents, teachers, **psychologists**, and other team members can complete the ABLLS as long as they know the student. The Scoring and Instruction Guide has strategies for teams to use to develop **Individualized Education Programs** for students.

REFERENCE

Partington, J., & Sundberg, M. (1998). *The assessment of basic learning and language skills.* Pleasant Hill, CA: Behavior Analysts, Inc.

BROOKE YOUNG

ASSISTIVE TECHNOLOGY

Several legislative acts or amendments have defined assistive technology (AT), **assistive technology device**, and **assistive technology service**. These include (a) Technology Related Assistance for Individuals with Disabilities Act of 1988 (PL 100-407) (Tech Act), (b) Individuals with Disabilities Education Act of 1990, (c) **Americans with Disabilities Act** of 1990, (d) Tech Act Amendments of 1994, and (e) Individuals with Disabilities Education Act Reauthorization of 1997.

First defined by the Technology Related Assistance for Individuals with Disabilities Act of 1988 (PL 100-407), AT means "any item, piece of equipment, or product system, whether acquired commercially, off the shelf, modified or customized, that is used to increase, maintain, or improve functional capabilities of individuals with disabilities." AT can be anything that makes it easier for the student to participate in class, complete homework, get around, turn things on, and communicate with friends and more (Assistive Technology Training Online, n.d.). AT should also be a required consideration in vocational training and in the workplace to increase independence. The Individuals with Disabilities Education Act of 1990 confirmed that AT is to be considered as part of a related service under special education and began the need for specific assessments in the area of AT for identification and selection.

The Americans with Disabilities Act of 1990 ensures access to buildings and employment; ADA ensures that employers could not and cannot discriminate due to disability, and that a reasonable accommodation must be made to allow for the individual to work. In addition ADA ensures that AT devices and services are included under this legislation to provide that reasonable accommodation.

The Tech Act of 1994 offers further clarification to what AT can do specifically related to vocational supports, natural environments, and workplace supports. It follows up on the provisions of ADA and further supports AT considering the advances in technology.

In the Reauthorization of IDEA 1997, AT is seen as a critical tool to provide further access to the general education classroom for all students. IDEA 1997 requires that AT must be considered as an option for all students that receive an IEP.

These acts ensure that AT needs must be identified on an individual basis and considered along with the child's other educational needs. Identification of AT needs must involve family members and a multidisciplinary team. Parents or IEP members can ask for additional evaluation or an independent evaluation to determine AT needs. When an evaluation is being conducted, the team should consider the following: fine-motor skills, communication, and alternatives to traditional learning approaches. Lack of availability of equipment or cost alone cannot be used as an excuse for denying an assistive technology service. If included in the IEP, assistive technology services and assistive technology devices must be provided at no cost to the family and, if so indicated, devices must be allowed to go home with the student. Parents always have the right to appeal if assistive technology services are denied.

REFERENCES

Americans with Disabilities Act, 42 U.S.C. §§ 12101-12213 (1990).

Assistive Technology Training Online. (n.d.). *Introduction to AT*. Retrieved November 29, 2006, from http://atto.buffalo.edu/registered/ATBasics/Foundation/intro/index.php.

Individuals with Disabilities Education Act Reauthorization of 1997 (Public Law 105-17).

Technology Related Assistance to Individuals with Disabilities Act of 1988 (P.L. 103-218).

Technology Related Assistance to Individuals with Disabilities Amendment Act of 1994 (P.L. 103-218).

FURTHER INFORMATION

Assistive Technology Training Online: http://atto.buffalo.edu.

Edyburn, D., Higgins, K., & Boone, R. (2006). *The handbook of special education technology research and practice*. Whitefish Bay, WI: Knowledge by Design, Inc.

TERRI COOPER SWANSON

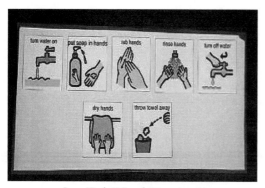

Low Tech "Visual Directions"

Mid Tech "Big Mac"

ASSISTIVE TECHNOLOGY DEVICE

There are a wide variety of assistive technology devices ranging from low tech to high tech. Low-tech devices, which do not involve batteries or any type of electronics, may include: (a) visual support strategies—typically low cost, hand made, and easy to use such as dry erase boards, clipboards, 3-ring binders, manila file folders, and photos; (b) tools to aid in writing, such as pencils or pens with a special grip; and (c) communication boards—portable communication boards allow the nonverbal student the means to be able to express their wants and needs. Mid tech includes battery-operated devices or simple electronic devices requiring limited advancements in technology, such as a tape recorder, Language Master, overhead projector, timer, calculator, or simple voice output device. High-tech devices are complex technological support strategies—typically "high" cost equipment. Examples include video cameras, computers and adaptive hardware, and complex voice output devices.

FURTHER INFORMATION
Assistive Technology Training Online: http://atto.buffalo.edu.
TERRI COOPER SWANSON

ASSISTIVE TECHNOLOGY SERVICE

Any individual with an **Individualized Education Program** can receive assistive technology services. Assistive technology service means any service that directly assists an individual with a disability in the selection, acquisition, or use of an **assistive technology device**. This may also include the evaluation of the needs of an individual with a disability, including a functional evaluation of the individual in the individual's customary environment; purchasing, leasing, or otherwise providing for the acquisition of assistive technology devices by individuals with disabilities; selecting, designing, fitting, customizing, adapting, applying, maintaining, repairing, or replacing of assistive technology devices; coordinating and using other therapies, interventions, or services with assistive technology devices, such as those associated with existing education and rehabilitation plans and programs; training or technical assistance for an individual with disabilities, or, where appropriate, the family of an individual with disabilities; and training or technical assistance for professionals (including individuals providing education and rehabilitation services), employers, or other individuals who provide services to, employ, or are otherwise substantially involved in the major life functions of individuals with disabilities.

FURTHER INFORMATION
Assistive Technology Training Online: http://atto.buffalo.edu.

TERRI COOPER SWANSON

ASSOCIATION METHOD

The Association Method is a phonics-based, multisensory, and multilevel curriculum designed to teach oral and written communication to people with severe communication disorders (Kotler, 2004), including autism spectrum disorders. This method develops and systematically associates each of the specific skills that must be coordinated for the development of the ability to understand and use oral communication. Multisensory teaching includes the use of auditory, visual, tactile, and motor-kinesthetic cues for learning.

Matched to the strengths and needs of each individual child, the curriculum progresses from sounds to syllables, to words of gradually increasing length, to basic sentences and questions, and then more advanced sentence structures. Ultimately, when sufficient language skills have been achieved, a transition is made to traditional textbook formats for instruction.

REFERENCE

Kotler, M. (2004). What is the association method? Retrieved October 17, 2006, from http://www.apraxia-kids.org/faqs/responsefromJcotler.html.

JAN L. KLEIN

ATTENTION DEFICIT HYPERACTIVITY DISORDERS (ADHD)

Attention deficit hyperactivity disorders (ADHD) are **developmental disorders** that include attention deficit/hyperactivity disorder, conduct disorder, and oppositional defiant disorder. There have been some arguments that hyperactivity disorders are part of the autism spectrum. While attention difficulties are seen in many children with autism spectrum disorders, this does not indicate that these disorders in their own right are part of the autism spectrum. In fact, presentation of difficulties in "pure" ADHD, conduct disorder and oppositional defiant disorder, while overlapping with behaviors seen in autism spectrum disorders (ASD), often have very different underlying motivations and a different quality to them. Also, such behaviors when seen in children with ASD do not necessarily require an additional diagnosis. This is dependent on the degree to which difficulties and behaviors interfere with functioning over and above the ASD. However, research does indicate the prevalence of such difficulties among children diagnosed with ASD. Gillberg (2002, p. 48) reports that the majority of children meeting diagnostic criteria for Asperger syndrome also met criteria for ADHD. In a recent Swedish study, Tonge, Brereton, Gray, & Stewart (1999) found that children and adolescents with autism spectrum conditions presented with more psychopathology, and were more disruptive, more antisocial, and more anxious than their nonspectrum peers.

CHARACTERISTICS OF ADHDS

Hyperactivity disorders are characterized by substantial restlessness, impulsiveness, and inattentiveness (Goodman & Scott, 2005). The key issue is in the lack of control over levels of activity, rather than the activity itself. Behaviors include fiddling with objects or clothing, getting up and walking about when the child should be seated, fidgeting or squirming when seated, being easily distractible and having difficulty staying on task, or a tendency to switch activities frequently. Commonly associated features include aggressive, antisocial, or defiant behaviors such that classification with the ***Diagnostic and Statistical Manual of Mental Disorders*** (DSM-IV-TR; APA, 2000) can often lead to a dual diagnosis of ADHD and conduct disorder or ADHD and oppositional defiant disorder in many children (Goodman & Scott, 2005). However, both hyperactivity disorders and "pure" conduct or oppositional disorders are characterized by impulsive behaviors, and by wandering in the classroom.

Children with hyperactivity disorders often have difficulties with social relationships. They may be rejected by peers who find the impulsive behaviors and interruptions during class and other activities a nuisance. There may be inappropriate calling out or rude or cheeky comments to adults and authority figures.

Other associated difficulties in some children with hyperactivity disorders include specific learning difficulties, soft neurological signs such as general clumsiness, and a history of developmental delay.

Conduct disorder and oppositional defiant disorder are characterized by antisocial behavior, failure to control behavior in a socially acceptable way, aggression, and defiance. Criteria for conduct disorder according to the DSM-IV-TR (APA, 2000) is that the child has shown at least four of the following behaviors for at least 6 months: (a) often losing temper, (b) often arguing with adults, (c) often defying adult requests or rules, (d) often deliberately annoying others, (e) often shifting blame to others, (f) often touchy or easily annoyed, (g) often angry and resentful, and (h) often spiteful or vindictive.

Criteria for oppositional defiant disorder according to the DSM-IV-TR (APA, 2000) is that there has been at least 12 months with at least three of the following behaviors: (a) often bullying, threatening, or intimidating; (b) often starting fights; (c) using serious weapons in fights; (d) being physically cruel to people; (e) being physically cruel to animals; (f) stealing with force; (g) forcing someone into sexual acts; (h) fire-setting to cause damage; (i) destroying other's property; (j) breaking into cars or houses; (k) conning others; (l) stealing without force; (m) often going out at night without permission; (n) running away from home overnight at least twice; and (o) often truanting, with truanting beginning before age 13.

REFERENCES
American Psychiatric Association. (2000). *Diagnostic and statistical manual of mental* disorders (4th ed., text rev.). Washington, DC: Author.
Gillberg, C. (2002). *A guide to Asperger syndrome.* Cambridge: Cambridge University Press.
Goodman, R., & Scott, S. (2005). *Child psychiatry* (2nd ed.). Oxford: Blackwell Publishing.
Tonge, B. J., Brereton, A. V., Gray, K. M., & Stewart, L. E. (1999). Behavioural and emotional disturbance in high-functioning autism and Asperger Syndrome. *Autism: International Journal of Research and Practice, 3,* 117–130.

FURTHER INFORMATION
Rutter, M. (1998). *Antisocial behaviour by young people.* Cambridge: Cambridge University Press.
Taylor, E. (1998). Clinical foundations of hyperactivity research. *Behavioural Brain Research, 94,* 11–24.

FIONA J. SCOTT

ATTRIBUTION

According to Frith (1991), the ability to represent mental states such as thoughts, feelings, or beliefs is impaired among individuals with autism. Such perspective-taking deficits are a basis for the quality of social behaviors most frequently observed for this population (Meyer & Minshew, 2002; Jolliffe & Baron-Cohen, 1999). It is also interesting to note that when parents are asked about their children's performance in these areas, they consistently share significant concerns about their children's skills. However, when the children are asked to rate themselves in the same areas, they show no significant concerns (Barnhill, Hagiwara, Myles, & Simpson, 2000). Further review of current research shows that individuals with Asperger syndrome have a heightened awareness for details coupled with deficits in organization of information, increasing the potential to severely affect problem solving and reasoning skills (Minshew, Goldstein and Siegel, 1997). Just from this sampling of research findings, it is not impossible to see how individuals with autism spectrum disorders (ASD) are challenged daily in many ways as they attempt to successfully interact in the social world around them. One area that holds promise for improving social function is that of attribution retraining.

Attribution patterns can be defined as how individuals under differing circumstances assume causation of words or deeds. A substantial research effort in the early 1970s resulted in the Attributional Theory of Achievement Motivation pioneered by Weiner et al. (1971). Originally tested in the learning disabilities community to determine factors influencing academic achievement, researchers were looking to explain the link between the children's causal ascriptions for achievement outcomes and their behavioral responses to academic success and failure. The results concluded that attributions are clearly related to motivation and affect performance (Weiner, 1986). Our ability to manipulate these attributional beliefs about the sources and causes of success and failure allows us to maintain some control over our own experiences and is directly related to our self-esteem and successful self-determination (Covington, 1985).

It is reasonable to suggest that if a person does not correctly attribute someone else's thoughts, words, or deeds on a regular basis that it may cause frequent misunderstandings during social interactions, and if left untreated could cause that person to become defensive or develop "hostile" attribution over time in an effort to avoid unpleasant interactions. These aggressive or hostile attribution patterns can be maladaptive when considering the potential for future behavior changes (Baumeister, 1989; Weiner, 1986) and lend itself to the development of clinical depression as proposed in the reformulated Learned Helplessness Theory (Metalsky, Abramson, Seligman, Semmel, & Peterson, 1982).

So where is the connection between attribution and the world of autism? One study shows that a third of adolescents with Asperger syndrome have pessimistic, maladaptive attribution styles; Barnhill (2001) and Baron-Cohen have spent a considerable amount of time advancing research that individuals with autism spectrum disorders are universally affected by deficits in theory of mind, which is our ability as a person to assume the emotions or activities going on in another person's head. Baron-Cohen refers to these activities as *mentalizing* and on numerous occasions has found that individuals with ASDs are not able to take on the perspective of others and accurately determine their thoughts or motivations. It is widely thought that people with autism do not enjoy what is referred to as the *Shared Attention Mechanism*. A key component of our theory of mind, it is the drive we should have toward establishing what is a shared interest between oneself and another person. It is a way to get on the same "wave length" with each other (Baron-Cohen, 1997, p. 66). Along with the previously mentioned deficits, if those with autism are not "hard wired" necessarily to have that ability or interest in establishing a common ground socially with others, it is easier to imagine that misunderstanding or perceiving social situations could occur regularly.

To incorporate attribution retraining as the first of many steps to increase social fluidity, example diagrams illustrate the following three variables in attribution retraining as identified by Weiner (1986):

1. Is the issue internal or external in locus? Did it happen because of something about you or something else?
2. Is the issue stable or unstable? Is it something you think will always happen?
3. Is it controllable or uncontrollable? Can you do anything about it?

Here is a real life example:

You are sitting in a restaurant and there is a screaming baby at the table next to you! The average individual with Asperger syndrome or PDD-NOS is likely to think that the screaming is internal to them because it hurts their ears, that it will NEVER stop and that they have no control over it, essentially coming up with a depressing or negative assessment of the situation.

The solution using attribution retraining would go something like this:

1. The problem is outside of me. A baby near me is having trouble and crying.
2. The situation really isn't stable. Sooner or later the baby will have to stop crying.
3. I do have some control over the situation in that I can ask to leave the room, use self-calming strategies or maybe change the table in order to make it less offensive to me.

As you can see, this assessment is still an uncomfortable situation but much more positively assessed, leaving room for the possibility of resolution to everyone's benefit without notions of purposeful or hurtful behaviors and emotionally charged responses. It is possible to use this methodology to improve the person's attribution pattern so that they are more consistently able to assess their circumstances and then select an appropriate response. While attribution is not the entire process of social problem solving, it should be thought of as an integral part of the successful problem solving experience.

REFERENCES

Barnhill, G. (2001). Social attributions and depression in adolescents with Asperger syndrome. *Focus on Autism and Other Disabilities, 16,* 45–53.

Barnhill, G., Hagiwara, T., Myles, B. S., & Simpson, R. L. (2000). Asperger syndrome: A study of the cognitive profiles of 37 children and adolescents. *Focus on Autism and Other Developmental Disabilities, 15,* 146–153.

Baron-Cohen, S. (1997). *Mindblindness: An essay on autism and theory of mind.* Cambridge, MA: MIT Press.

Baumeister, R. F. (1989). *Masochism and the self.* Hillsdale, NJ: Lawrence Earlbaum Associates.

Covington, M. V. (1985). Anatomy of failure-induced anxiety: The role of cognitive mediators. In R. Schwarzer (Ed.), *Self-related cognitions in anxiety and motivation.* Hillsdale, NJ: Lawrence Erlbaum Associates.

Frith, U. (1991). *Autism and Asperger syndrome.* Cambridge: Cambridge University Press.

Jolliffe, T., & Baron-Cohen, S. (1999). The Strange Stories Test: A replication with high-functioning adults with autism or Asperger syndrome. *Journal of Autism and Developmental Disorders, 29,* 395–406.

Metalsky, G. I., Abramson, L. Y., Seligman, M. E., Semmel, A., & Peterson, C. (1982). Attributional styles and life events in the classroom: Vulnerability and invulnerability to depressive mood reactions. *Journal of Personal and Social Psychology, 43,* 612–617.

Meyer, J., & Minshew, N. (2002). An update on neurocognitive profiles in Asperger syndrome and high-functioning autism. *Focus on Autism and Other Disabilities, 17,* 152–160.

Minshew, N., Goldstein, G., & Siegel, D. J. (1997). Neuropsychological functioning in autism: Profile of a complex information processing disorder. *Journal of the International Neuropsychological Society, 3,* 303–316.

Weiner, B. (1986). *Attribution theory of motivation and emotion.* New York: Springer-Verlag.

Weiner, B., Frieze, I., Kukla, A., Reed, L., Rest, S., & Rosenbaum, R. M. (1971). *Perceiving the causes of success and failure.* New York: General Learning Press.

FURTHER INFORMATION

Ozonoff, S., Rogers, S., & Pennington, B. (1991). Asperger syndrome: Evidence of an empirical difference from high functioning autism. *Journal of Child Psychology and Psychiatry, 32,* 1081–1105.

Szatmari, P. (1991). Asperger's syndrome: Diagnosis, treatment and outcome. *Psychiatric Clinics of North America, 14,* 1, 81–92.

SHERRY MOYER

ATYPICAL BEHAVIOR

Atypical behavior refers to any behavior or combination of behaviors found to be extreme. Areas of atypical behaviors commonly presented by individuals with autism spectrum disorders include temperament, attention, attachment, social behavior, play, vocal and oral behavior, senses and movement, self-stimulation and self-injury, and neurobehavioral state.

MELANIE D. HARMS

AUDIOLOGIST

The role of an audiologist is to evaluate an individual's hearing to determine if there is a hearing loss. Once a hearing loss has been detected, the audiologist will make recommendations for services needed, which might include **speech therapy**, assistance from a medical professional, or an amplification device.

KATHERINE E. COOK

AUDITORY INTEGRATION TRAINING

Auditory Integration Training (AIT) is an intervention designed to help those with auditory processing problems. Consisting of 10 hours of listening to electronically modified music on headphones, typically done in two half-hour sessions a day over 10–12 days, AIT is intended to decrease auditory sensitivities and slightly improve overall hearing. It is also thought to positively influence behavior, social interactions, attention, and communication. It is purported to aid individuals with a variety of disabilities including ADHD, ADD, central auditory processing disorder, autism, and dyslexia. It can be used for both children and adults, but it is not recommended to be given prior to age 5 as the ear is not fully developed until then.

AIT was created by ear, nose, and throat physician Dr. Guy Bérard in France in the 1960s, as he dealt with his own loss of hearing. Having studied briefly under

Dr. Alfred Tomatis but unsatisfied with his approach, Dr. Bérard's idea was to develop a sort of physical therapy for the auditory system. Over 5 years, he built his first AIT device, then came to produce the AudioKinetron and the Earducator. There are now other AIT devices on the market as well. Dr. Bérard administered AIT to over several thousand individuals before retiring and reports great success; however, he never carried out any research or took data. He published a book explaining AIT and the theory behind it titled *Hearing Equals Behavior* (originally published in French in 1982 as *Audition égale comportement,* translated and published in English in 1993). However, it was the book *Sound of a Miracle* by Annabel Stehli (1991) that brought public attention to this intervention. Stehli wrote about her daughter, Georgianna, diagnosed with autism, who was "cured" after receiving AIT from Dr. Bérard.

Before intervention is begun, a child is given an audiogram to determine the frequencies to which the child is hypersensitive, represented by auditory peaks in their performance on the test. Other tests may also be conducted to find the decibel level to be used as well as other measurements of hearing and auditory sensitivities. Based on these tests the child then listens to music through headphones, which is electronically processed in two possible ways (can be used separately or both simultaneously). One is through modulation, whereby using wide-band filters the AIT device randomly dampens different frequencies of the music as it plays. The dulling of one frequency may last from a fraction of a second to a few seconds. Although not always done, the music may also be modified through narrow-band filters. These filters dampen the frequencies to which the child is hypersensitive. However, this requires accurate audiometric measures that may be difficult to attain depending on the functioning level of the child. If there is any doubt of the accuracy of audiometric tests, it is better to not use the narrow-band filters rather than risk using the wrong ones. Audiograms are usually given again in the middle of treatment and finally 3 months after treatment has finished. The delay in giving the final exam is Bérard's observation that results often take up to 3 months to appear. Bérard also reports that during, and for several weeks after the intervention, a client's behavior may worsen.

Although Bérard himself never carried out any research regarding the efficacy of AIT, there have been over 20 studies conducted since the early 1990s. Nonetheless, there is still a great deal of controversy regarding this technique and its efficacy. Proponents and skeptics alike, including the American Speech-Hearing-Language Association (ASHA) and the American Academy of Audiology, emphasize that AIT is still in the investigative stages and should only be undertaken if this is clearly understood by the family or individual seeking therapy. Both sides of the debate find serious flaws in opposing studies and there is certainly a lack of studies that can stand up to rigorous scientific scrutiny. Frequent critiques arise because of the lack of sufficient numbers of participants, control groups, and adequate, objective assessments. Finally, much skepticism finds its justification in the lack of understanding of how and why AIT is effective. Some critics assert that explanations given by Bérard are contrary to current accepted science in the field. While there are several proposed explanations for improvement as a result of AIT, there is no proof for any of them.

It should be noted that the Food and Drug Administration (FDA) has not yet approved AIT devices for marketing. Therefore, by law no claim can be made as to the effectiveness and safety of AIT. Practice of AIT requires a special investigative device exemption (IDE) filed with the FDA, and charges should be nominal and not result in profit for the professional administering AIT.

REFERENCES

Bérard, G. (1993). *Hearing equals behavior.* New Canaan, CT: Keats Publishing.

Stehli, A. (1991). *Sound of a miracle.* New York: Doubleday Dell.

FURTHER INFORMATION

American Speech-Language-Hearing Association. (2004). Auditory Integration Training. *ASHA Supplement 24,* in press. Retrieved June 27, 2005, from http://www.asha.org/NR/rdonlyres/A0067509-9F38-458A-A065-1B9312ECF990/0/v1PSAIT.pdf.

Dawson, G., & Watling, R. (2000). Interventions to facilitate auditory, visual, and motor integration in autism: A review of the evidence. *Journal of Autism and Developmental Disorders, 30*(5), 415–421.

Edelson, S., Arin, D., Bauman, M., Lukas, S., Rudy, J., Sholar, M., & Rimland, B. (1999). Auditory integration training: A double-blind study of behavioral and electrophysiological effects in people with autism. *Focus on Autism and Other Developmental Disabilities, 14*(2), 73–81.

Gravel, J. S. (1994). Auditory integration training: Placing the burden of proof. *American Journal of Speech-Language Pathology: A Journal of Clinical Practice, 3*(2), 25–29.

Mudford, O., Cross, B., Breen, S., Cullen, C., Reeves, D., Gould, J., & Douglas, J. (2000). Auditory integration training for children with autism: No behavior benefits detected. *American Journal on Mental Retardation, 105*(2), 118–129.

Rimland, B., & Edelson, S. (1994). Is theory better than chicken soup? *American Journal of Speech-Language Pathology, 3*(2), 38–40.

Rimland, B., & Edelson, S. (1994). The effects of auditory integration training on autism. *American Journal of Speech-Language Pathology, 3*(2), 16–24.

Tharpe, A. M. (1999). Auditory integration training: The magical mystery cure. *Language, Speech & Hearing Services in Schools, 30*(4), 378–383.

KATIE BASSITY

AUGMENTATIVE AND ALTERNATIVE COMMUNICATION

Augmentative and alternative communication (AAC) refers to an array of systems designed to compensate for oral or written communication impairments (American Speech-Language-Hearing Association [ASHA], 2005). The systems either supplement the existing communication modality or are the primary form of communication. The purpose of AAC is to enable individuals to express wants and needs, transfer information, support interpersonal closeness, and establish social etiquette (Light, 1988; Light, Parsons, & Drager, 2002) so that they can "efficiently and effectively engage in a variety of interactions and participate in activities of their choice" (Beukelman & Mirenda, 2005, p. 8). AAC systems include symbols, aids, techniques, and strategies (ASHA, 2004, 2005).

Individuals with autism spectrum disorders demonstrate an array of communication difficulties including limited comprehension and use of language and the nonverbal aspects of interactions. Frequently these difficulties coincide with the emergence of behavioral difficulties, frustration, and/or withdrawal. The varied AAC options currently available allow for individualization in the selection and design of an AAC system for a child or an adult with autism spectrum disorders (ASD). A system can be developed to meet the needs of a child who is just beginning to understand cause-and-effect relationships and the turn-taking aspects of human communication. Systems can also change over time to address the communicative ability of individuals who are able to express wants and needs as well as construct unique utterances specific to educational, vocational, or leisure contexts. Therefore, AAC systems for individuals with ASD address behavioral, language, social, learning, and literacy needs. Interdisciplinary team assessment and intervention practices guide professionals and families in identifying, developing, and utilizing AAC systems. Teams should monitor progress and modify the system based on therapeutic evidence in order to address the changing needs of the individual.

SYMBOLS

Many AAC systems use symbols that represent ideas, events, or objects. The level of abstraction, or representation, varies across symbols. Symbols can be concrete, or transparent, clearly representing an idea, event, or object. These types of symbols include natural gestures and signs, life-size or miniature objects, graphic representations such as photos, or color pictures, as well as some line drawings and Rebus symbols (Beukelman & Mirenda, 2005). Other symbols are abstract, or opaque, where the referent or relationship between the symbol and the event is not immediately apparent. These types of symbols include words, some gestures, iconic line drawings, and Rebus symbols, as well as more abstract and complex iconic systems such as Blisssymbols (Silverman, 1995). Some commercially available symbol programs include Boardmaker (Mayer Johnson LLC, 2004) and DynaSyms (Poppin & Company, 2005).

The comprehension and use of symbols is integral and essential to language development and thus successful use of an AAC system. Given that people with ASD possess difficulties with symbolic thought or language (APA, 2000), it is important to consider the available array of concrete objects and oral, gestural, and graphic symbols so that representation of ideas within the system best matches the individual's ability. In the process of developing and implementing an AAC system, symbol comprehension and use is taught and enhanced. Consequently, the level of representation can change over time from concrete objects to iconic symbols or gestures as the individual's symbolic thought or language ability grows. Systems can integrate multiple sensory components where an object or graphic symbol is paired with texture and/or an auditory dimension. Doing so can support comprehension and learning and result in increased meaningful use of the system. For example, a young child with minimal language skills may use a miniature bus affixed to a voice output device that sings "the Wheels on the Bus" when depressed. The concrete object paired with the verbal cue provides the child with comprehension support. Over time and with consistent presentation, the child is more likely to spontaneously use the device to signal "time for the bus."

AIDS

AAC systems also include a variety of aids or devices referred to as low (unaided), medium, or high (aided) technology, depending upon the level of computer technology involved. Low-technology, electronically unaided systems include natural forms of communication such as functional gestures, sign language, and facial expressions. Medium-technology aids consist of physical and graphic symbols in the absence of electronic technology. Objects or photographs, color or black and white line drawings, iconic representations, alphabet boards, or words organized on concrete displays such as poster boards, wallets, flip charts, vests, or within binders are all medium-technology aids (Beukelman & Mirenda, 2005).

Finally, high-technology devices utilize electronic and/or computer technology and voice output. Speech-generating devices (SGD) produce speech via synthesized (electronic) or digital (recorded) productions paired with some type of symbol represented on either a fixed, dynamic, or hybrid visual display. Fixed displays include overlays where symbols occupy a fixed location. Dynamic display devices use LCD screens that allow the symbols to be manipulated using various functions on the device. Hybrid systems incorporate both fixed and dynamic symbol displays. Results of research on the effect of SGDs on the behavioral, linguistic, and social functioning of children with ASD have been positive (Beukelman & Mirenda, 2005). Some contemporary high-technology SGDs include Tech Speak (Liberator Co., 2005), Chat PC (Saltillo, 2005), Macaw (ZYGO Industries, 2005), Dynamo (DynaVox Technologies, 2005), and ChatBox (Prentke Romich Co., 2005).

TECHNIQUES

The technique used to activate symbols on medium- and high-technology systems varies across devices. Symbol selection depends upon the individual's visual, auditory, and motor skills. Direct selection options include physical pressure, touch, or removal of symbols; use of eye gaze or index finger to point to the symbol; as well as speech recognition systems (Beukelman & Mirenda, 2005). Various activation options include timed activation, release activation, visual or auditory scanning, and enlarged pictures. Timed and release activation options can be adjusted to assist individuals who tap repeatedly or those with low muscle tone that results in difficulty depressing symbols (Beukelman & Mirenda, 2005). Visual scanning uses a light to highlight symbol options and auditory scanning uses a tone; these systems can also be combined. Finally, tactile options such as raised grids to separate symbols can support successful activation of desired symbols.

STRATEGIES

The strategy with which specific symbols are stored affects the timing of the communicative act, formulation of ideas, and the rate of communication (Beukelman & Mirenda, 2005). Strategy refers to the amount of information or number of messages an SGD can hold, which ranges from a single message (single-hit device) to hundreds of messages arranged according to topics. Messages can be arranged by levels, or overlays, similar to computer files and stored within the device's electronic system. Complete messages can be stored individually within one symbol. Symbols representing single- or multiple-word messages may be sequenced together or "chained" in order to formulate more novel ideas, and some SGDs integrate a spelling keyboard function. Many devices allow flexibility in moving from single-hit productions of complete utterances to chaining of ideas and spelling options.

SELECTION OF AAC DEVICE

AAC must address the individual's changing needs. Light (1989) provides a framework that includes analysis of the individual's linguistic, operational, social, and strategic competence. Linguistic competence involves identifying the individual's ability to understand and use symbol systems. Some AAC experts (Beukelman & Mirenda, 2005; Cress, 2002; Harwood, Warran, & Yoder, 2002; Light et al., 2002) discuss linguistic competence by separating the beginning communicator who does not understand or use symbols and the beginning communicator with emerging symbolic understanding from the communicator with more advanced academic needs. Given the severity and range of language impairments found among individuals with ASD, this distinction is important.

Individuals who are beginning communicators with minimal symbolic understanding require support to develop foundational communication skills including cause-effect and object permanence awareness, imitation, joint attention, and use of a natural gestural system. Successful communication development at this stage requires that the communicative partner learn facilitative strategies such as optimizing responsiveness, focusing on what the child is attending to, recognizing and interpreting communicative attempts, creating predictable routines, and modeling language using simplified utterances, commenting, expansions, and elaborations (Siegle & Cress, 2002). At this stage, low- and medium-technology AAC is initially beneficial (Beukelman & Mirenda, 2005).

As children develop into beginning communicators with emerging symbolic skills, medium-technology AAC may be beneficial. These children are ready to use object and graphic symbols to make choices and requests, gain attention, protest or reject, and self-select symbols (Beukelman & Mirenda, 2005). At this point, social and strategic competence as defined by Light (1989) emerges and can be therapeutically addressed. That is, children are ready to learn how to initiate, maintain, develop, repair, and end conversations using the AAC device. Turn-taking ability and use of the device to ask questions, comment, answer, and acknowledge emerges along with communication breakdown coping strategies (Light, 1989). As mentioned earlier, careful selection of symbols, messages, and aids that support social and strategic competence is critical for individuals with ASD.

Since adaptive social functioning is essential to programming for children with ASD, consideration of the behaviors a child with ASD uses to protest and gain attention is important. AAC systems can assist individuals with ASD in developing adaptive protesting behaviors using messages such as "I want to be alone"; "don't touch me"; "it is too loud in here"; "no thanks"; or "not yet." Additionally, the inherent human behavior of gaining attention can be addressed. Indeed, research has shown that integrating AAC with Functional Communication Training (FCT) is effective in reducing maladaptive, while increasing adaptive, attention gaining behaviors (Durand, 1993, 1999; Mirenda, 1997).

Operational competence considerations balance the demands of the individual's developmental and chronological ages in order to support functional and meaningful interactions. Systems must be adaptable to account for anticipated growth but be useable in the present. Portability and durability of the device are critical considerations affecting access across communicative contexts. Increased access translates to increased opportunity for use, which promotes increased skill, and is therefore an essential programming component. Additionally, the cultural background, age, and gender of the individual must be considered. For example, the wording of messages and the voice used to transmit the message on the SGD must match that of the individual using the system and his/her social network (Beukelman & Mirenda, 2005).

TRANSDISCIPLINARY TEAM

Assessment and intervention requires a transdisciplinary approach. Beukelman and Mirenda (2005) propose use of the Participation Model, which considers intrinsic and extrinsic variables influencing AAC use. With this model, individual independence, personal characteristics, and opportunities of use are cohesively addressed. Individual independence involves analysis of the level of support and prompts needed for successful utilization of the AAC system. Addressing personal characteristics involves formal and informal analysis and treatment of the individual's cognitive, language, social, hearing, vision, behavioral, motor, and literacy abilities. The team must also consider and plan for extrinsic strengths and challenges. For example, studies (Angelo, Jones, & Kokoska, 1995; Angelo, Kokoska, & Jones, 1996) examining parental concerns have identified that parents of children who use AAC worry about acquiring additional knowledge of and training in the use, maintenance, and programming of AAC devices along with the ability to plan for the future and integrate the device across settings. Community awareness and support, funding, parent and professional training and accessibility to devices are other concerns expressed by parents (Angelo, Jones, et al., 1995; Angelo, Kokoska, et al., 1996). Assessment tools such as the Wisconsin Assistive Technology Initiative Assistive Technology Assessment (WATI, 2004) and the Augmentative Communicative Assessment Profile (Goldman, 2002) allow for analysis of intrinsic and extrinsic variables when considering high- and low-technology systems for children.

AAC METHODS FOR INDIVIDUALS WITH ASD

Various AAC methods have been discussed in the literature specifically for use with individuals with ASD. One method, **Facilitated Communication** (FC), involves the use of a second person who manually supports or facilitates the use of the AAC system with the person with ASD (Biklen, 1990). Controversy surrounding this method has focused on the authenticity of the messages produced. Given the research, numerous professional organizations, including ASHA, have issued position statements indicating that FC should be viewed as an experimental method.

Another method used with children with ASD is the **Picture Exchange Communication System** (PECS; Frost & Bondy, 2002). This method utilizes prescribed applied behavioral analysis (ABA), whereby very systematic verbal productions are paired with the use of tangible symbols. PECS requires use of a supportive third person, or assistant, who prompts the individual to physically remove a symbol and give it to the communicative partner, or facilitator. Thus, sharing communication with a partner is emphasized. Over time, the level of prompts and reliance on the assistant is faded, and use of symbols for a variety of social-communicative purposes is expanded.

AAC systems, or **assistive technology**, also support more advanced academic and communicative needs, specifically access to written communication and literacy support. For example, **assistive technology devices**, like label makers, allow the individual to type out short answers and affix them to worksheets. Word processors are considered assistive technology when used to compensate for fine-motor difficulties. Touch screens provide access to computer technology and are an effective tool in supporting teaching of concepts, literacy development, and computer access. Finally, speech-recognition word processing systems are also available and may prove to be an effective tool for some individuals with ASD.

AAC systems used to organize time and create predictability include various schedule boards, which are different and separate from systems used for oral communication. Schedule boards can integrate objects, pictures, or print (Quill, 1989). Some higher functioning individuals with ASD can benefit from using high technology, computerized scheduling systems such as a Palm Pilots or Blackberries. Schedule systems used to represent part of or an entire day are referred to as macroschedules. Schedules can also represent steps needed to complete a particular task, such as hand washing, and are referred to as microschedules (Quill, 1989).

Varied AAC systems are available to enhance the social, communicative, linguistic, behavioral, academic, and vocational lives of individuals with ASD. An interdisciplinary team approach is necessary to assist in identifying the AAC system best suited to meet an individual's current needs. Initially, an assessment of the individual's cognitive, motor, language, and social skills is essential to identifying a system that matches his/her current ability. Additionally, planning must consider strategies that will support the individual's further growth as a communicator and learner. AAC systems are not static and should be modified as the individual grows and gains skills. Successful and consistent integration of AAC systems across the multiple environments a person encounters can elicit and support adaptive functioning and consequently learning and socialization.

REFERENCES

American Psychiatric Association. (2000). *Diagnostic and statistical manual of mental disorders* (4th ed., text rev.). Washington, DC: Author.

American Speech-Language-Hearing Association. (2004). Roles and responsibilities of speech-language pathologists with respect to augmentative and alternative communication: Technical report. *ASHA Supplement, 24*, 1–17.

American Speech-Language-Hearing Association. (2005). *Roles and responsibilities of speech-language pathologist with respect to alternative communication: Position statement.* Retrieved June 1, 2006, from http://www.asha.org.

Angelo, D., Jones, S., & Kokoska, S. (1995). Family perspective on augmentative and alternative communication: Families of young children. *Augmentative and Alternative Communication, 11*, 193–201.

Angelo, D., Kokoska, S., & Jones, S. (1996). Family perspective on augmentative and alternative communication: Families of adolescents and young adult. *Augmentative and Alternative Communication, 12*, 13–22.

Beukelman, D. R., & Mirenda, P. (2005). *Augmentative and alternative communication: Supporting children and adults with complex communication needs* (3rd ed.). Baltimore: Brookes Publishing Co.

Biklen, D. (1990). Communication unbound: Autism and praxis. *Harvard Educational Review, 60*, 291–314.

Cress, C. J. (2002). Expanding children's early augmented behaviors to support symbolic development. In J. Reichle, D. R. Beukelman, & J. C. Light (Eds.), *Exemplary practice for beginning communicators: Implications for AAC* (pp. 219–272). Baltimore: Brookes Publishing Co.

Durand, V. M. (1993). Functional communication training using assistive devices: Effects on challenging behavior. *Augmentative and Alternative Communication, 9*, 168–176.

Durand, V. M. (1999). Functional communication training using assistive devices: Recruiting natural communities of reinforcement. *Journal of Applied Behavior Analysis, 32*, 247–267.

DynaVox Technologies. (2005). *Dynamo.* Pittsburgh, PA: Author.

Frost, L., & Bondy, A. (2002). *Picture exchange communication system training manual* (2nd ed.). Newark, DE: Pyramid Education Products.

Goldman, H. (2002). *Augmentative Communication Assessment Profile*. London: Speechmark Publishing.

Harwood, K., Warren, S., & Yoder, P. (2002). The importance of responsivity in developing contingent exchanges with beginning communicators. In J. Reichle, D. R. Beukelman, & J. C. Light (Eds.), *Exemplary practice for beginning communicators: Implications for AAC* (pp. 59–96). Baltimore: Brookes Publishing Co.

Liberator Company. (2005). *Tech Speak*. London: UK: Author.

Light, J. (1988). Interaction involving individuals using augmentative and alternative communication systems: State of the art and future directions. *Augmentative and Alternative Communication, 4,* 66–78.

Light, J. (1989). Toward a definition of communicative competence for individuals using augmentative and alternative communication systems. *Augmentative and Alternative Communication, 5,* 137–144.

Light, J. C., Parsons, A. R., & Drager, K. (2002). "There's more to life than cookies": Developing interactions for social closeness with beginning communicators who use AAC. In J. Reichle, D. R., Beukelman, & J. C. Light (Eds.), *Exemplary practice for beginning communicators: Implications for AAC* (pp. 187–218). Baltimore: Brookes Publishing Co.

Mayer Johnson LLC. (2004). *Boardmaker*. Solana Beach, CA: Author.

Mirenda, P. (1997). Supporting individuals with challenging behavior through functional communication training and AAD: Research review: *Augmentative and Alternative Communication, 13*(4), 207–225.

Poppin & Company. (2005). *DynaSyms*, Unity, ME: Author.

Prentke Romich Company. (2005). *ChatBox*. Wooster, OH: Author.

Quill, K. (1989). *Educating children with autism*. Albany, NY: Delmar.

Saltillo. (2005). *Chat PC*. Millersburg, OH: Author.

Siegle, E. B., & Cress, C. J. (2002). Overview of the emergence of early AAC behaviors: Progression from communicative to symbolic skills. In J. Reichle, D. R. Beukelman, & J. C. Light (Eds.), *Exemplary practice for beginning communicators: Implications for AAC* (pp. 25–57). Baltimore: Brookes Publishing Co.

Silverman, F. (1995). *Communication for the speechless* (3rd ed.). Needham Heights, MA: Allyn & Bacon.

Wisconsin Assistive Technology Initiative. (2004). *W.A.T.I. Assistive Technology Assessment*. Retrieved June 1, 2006, from http://www.wati.org.

Zygo Industries. (2005). *MacCaw*, Portland, OR: Author.

LISA R. AUDET

AUTISM. *See* Autistic Disorder

AUTISM BEHAVIOR CHECKLIST (ABC)

The Autism Behavior Checklist (ABC; Krug, Arick, & Almond, 1993) is an independent autism screening tool of 57 items completed by parents. The assessment relies on **direct observation** of the student and historical information provided by parents and other people knowledgeable about the student. This tool is designed to assist in the diagnosis of autism rather than provide programming information about treatment. The ABC is a subtest of the *Autism Screening Instrument for Educational Planning* (ASIEP-2).

REFERENCE
King, D. A., Arick, J. R. & Almond, P. J. (1993). *Autism screening instrument for educational planning*. Austin, TX: Pro-Ed.

BROOKE YOUNG

AUTISM DIAGNOSTIC INTERVIEW–REVISED (ADI-R)

The Autism Diagnostic Interview–Revised (ADI-R; Lord, Rutter, & LeCouteur, 1994; Rutter, LeCouteur, & Lord, 2003) is a detailed parental history interview designed to identify individuals with autism. The interview covers early developmental history and current and early behavior presentation in each of the triad areas of the autism spectrum, and includes algorithms that allow the assessor to categorize presentation of autism features as measured against DSM-IV-TR and ICD-10 requirements, as well as provides extra non-algorithm information to enable appropriate diagnostic subtypes on the spectrum to be identified, and severity of presentation of symptoms. The ADI-R has been shown to be good at distinguishing autism from non-autism in clinical populations, but it does not in itself differentiate between core autism and the broader autism spectrum presentations. It was designed to be used in conjunction with the **Autism Diagnostic Observation Schedule**, with research indicating a positive result on both instruments is 99 percent accurate for diagnosis of autism. Both instruments require training before use.

REFERENCES

Lord, C., Rutter, M., & LeCouteur, A. (1994). Autism Diagnostic Interview–Revised: A revised version of a diagnostic interview for caregivers of individuals with possible pervasive developmental disorders. *Journal of Autism and Developmental Disorders, 24,* 659–685.

Rutter, M., LeCouteur, A., & Lord, C. (2003). *ADI-R Autism Diagnostic Interview–Revised.* Los Angeles: Western Psychological Services.

FIONA J. SCOTT

AUTISM DIAGNOSTIC OBSERVATION SCHEDULE (ADOS)

The Autism Diagnostic Observation Schedule (ADOS; Lord et al., 2000; Lord, Rutter, DiLavore, & Risi, 2002) is designed to measure presentation of behavioral response and communicative attempt as compared to the triad features of autism. It has four modules depending on the child's level of communicative functioning, covering (a) preverbal/single words, (b) phrase speech, (c) fluent speech child, and (d) fluent speech adolescent/adult. It enables the examiner or clinician to record the range of various presentations of the core triad features of autism spectrum disorders—namely impairments in social interaction, impairments in communication, and presentation of repetitive and stereotyped behaviors coupled with poor imagination or symbolic play skills. Like the **Autism Diagnostic Interview–Revised** (ADI-R), the ADOS uses algorithms to classify individuals, but unlike the ADI-R it covers both autism and autism spectrum. The ADOS was designed for use alongside the ADI-R, and combined use offers 99 percent accuracy in classifying autism. The ADOS requires training prior to use.

REFERENCES

Lord, C., Risi, S., Lambrecht, L., Cook, E. H., Jr., Leventhal, B. L., DiLavore, P. C., et al. (2000). Autism Diagnostic Observation Schedule: Generic: A standard measure of social and communication deficits associated with the spectrum of autism. *Journal of Autism & Developmental Disorders, 30*(3), 205–223.

Lord, C., Rutter, M., DiLavore, P. C., & Risi, S. (2002). *The Autism Diagnostic Observation Schedule: Generic.* Los Angeles: Western Psychological Services.

FIONA J. SCOTT

AUTISM SCREENING INSTRUMENT FOR EDUCATIONAL PLANNING–SECOND EDITION

Autism Screening Instrument for Educational Planning–Second Edition (ASIEP-2; Krug, Arick, & Almond, 1996) is an individually administered instrument designed to help professionals evaluate autistic individuals (18 months of age through adulthood) and develop appropriate instructional plans in accordance with the **Individual with Disabilities Education Act** (PL 94–142). It can also be used for differential diagnosis, as it distinguishes individuals with autism from those with other severe handicaps. The scale looks at five aspects of behavior, which together provide a clear picture of the individual's functional abilities and instructional needs.

The ASIEP is composed of five subtests: Autism Behavior Checklist (sensory, relating, body concept, language, and social self-help behaviors); a sample of vocal behavior (spontaneous verbal behavior); interaction assessment (social interaction based on observable behaviors); educational assessment (language performance and communicative abilities through signed or verbal responses); and prognosis of learning rate. Each subtest employs a different format, and each is individually normed. The entire test can be administered by a professional with experience with children with autism in $1^1/_2$ to 2 hours. It yields percentiles and summary scores for each subtest.

REFERENCE
Krug, D., Arick, J., & Almond, P. (1996). *Autism screening instrument for educational planning.* Los Angeles: Western Psychological Services.

JEANNE HOLVERSTOTT

AUTISM SCREENING QUESTIONNAIRE. *See* Social Communication Questionnaire

AUTISTIC DISORDER

Autistic disorder, or autism, is currently understood as a developmental disability that begins before the age of three. Autism's three main areas of impact are in the domains of social interaction, communication, and restricted, repetitive, and stereotyped interests and behaviors. The psychiatric handbook of mental disorders, the ***Diagnostic and Statistical Manual of Mental Disorders*** (DSM-IV-TR: APA, 2000), classifies autism as a **pervasive developmental disorder** (PDD). This PDD term refers to a group of disabilities with similar core characteristics and a wide range of manifestation and prognosis. The other four diagnostic PDD labels include *Asperger syndrome* (AS), **Childhood Disintegrative Disorder** (also known as Heller's syndrome), **Rett's Disorder** (also known as Rett syndrome), and **Pervasive Developmental Disorder–Not Otherwise Specified** (PDD-NOS, also known as atypical autism).

Autism has been known by several other names over the past decades including: early infantile autism, childhood autism, Kanner's autism, and classical autism.

Individuals with autism present on a continuum of expression with cognition across all IQ levels and possession of individual strengths and needs. Some with autism have no language, have significant cognitive impairment, and are in need of constant care. Others have limited language and mild cognitive impairments, but are in need of significant support. Still others have average to above-average intelligence and their difficulties are less noticeable. Common strengths in autism include visual/spatial abilities, systemizing skills, proclivity for routine-oriented behaviors, rote learning, and physical development. Some with autism have splinter skills, or unique talents and abilities that seem unusual when compared to adaptive or other functioning levels. For example, an 8-year-old child with autism may not be toilet trained but be able to do puzzles at amazing speed. Or an adult with autism may be nonverbal but be able to play a musical instrument with expertise.

Generally, those with autism have challenges with verbal and nonverbal communication, relating to others, difficulty learning by traditional methods, are resistant to change, and insist on familiarity. Other concerns include possible co-occurring medical conditions, sensory processing difficulties, and behavioral deficits and/or excesses. Approximately one-third of those with autism experience seizures at some point. Some individuals with autism exhibit odd repetitive behaviors such as hand flapping, finger twisting, light filtering, body posturing, or complex movements of the body. It has been inferred that these behaviors are due to a need to respond to sensory input or as a means to deal with stress, anxiety, or confusion. Others with autism may have self-injurious or aggressive behaviors. These behaviors are often the result of inappropriate teaching, lack of positive supports, and the difficulties facing a person who may have limited communication and/or means to have needs met.

Today, many use the term autism to refer to an autism spectrum disorder (ASD) or the clustering of three of the most common PDDs (autism, AS, and PDD-NOS). The distinctions between these labels can be subtle, but generally those with PDD-NOS meet at least one of the criteria of autism but lack other criteria to qualify for the autism diagnosis. For example, a child with PDD-NOS might have average IQ, good social skills, but significant and pervasive communication issues. Those with AS have average to above-average cognition and speech development that is typical, but have social and behavioral impairments. For example, an adult with AS might have a high IQ, hold a job in a computer company, be married, but have intense social needs and anxieties as well as some repetitive and stereotyped behaviors. Autism tends to be the most challenging of the group, with many having cognitive impairment (IQ less than 70), less or no verbal language ability, and more medical, sensory, and behavioral needs. For example, a teenager with autism might have cognitive impairment and limited adaptive skills, no language ability, use limited sign language to communicate, have epilepsy, and self-injurious behaviors. The previous examples are merely attempts at detailing the wide range of presentations for similar disabilities. Although each individual with autism has impairments in the three main areas (social, communication, and behaviors), each is unique in how the impairments and strengths are expressed, in personality and in potential. Today, many professionals use the terms PDD and ASD interchangeably.

Another ongoing debate in the field is whether or not AS is a distinct disability or just a form of **high-functioning autism** (HFA). The term HFA has been used to describe those with autism who are less impaired compared to those with severe cognitive impairment, individuals with autism who have an IQ above 70, or those with average or even superior IQ. Since AS was added to the *Diagnostic and Statistical Manual of Mental Disorders* in 1994 (APA), there has been debate about whether AS and HFA are the same or different diagnoses.

Although autism has been one of the most studied disabilities of childhood, it remains one of the most perplexing. What causes autism is still beyond the understanding of scientists, although they are much closer today than when autism was first described in the literature by **Leo Kanner** in 1943. Autism has been conceptualized in a number of ways over the past 60 years. From the mid-1940s into the 1960s, autism was thought to be a psychogenic condition of childhood caused by parents' inability to bond with their children, and the negative term "refrigerator parent" (often the mother was implicated) was used to label the parents of children with autism. Although Kanner and others first posited that autism was a condition that was present at birth or developed soon after, professionals missed some telltale signs (such as if parents could not bond with their child with autism, why did they have other children who developed without having autism?), and chose rather to blame the parent. From the 1960s onward, evidence was presented that began to overturn this unfortunate beginning. This evidence came in the form of family and **twin studies**, brain research, and other designs that described autism as a biological disorder that had genetic roots.

Even though most today agree that autism is a spectrum of disorders that range from mild to severe presentations, there is still debate on how autism develops. Some believe that autism is predetermined genetically and that the impact of the disability will depend on the number of genes affected in any one individual. Others believe that autism is caused by environmental factors that combine with affected genes to cause the disability. Still others believe that autism is caused when various environmental toxins get into a child's body, and the immune system is unable to process these materials. What most agree on is that the behavior, learning, and characteristics of individuals with autism are different from typically developing individuals because the biology of the brain is different due to genetic and/or environmental influences. Although biological in nature, there is currently no medical test for autism and it is diagnosed only after observations of the child and interviews with caregivers.

Autism was once thought an extremely rare condition of childhood. Initial prevalence statistics estimated that 4 to 5 out of 10,000 children had autism. Currently, autism is one of the most diagnosed disabilities of childhood with a prevalence rate of approximately 2 to 6 per 1,000. How and why the prevalence rate is changing are controversial questions; some blame the environment and others conclude that the broadening of the autism spectrum accounts for the increase. Today the total autism population in the United States has been estimated at approximately 1.5 million children, youth, and adults (Autism Society of America, 2006). Both historically and currently autism is much more common in males than females (4 to 1 for autism, as high as 9 to 1 for AS).

In the middle of the 1900s, psychotherapy and/or removal of the child with autism from the home were seen as possible treatments. Since that time, **applied behavior analysis** (ABA), special education, **cognitive behavior modification**, visual/environmental supports, **structured teaching**, **positive behavior support**, speech-language therapy, **occupational therapy, physical therapy**, counseling, and **social skills training** have all become avenues to teach individuals with autism. Historically, many individuals with autism were placed in institutions. Since the inclusion and deinstitutionalization movements and passage of national laws, most individuals with autism now live at home and go to public schools. However, some children are home-schooled or attend special schools, and many families augment public school education by providing their children with private services at home.

The future for individuals with autism remains variable depending on education, supports, availability of services, early intervention, degree of strengths and impairments, and other factors. Although considered a lifelong disability, many with autism have made significant progress and contributions. For example, Temple Grandin, Professor of Animal Sciences at Colorado State University, is one of the most well known adults with autism in the United States. Grandin has become an expert in livestock handling and is well known internationally for her expertise in this area as well as being a speaker and advocate for those with autism.

Since the controversy over the increased diagnosing of autism and related disorders in the 1990s to today, autism has become better known to the public. Television shows, magazine articles, newspaper stories, motion pictures, documentaries, and so forth have all helped to spread awareness about autism and its impact on individuals, families, educators, other professionals, and communities. For example, many people have seen or heard of the award-winning motion picture *Rain Man*, which was produced in 1988, a portrayal of an adult with autism and his brother as they journeyed across the country.

One of the biggest and later controversies in autism pertains to the question of potential cures for this disability. Some believe that those with autism can and should be cured. This remains highly controversial, and the ethical question of whether or not autism should be cured has been asked. Others, both those with autism and their advocates, have spoken out against curing autism. They believe that autism is a culture and that curing autism would be eradicating these persons and their way of life. They aren't arguing against helping and teaching persons with autism, however they argue that curing autism would take away the uniqueness and future contributions of those with autism.

In the early twenty-first century, the autism research community was focusing on a number of areas including, genetics, brain research, treatment and education, possible environmental contributors, and how autism develops. It is very possible that in the next 50 years the specific genes responsible for autism will be located and that therapies will be created to address these chromosomal differences both in utero and postnatally. Furthermore, continued advances in the field of brain studies may also bring about treatments to change neurology. Environmental factors may also be identified as contributors to autism with appropriate responses following. Other new or existing methodologies will be identified as best practice for teaching those with autism. If an eventual cure for autism is discovered, the ethical question of whether or not autism should be cured will continue to be debated. Included within this discussion will be the moral imperative to treat those with this disability with dignity and respect.

See also self-injurious behavior; speech therapy; visual supports.

REFERENCES

American Psychiatric Association. (1994). *Diagnostic and statistical manual of mental disorders* (4th ed.). Washington, DC: Author.

American Psychiatric Association. (2000). *Diagnostic and statistical manual of mental disorders* (4th ed., text rev.). Washington, DC: Author.

Autism Society of America [ASA]. (2006). *What is autism?* [Brochure]. Bethesda, MD: Author.

FURTHER INFORMATION

Frith, U. (Ed.). (1989). *Autism: Explaining the enigma*. Oxford: Blackwell.

Gillberg, C., & Coleman, M. (2000). *The biology of the autistic syndromes* (3rd ed.). London: Keith Mac Press.

Grandin, T. (1995). *Thinking in pictures and other reports from my life with autism*. New York: Vintage Books.

Herbert, M. R. (2005). Autism: A brain disorder, or a disorder that affects the brain [Electronic Version]. *Clinical Neuropsychiatry, 2*, 354–379.

Johnson, M. (producer), & Levinson, B. (director). (1988). *Rain Man* [Motion Picture]. United States: United Artists.

Kanner, L. (1943). Autistic disturbances of affective content. *The Nervous Child, 2*, 217–250.

National Research Council. (2001). *Educating children with autism*. Committee on Educational Interventions for Children with Autism. Division of Behavioral and Social Sciences and Education. Washington, DC: National Academy Press.

Powers, M. D. (2000). *Children with autism* (2nd ed.). Rockville, MD: Woodbine House.

Quill, K. A. (2000). *Do watch listen say: Social communication intervention for children with autism*. Baltimore: Brookes Publishing Co.

PAUL G. LaCAVA

B

BASELINE

"Baseline conditions serve as the background or context for viewing the effects of a second type of condition" (Johnston & Pennypacker, 1993, p. 225). Kennedy (2005) further explained, "The starting point for most experimental analyses of behavior is the establishment of a baseline" (p. 35). In other words, baseline refers to the occurrence of a response in its freely occurring or natural state. It is the observations of a dependent variable response prior to the administration of a treatment condition, which may or may not change this response. It is the measure against the result of the treatment to see whether the dependent variable changes or not. The recording of a baseline is very important because the baseline data serves as the standard against which change elicited by the experimental treatment is assessed.

REFERENCES

Johnston, J. M., & Pennypacker, H. S. (1993). *Strategies and tactics of behavioral research* (2nd ed.). Hillsdale, NJ: Lawrence Erlbaum Associates.

Kennedy, C. H. (2005). *Single-case designs for educational research.* Boston: Pearson Education, Inc.

KAI-CHIEN TIEN

BEHAVIOR

Behavior is the observable manifestation of internal functioning. This means that behavior is a form of communication and can be a reaction to either an external or internal situation. For example, self-stimulatory behavior is widely considered to serve the function of stimulating the individual's mind and senses, as well as serving a self-regulating function. These behaviors would be a response to internal conditions. On the other hand, if a room is noisy and the child covers his ears, he is reacting to the external situation. It is important to remember that all behavior, including undesired or inappropriate behavior, is a form of communication. Any intervention for a targeted behavior will be unsuccessful if it does not address what the individual intended the behavior to communicate.

KATIE BASSITY

BEHAVIORAL ASSESSMENT OF THE DYSEXECUTIVE SYNDROME (BADS)

The Behavioral Assessment of the Dysexecutive Syndrome Battery (BADS; Wilson, Alderman, Burgess, Emslie, & Evans, 1996) is designed to assess adolescents and adults with dysexecutive syndrome (DES). DES includes disorders of planning, organization, problem solving, and attention, closely resembling what was once called "frontal lobe syndrome." The BADS includes items that are specifically sensitive to frontal lobe damage and to those skills involved in problem solving, planning, and organizing behavior over an extended period of time. It assesses capacities for everyday living that reflect the real-life demands that occur when people need to solve problems, set priorities in the face of competing demands, and adapt behavior to changing situations. The BADS helps determine whether an individual has a general impairment of executive functioning or a specific kind of executive disorder.

REFERENCE

Wilson, B. A., Alderman, N., Burgess, P. W., Emslie, H., & Evans, J. J. (1996). *Behavioural assessment of the dysexecutive syndrome.* Bury St. Edmunds, UK: Thames Valley Test Company.

JEANNE HOLVERSTOTT

BEHAVIORAL OBJECTIVE

A behavioral objective is a definition of a desired behavior toward which a child is working. It should be observable and measurable, such that anyone reading it would be able to clearly identify the behavior being addressed, as well as assess if the **objective** has been met. Therefore, a behavioral objective must also include criteria that define what it means to accomplish or meet the objective. Behavioral objectives should also be stated in positive terms and should be socially valid, helping an individual reach maximum independence and integration.

KATIE BASSITY

BEHAVIORAL REHEARSAL

Behavioral Rehearsal is a method employed for the acquisition of skills, particularly one related to **social competence**. To utilize behavioral rehearsal, a desired objective (behavior) is identified; for example, an individual will appropriately gain and sustain the attention of peers. Positive manifestations of this skill are then described (visually with pictures, television clips, etc., and verbally) and demonstrated. For the child with difficulties asking other students to play, desirable behavioral outcomes might be specific phrases ("Can I play with you?" or "Do you want to play?"). After observing these demonstrations, the individual engages in structured practice of this skill while coaching and feedback guide performance. Several modalities of behavioral rehearsal can assist in the acquisition of the skill in this context. *Covert* rehearsal presents a situation for the individual to mentally practice, while *verbal* rehearsal incorporates verbal processing of the situation. *Overt* rehearsal involves role-playing or modeling the skill. The individual should be encouraged to implement this skill in real-world situations to promote generalization.

JEANNE HOLVERSTOTT

BEHAVIOR ANALYSIS. *See* Applied Behavior Analysis

BEHAVIOR ANALYST CERTIFICATION BOARD (BACB)

The Behavior Analyst Certification Board (BCBA) is a nonprofit corporation that sets international standards for certification in behavior analysis. The certification process is voluntary, which means a practitioner may practice behavior analysis without certification from the BACB. However, the board and its certification process are intended to promote high quality practitioners in the field of behavior analysis as well as standards for consumers. The BACB currently offers two levels of certification: **Board Certified Associate Behavior Analyst**, and **Board Certified Behavior Analyst**.

FURTHER INFORMATION
Board Analyst Certification Board: http://www.bacb.com.

KATIE BASSITY

BEHAVIOR ASSESSMENT SCALE FOR CHILDREN (BASC)

Behavior Assessment Scale for Children (BASC) is an assessment tool designed to identify emotional disturbances and problem behaviors in children and adolescents (Manning & Miller, 2001). As such, the BASC is used to make educational evaluations, clinical diagnoses, and intervention plans. BASC encompasses five components: a Teacher Rating Scale (TRS); a Parent Rating Scale (PRS); a Self-Report Inventory; a Student Observation System (SOS); and a Structured Developmental History (SDH; Reynolds & Kamphaus, 1992). This multidimensional assessment is thought to include many aspects of behavior, not only problem behaviors, but also strengths and **adaptive behaviors**.

REFERENCES
Manning, S. C., & Miller, D. C. (2001). Identifying ADHD subtypes using the parent and teacher rating scales of the behavior assessment scale for children. *Journal of Attention Disorders*, 5(1), 41–51.
Reynolds, C. R., & Kamphaus, R. W. (1992). *Behavior Assessment System for Children–Manual*. Circle Pines, MN: American Guidance Service.

YU-CHI CHOU

BEHAVIOR CONTRACT. *See* Contingency Contracting

BEHAVIOR HEALTH REHABILITATION SERVICES (BHRS)

Behavioral Health Rehabilitation Services (BHRS), sometimes called wraparound services, are behavioral services provided in home, school, and community settings based on the recommendation of a **psychiatrist** or **psychologist**. Generally, these services are provided through the Office of Medical Assistance Programs and are put in place for those individuals who require more than outpatient services and otherwise might need a more restrictive environment. BHRS is composed of three levels of support: Behavioral Specialist Consultants (BSC), Mobile Therapists (MT), and Therapeutic Staff Support (TSS), in addition to the psychologist or psychiatrist.

KATIE BASSITY

BEHAVIOR INTERVENTION PLAN

A Behavior Intervention Plan (BIP) is a detailed plan that identifies the student's **maladaptive behavior**, the **function of behavior**, and strategies to teach new socially appropriate behaviors. A BIP is framework to assist educators in using proactive teaching strategies when confronted with a **target behavior**.

KATHERINE E. COOK

BEHAVIORISM

Behaviorism is the philosophy regarding the science of behavior and is considered one aspect of study within the science of behavior. Beginning as a school of thought within the field of psychology, behaviorism finds its greatest influence from the work of B. F. Skinner. There are several different kinds of behaviorism, some of which acknowledge the existence and influence of internal states and processes; others do not. It is this aspect of behaviorism that has created controversy. This controversy continues today, particularly as the application of **applied behavior analysis** in education with individuals with autism and other disabilities and disorders has found substantial research support.

FURTHER INFORMATION
Cooper, J., Heron, T., & Heward, W. (1987). *Applied behavior analysis*. Upper Saddle River, NJ: Pearson Education.

KATIE BASSITY

BEHAVIOR MODIFICATION

Behavior modification is the application of **operant conditioning** principles in everyday situations. However, behavior modification is a widely used term, particularly by educational practitioners, which generally refers to any interventions that seek to change behavior. This may include the use of proactive or antecedent interventions. These interventions focus on occurring prior to a behavior in order to prevent it.

KATIE BASSITY

BEHAVIOR PRINCIPLES

Behavior principles are the main findings on which behaviorism is based. These principles express a functional relationship between behavior and something that controls it. For example, reinforcement and **punishment** are two principles of behavior. Behavior principles have been shown to be true across thousands of situations and people, but across other species as well. In other words, these may be considered laws of behavior. Although there are few behavior principles, each has many forms of application in practice. A method that puts a principle of behavior into practice is referred to as a behavior change procedure.

FURTHER INFORMATION
Cooper, J., Heron, T., & Heward, W. (1987). *Applied behavior analysis*. Upper Saddle River, NJ: Pearson Education.

KATIE BASSITY

BETTELHEIM, BRUNO (AUGUST 28, 1903–MARCH 13, 1990)

Bruno Bettelheim rose to prominence as a psychologist in the United States. Bettelheim's significant theory claimed that unemotional and cold mothering was the essential cause of childhood autism. This theory, often called the "refrigerator mother" theory and now soundly repudiated by science, caused severe damage to thousands of families who believed his untested claims. He was convinced that autism had no organic basis, but that it instead was mainly influenced by the upbringing of mothers who did not want their children to live, either consciously or unconsciously, which in turn caused them to restrain contact with them and fail to establish an emotional connection.

VIRGINIA L. COOK

BIAS

Shadish, Cook, and Campbell (2002) define bias as systematic errors in an estimate or an inference (p. 505). To be more specific, a bias is a prejudice in a general or specific sense, usually in the sense of having a predilection to one particular point of view or ideology. Any mental condition that would prevent an individual from being objective and impartial is called bias. In statistics, the word *bias* means that an estimator has been averaged over- or under-estimated (Cohen, 2001). It is a statistical sampling or testing error caused by systematically favoring a particular outcome over others. It has at least two different senses, one referring to something considered very undesirable and the other referring to something that is occasionally desirable.

REFERENCES

Cohen, B. H. (2001). *Explaining psychological statistics* (2nd ed.). Danvers, NY: John Wiley & Sons, Inc.

Shadish, W. R., Cook, T. D., & Campbell, D. T. (2002). *Experimental and quasi-experimental designs for generalized causal inference.* Boston: Houghton Mifflin Company.

KAI-CHIEN TIEN

BIOFEEDBACK

Biofeedback refers to a continuous auditory or visual feedback of changes in bodily reactions or functions brought about by changes in an individual's thoughts or emotions. Some examples of bodily functions could be breath, muscle tension, skin temperature, and heart rate. By providing information about a bodily state frequently, the individual can learn to recognize the link between thoughts, physical reactions, and feelings. Biofeedback is a form of self-management, and is developed to empower people to feel better about themselves. This is done by essentially changing destructive, problematic behavior and habits or inefficient patterns of coping into positive behaviors.

Biofeedback works when a person is hooked up to electromechanical equipment, such as a blood pressure monitor. The equipment measures and records physiological functions and provides the individual with information about them. For example, a visual display on a computer screen, a tone or both may be used to indicate when blood pressure is below the predetermined level. Heart rate can also be measured and individuals can learn the association between the pace of the heartbeat and relaxation. An individual would be hooked up to a heart rate monitor. The external electronic monitoring device (EKG) would give the individual an immediate and continuous readout of the beating heart.

Biofeedback is essentially a step-by-step process for self-control and makes use of many of the same techniques used by behavior therapists. Biofeedback involves providing the individual with information about physiological processes of which they are normally unaware. With the benefit of this additional information they can learn to bring voluntary control over physiological conditions that otherwise may have been potentially harmful to their health.

Biofeedback involves developing an increased awareness of body states, learning voluntary control over these states, and learning to use these new skills in everyday life. The goal is for the individual to use the new skill to control the bodily state without the biofeedback instruments. This learning occurs through the biofeedback training through increased awareness of other physical sensations. The feedback equipment informs the individual when their body is producing too little or too much of the state it is measuring. This learning increases the individual's self-control by returning the responsibility for one's health to the individual and allows the individual to control their own stress responses.

Biofeedback and relaxation training techniques have had efficacious applications and success for reducing anxiety, diabetes, tension and migraine headaches, insomnia, chronic pain, asthma, psoriasis, epilepsy, stroke, hypertension, and cardiac arrhythmia.

For example, an individual with high blood pressure can learn to regulate their heart rate by being hooked up to a heart rate monitor. An auditory tone or a visual display can indicate the current rate. The individual can use relaxation techniques to lower the blood pressure. Once they learn to lower their blood pressure by using the biofeedback, then they can achieve the same outcome without the equipment. This can involve increased knowledge and attunement with their bodily sensations of higher and lower blood pressure during the biofeedback training sessions.

STEPHANIE NICKELSON

BLEULAR, EUGEN

Eugen Bleular (April 30, 1857–February 9, 1940), a Swiss psychiatrist, was appointed professor of psychiatry at the University of Zürich in 1898 and director of the University Psychiatric Hospital from 1898 to 1927. Considered one of the most influential psychologists of his time, Bleuler is best known today for his introduction of the terms *schizophrenia* in 1908 and *autism* in 1912.

TERRI COOPER SWANSON

BOARD CERTIFIED ASSOCIATE BEHAVIOR ANALYST (BCABA)

The Board Certified Associate Behavior Analyst (BCABA) certification is a combination of coursework, experience supervised by a **Board Certified Behavior Analyst** (BCBA), and a standardized exam. In addition, a BCABA must have a minimum of a bachelor's degree. In practice, a BCABA may supervise behavior analytic intervention and train others in behavioral interventions in areas similar to his or her training. However, the **Behavior Analyst Certification Board** (BACB) strongly recommends that a BCABA practice under a BCBA according to the standards of the Board.

FURTHER INFORMATION
Behavior Analyst Certification Board: http://www.bacb.com.

KATIE BASSITY

BOARD CERTIFIED BEHAVIOR ANALYST (BCBA)

The Board Certified Behavior Analyst (BCBA) certification is a combination of coursework, experience supervised by a BCBA, and a standardized exam. This certification requires more credit hours and longer experience than the **Board Certified Associate Behavior Analyst** (BCABA). Additionally, certification requires a minimum of a master's degree. In practice, a BCBA may create and implement behavior analytic interventions based on current research, train others in behavioral principles and interventions, and conduct, analyze, and interpret a variety of behavioral assessments and data.

See also Behavior Analyst Certification Board.

FURTHER INFORMATION
Behavior Analyst Certification Board: http://www.bacb.com.

KATIE BASSITY

BOLLES SENSORY INTEGRATION

Bolles Sensory Integration, also known as Bolles Sensory Learning Method, was developed by Mary Bolles, an occupational therapist, to re-educate and remediate an individual's ability to process and integrate sensory information. This approach stimulates particular sensory systems to learn or relearn the ability to receive, process, and integrate sensory information. This specialized intervention combines specific visual, auditory, and vestibular stimuli into one sensory experience to facilitate effective sensory integration. To date, Bolles Sensory Integration is not supported by empirical data.

KELLY M. PRESTIA

BOWEL PROBLEMS

Fecal incontinence and **constipation** are the common symptoms of bowel problems. Fecal incontinence occurs when feces are passed involuntarily and inappropriately (Royal College of Physicians, 1995), which usually causes urgency or passive leakage (Boyd-Carson, 2003). Constipation, on the other hand, occurs when there is a reduction in the frequency of passing stools and increased straining in passing stools (Arnaud, 2003; Storrie, 1997). Approximately 20 percent of children with autism or **pervasive developmental disorders** reportedly experience constipation (O'Moore, 1978). Children who experience bowel problems may produce loose stools, move their bowels three times per week or less, strain to move their bowels, have difficulties producing stools, pass gas frequently, and burp or belch frequently (Kerwin, Eicher, & Gelsinger, 2005).

REFERENCES
Arnaud, M. J. (2003). Mild dehydration: A risk factor of constipation? *European Journal of Clinical Nutrition, 57*, Supplement 2, S88–S95.
Boyd-Carson, W. (2003). Faecal incontinence in adults. *Nursing Standard, 18*(8), 45–54.

Kerwin, M., Eicher, P., & Gelsinger, J. (2005). Parental report of eating problems and gastrointestinal symptoms in children with pervasive developmental disorders. *Children's Health Care*, 34(3), 221–234.

O'Moore, M. (1978). *Irish Journal of Psychology*, 4, 33–52.

Royal College of Physicians. (1995). *Incontinence: Causes, management and provision of services*. London: Royal College of Physicians.

Storrie, J. B. (1997). Biofeedback: A first-line treatment for idiopathic constipation. *British Journal of Nursing*, 6, 152–158.

YU-CHI CHOU

BRUSHING

Brushing refers to a general technique of applying gentle but firm, rhythmic pressure with a stiff brush in an attempt to reorganize an individual's sensory system to prepare them for learning. A specific protocol for brushing was developed by Patricia Wilbarger.

See also Wilbarger Protocol.

KELLY M. PRESTIA

BULLYING

Experts define bullying as repeated negative actions intended to harm or distress a target and characterized by a power imbalance, which can either be social, psychological, or physical in nature. Bullying can take many forms, including physical, verbal, social, or educational. "Educational bullying is when adults who perform as members of the school staff in some function use their power to either intentionally or unintentionally harm students, causing them distress" (Heinrichs, 2003, p. 27). Verbal bullying is the most common type of bullying for both boys and girls.

Bullying is pervasive in our schools and communities. Almost one third of students are involved in moderate to frequent bullying either as a target or aggressor (Nansel et al., 2001). According to anecdotal reports, nearly all students say they have been teased and harassed at school (National Association of Attorneys General, 2000). Furthermore, every school day, 160,000 students miss school because they are afraid of being bullied (Fried & Fried, 1996).

HIGH-RISK STUDENTS

For some students, bullying experiences are severe, chronic, and frequent. Approximately 10–15 percent of children who are targeted for bullying fall into this high-risk group. A smaller proportion (5–10 percent) are so seriously targeted that without significant support from adults and peers, they will most likely not be able to overcome the consequences of their experiences and progress positively (Pepler & Craig, 2000).

As a group, children with special needs are more frequent targets of bullying, and kids who talk, act, or think differently tend to suffer more bullying and exclusion than does someone with a physical challenge. Children and adults may have more difficulty understanding differences that cannot be seen such as significant social, behavioral, emotional, and/or sensory challenges, especially when these same individuals exhibit cognitive/academic strengths (Kavale & Forness, 1996; Little, 2002). For example, children with autism spectrum disorders (ASD) often make statements that are interpreted as rude because of their social deficits and tendency toward literal interpretations. Because these children may look "normal" physically, peers and adults may have little tolerance for this characteristic manifestation of their disorder (Heinrichs, 2003).

BULLYING AND CHILDREN/YOUTH WITH AUTISM SPECTRUM DISORDERS (ASD)

There is little research on bullying and children with ASD. Liza Little (2002) surveyed over 400 parents of children diagnosed with Asperger syndrome (AS) and **nonverbal learning disability** (NLD), ranging from 4 to 17 years, about bullying. Ninety-four percent of the parents indicated that their child had been bullied at least once during the previous year. Compared to studies of the general population, kids with AS were four times more likely to be bullied. The survey also indicated that children with Asperger syndrome and NLD experience a very high level of peer shunning that increases with age and peaks in high school—a time when peers are becoming more important in the lives of adolescents. Peer shunning is the act of ignoring or excluding children and includes such examples as not being invited to parties, sitting alone at lunch, and being picked last for activities. This study suggests that peer victimization and bullying of all kinds are pervasive among children diagnosed with AS.

Clearly, children and youth with autism spectrum disorders are at considerable risk for bullying due to the innate characteristics of their disability related to their social, communication, behavioral, and sensory challenges, which set them apart from their peers and make it more difficult for them to recognize and respond when targeted by others. Because of bullying and peer shunning, children with AS may be excluded or have negative experiences when involved with the activities that commonly make up the social lives of our children. They are more likely to experience frequent, severe, and chronic bullying, placing them in the 5–10 percent of high-risk students who will need a significant amount of support and intervention from adults to progress positively in their school and community (Heinrichs, 2003).

HOW CHILDREN COPE WITH BULLYING

Recent research on bullying experiences in school that explore the social world of students indicates that our children do not feel safe (Garbarino & deLara, 2002; National Association of Attorneys General, 2000; Rigby, 1996). Garbarino and deLara's work with teenagers found that the students did not feel safe in school and that their main coping mechanism is trying to predict the behavior of their peers and teachers. In other words, when they could predict someone's behavior based on past experiences, they felt safer and could determine how to stay out of harm's way. This included identifying "unowned spaces" or "hot spots" that should be avoided—typically less-supervised areas identified by students as being potentially unsafe (e.g., restrooms, hallways, and locker areas).

Garbarino and deLara (2002) determined that students are "overfunctioning" trying to stay safe in school while adults seem to be "underfunctioning." Students are expending energy on trying to predict behaviors in order to feel safe. This is energy that detracts from their ability to learn. The authors concluded that adults need to take more responsibility for providing a safe learning environment so students can attend to learning.

IMPLICATIONS FOR CHILDREN WITH AUTISM SPECTRUM DISORDERS

If typical students are spending too much time and energy trying to predict behaviors so they can feel safe, we can assume that children with ASD expend even more time and energy predicting behavior. They are more frequently targeted for bullying and exclusion, and because of the innate characteristics of their disability will have more difficulty predicting the behaviors of others. Characteristically, individuals with ASD have difficulty taking the perspective of others or predicting what others may be thinking or feeling in social situations (**Theory of Mind**). This puts them at a great disadvantage, and as a result they will expend a great deal of time and energy trying to stay safe with very little success. Consequently, this may increase their already higher levels of anxiety and may eventually lead them to express negative feelings about school or even begin to exhibit school refusal (Heinrichs, 2003).

KEY COMPONENTS OF A SUCCESSFUL BULLYING PREVENTION PROGRAM

Successful bullying prevention programs must include a strong emphasis on awareness, understanding, and willingness on the part of all adults to be proactive and do what is necessary to provide a safe environment for all children. Ultimately, "we cannot expect the least empowered person, the targeted child, to bear the burden of 'beating the bullies' or to somehow figure out how to change his or her behavior in order to create a safer school environment" (Heinrichs, 2003, p. 15). This is especially true for high-risk students with ASD "because compared to their neurotypical peers, their social-communication disability renders them less skilled at effectively protecting themselves when bullying occurs" (Heinrichs, 2003, p. 15).

Effective bullying prevention needs to involve the entire community of children/youth and adults and include steps at the school, class, and individual level. Special attention and modifications must be considered when dealing with students with exceptionalities so they can be safe and continue to learn. Using special assessment tools such as the Modified Inventory of Wrongful Activities to accurately identify the extent of bullying in children with ASD, along with periodic social interviews, can help provide an accurate picture of their bullying and social experiences (Heinrichs, 2003). Drawing on best practices that will enable children with ASD to have more success in the social arena is also of great importance.

Critical components of a successful bullying prevention program include: (a) identifying high-risk areas and increasing supervision with trained adults; (b) adults modeling appropriate behaviors; (c) promoting social-emotional learning for all students, involving parents; and (d) most importantly, a long-term commitment to making bullying prevention a priority. Adults are key to bullying prevention and our dedication to providing a safe environment for children to learn will ultimately make a difference for children with ASD and for all children.

REFERENCES

Fried, S., & Fried, P. (1996). *Bullies and victims: Helping your child survive the schoolyard battlefield.* New York: M. Evans and Company, Inc.

Garbarino, J., & deLara, E. (2002). *And words can hurt forever: How to protect adolescents from bullying, harassment, and emotional violence.* New York: The Free Press.

Heinrichs, R. (2003). *Perfect targets: Asperger syndrome and bullying: Practical solutions for surviving the social world.* Shawnee Mission, KS: Autism Asperger Publishing Co.

Kavale, K. A., & Forness, S. R. (1996). Social skills deficits and learning disabilities: A meta-analysis. *Journal of Learning Disabilities*, 29, 226–237.

Little, L. (2002). Middle-class mothers' perceptions of peer and sibling victimization among children with Asperger's syndrome and nonverbal learning disorders. *Issues in Comprehensive Pediatric Nursing*, 25, 43–57.

Nansel, T., Overpeck, M., Pilla, R., Ruan, W., Simons-Morton, B., & Scheidt, P. (2001). Bullying behaviors among U.S. youth: Prevalence and association with psychosocial adjustment. *Journal of the American Medical Association*, 285, 2094–2100.

National Association of Attorneys General. (2000). *Bruised inside: What our children say about youth violence, what causes it, and what we need to do about it*. Retrieved July 7, 2004, from http://www.ct.gov/ag/lib/ag/children/bruised.pdf.

Pepler, D. J., & Craig, W. (2000). *Report 60: Making a difference in bullying*. Toronto: LaMarsh Centre for Research on Violence and Conflict Resolution.

Rigby, K. (1996). *Bullying in schools: And what to do about it*. London: Jessica Kingsley Publishers.

FURTHER INFORMATION

Gray, C. (2004). Gray's guide to bullying. *Jenison Autism Journal*, Spring 2004.

Olweus, D. (1993). *Bullying at school: What we know and what we can do*. Oxford: Blackwell Publishers.

REBEKAH HEINRICHS

C

CAREER PLANNING

Prior to adulthood, it is essential that caregivers, teachers, and community supports ensure individuals with autism have the opportunities to acquire the skills necessary to be successfully employed in a desired profession. The **Individuals with Disabilities Education Act** (IDEA, 2004) mandates that each student with a disability will begin to transition from the classroom to the workforce no later than age 16. However, when the student reaches adulthood, the Vocational Rehabilitation Act and **Americans with Disabilities Act** mandate only equal access and not the provision of necessary services and supports once access is obtained.

The career planning process is based on individual needs, preferences, interests, and the individual's participation in job sampling, family input, comprehensive vocational assessments, and structured community experience (DeStefano and Wermuth, 1992). Literature on career/transition planning presents a consensus of best practices. Items are grouped in relation to (a) transition planning, (b) transition implementation, or (c) transition evaluation.

Transition planning includes development of long-term goals, short-term objectives, a plan for posttransition services, case management services, and a timeline for transition activities. Transition implementation includes vocational, leisure, and residential options; transportation training; money management; and vocational skills training. Transition evaluation comprises long-term support and follow-up of specific outcome evaluations (Stowitschek, 1992).

The most important contribution to transitioning is the parents' role as an advocate for their child (Friedlander, 1989). Parental advocacy, support, and input become more critical as their child enters into adulthood. Given the complexity and long-term needs of these individuals, comprehensive planning is a necessity and must include the individual, parents, educational staff, and agency representatives (IDEA, 2004). Considerations for ongoing support services throughout adulthood must include a structured community experience, community-referenced behavior management and social skills training (Berkell, 1992), and the incorporation of individual choice (Winking, O'Reilly, & Moon, 1993).

To obtain suitable employment there are several routes that an individual with ASD can choose. First, attend a two- or four-year college to receive the necessary training for a professional career. Second, prepare a portfolio for potential employers and seek out mentors in the business community that recognize their abilities and potential to enhance their skill base. Third, contact **vocational rehabilitation** services to set up a work evaluation for assessment of job skills, job sampling, and job training. Fourth, contact a local vocational training center to apply for services in a sheltered workshop setting. Most importantly, all of these options can be incorporated into a student's Individual Service Plan and begin working on discovering the best career option when they turn 16.

REFERENCES

Berkell, D. E. (1992). Transition issues for secondary school students with autism and developmental disabilities. In F. R. Rusch, L. DeStefano, J. Chadsey-Rusch, L. A. Phelps, & E. Szymanski (Eds.), *Transition from school to adult life: Models, linkages, and policy* (pp. 460–472). Sycamore, IL: Sycamore.

DeStefano, L., & Wermuth, T. R. (1992). IDEA (PL 101–476): Defining second generation of transition services. In F. R. Rusch, L. DeStefano, J. Chadsey-Rusch, L. A. Phelps, & E. Szymanski (Eds.), *Transition from school to adult life: Models, linkages, and policy* (pp. 537–549). Sycamore, IL: Sycamore.

Friedlander, B. (1989). Becoming an advocate. In M. Powers (Ed.), *Children with autism: A parent's guide* (pp. 231–252). Rockville, MD: Woodbine House.

Individuals with Disabilities Education Improvement Act of 2004. Public Law 108–446. U.S. Code. 20 2004. [section] 1400 et seq.

Stowitschek, J. J. (1992). Policy and planning in transition programs at the state agency level. In F. R. Rusch, L. DeStefano, J. Chadsey-Rusch, L. A. Phelps, & E. Szymanski (Eds.), *Transition from school to adult life: Models, linkages, and policy* (pp. 519–536). Sycamore, IL: Sycamore.

Winking, D. L., O'Reilly, B., & Moon, M. S. (1993). PREFERENCE: The missing link in the job match process for individuals without functional communication skills. *Journal of Vocational Rehabilitation, 3,* 27–42.

STACEY L. BROOKENS

CARTOONING

Cartooning is a visual interactive strategy that can be designed to assist a person in his understanding a social situation. Talking bubbles, which are drawn from the character's mouth, and thinking bubbles, drawn from the character's head, are used to illustrate verbal expression, unspoken thoughts, and cues about what is going on. This is done in the same way as in traditional comics. Cartooning may be used to illustrate the order in which certain events will happen, to tell a story, to assist in organizing tasks, to clarify what people mean when they use certain words, or to problem solve a particularly difficult social conflict. Examples of cartooning include comic strip conversations (Gray, 1994), cognitive picture rehearsal (Groden & LeVasseur, 1995), and Social Mapping (Curtis & Dunn, 1999).

The social disorder in autism is perhaps the least understood aspect of the autism disorder (Klin & Volkmar, 1993). Children on the autism spectrum do not appear to understand why people do what they do, why they think the way they think, or why they make the decisions they make (Baron-Cohen & Howlin, 1993). Simon Baron-Cohen refers to this as an inability to "mind read" (Baron-Cohen, 1995). Tony Attwood explains this as "lacking the ability to think about thoughts" (Attwood, 1998). A person who has difficulty in this area of social understanding is likely to find school and other social settings threatening and difficult to interpret. Why does a teacher make the decisions she makes? Why does a peer play with you one day on the playground but not the next day? Why do some teachers ignore misbehavior and others promptly call attention to it? When, if ever, is it okay to swear? Why do people want me to say "hi" to them in the hallway? These and other everyday questions surrounding social behavior can be directly taught through the use of cartooning.

COMIC STRIP CONVERSATIONS

A way of making social language and social behavior more concrete, cartooning is best used proactively, or as a teaching tool prior to a situation that typically causes problems. Cartooning can be used to teach new or alternative behavior. When confronted with a social problem, students with autism often become anxious and frustrated. This frustration can heighten when a parent or teacher attempts to correct the problem, and a face-to-face confrontation can increase the frustration and stress even more. Using cartooning strategies to explain what went wrong and to offer solutions can take the "edge" off such otherwise volatile situations. When using cartooning strategies, it is important to recognize and validate the perspective of the person with ASD even if you consider that perspective irrational. Perspective taking is a two-way street, and without mutual understanding and respect, it can be difficult to motivate the person with ASD.

Behavioral conflicts between individuals with ASD and their parents, teachers, or peers often occur because of a communication breakdown or a misinterpretation. For example, the person with ASD may misinterpret a person's nonverbal social language (facial expression, tone of voice, etc.) or her reaction to a particular situation. A comic strip conversation as defined by Gray (1994) can be used to visually review the conflict situation.

For example, while John was at his fifth-grade environmental retreat, he decided to take off all of his clothes and run naked through the cabin. The other boys in John's cabin were mortified, embarrassed, and confused, so they laughed. John misinterpreted their laughter to mean that his behavior was funny. He continued to do it even though his counselor told him that the behavior was inappropriate. A comic strip conversation was used to clarify for John what had happened. As illustrated in Figure 1, stick figures

Figure 1 Comic Strip Conversations for the Individual's Perspective

Figure 2 Comic Strip Conversations for the Peers' Perspectives

Cabin #3- Pinewood - Another perspective

were drawn to illustrate the situation. The environment was labeled, and the words of each person were written in their talking bubbles. John was then asked to fill in his thinking bubble. Now the counselor was able to acknowledge John's perspective. John was then asked to guess what might have been in the other campers' thinking bubbles when he ran naked (see Figure 2). He was able to fill in the thinking bubbles with his ideas. Again, this enabled the counselor to acknowledge John's perspective and give him more information by filling in other ideas about how others felt about his behavior. This method of processing an incident increased the accuracy of John's thinking about what happened and how others were affected.

Gray (1994) expands on the comic strip conversation by suggesting that color be added to help clarify the intent of someone's words (see Figure 3). This can be particularly helpful for the student who has difficulty "reading" nonverbal social cues such as tone of voice. For example, consider the example of John at camp. If one of the other boys had said to John that his behavior would make him really popular with the other boys, the adult working with John may consider the use of color to more clearly demonstrate the boy's motivation for saying those words. For example, teasing or sarcastic words may be defined prior to the conversation as being red. Honest or innocent words may be defined as being blue. When John tells the adult that he said, "How do you like me now?" he reports that he was serious and wanted an honest answer. In this case John's words should be blue to illustrate their honest motivation. On the other hand, Edward's words are red to clearly illustrate for John that he did not mean what he said literally, that he was being sarcastic.

Many individuals with ASD have difficulties understanding another person's perspective or how another person feels about certain situations. The ability to understand that your actions have an impact on those around you and that others can contribute to making your experiences pleasurable is at the core of social

Figure 3 How Color Can Clarify the Intent of Words

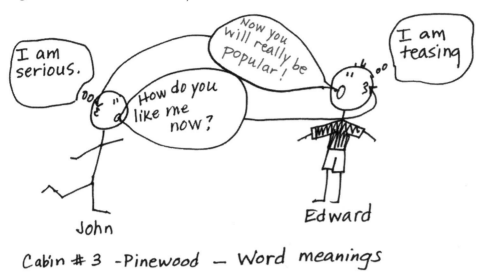

Cabin # 3 - Pinewood — Word meanings

understanding. If a person with autism does not understand another person's contribution to a social interaction, he may be less likely to seek out interactions or recognize the value of social interactions.

COGNITIVE PICTURE REHEARSAL

Cognitive picture rehearsal (Groden & LeVasseur, 1995) combines cartooning with repetitive practice to teach self-control. This method involves presenting a behavioral sequence in the form of cartoons with a written script. The goal is to teach a skill or response to replace an unwanted behavior. The method also builds in the direct teaching of relaxation by prompting the use of relaxation strategies when faced with a stressful situation.

Prior to using this method, it is important to analyze the behavior being addressed so that you can accurately describe when it typically happens, under what conditions it typically happens, what happens after the unwanted behavior is exhibited, and how do those around her react. An example of how this might work would be the situation with Claire, a 4-year-old with ASD who consistently screams and hits other children during morning groups (see Figure 4). The teacher has determined that the breakdown occurs while she is waiting for her turn. The teacher knows that allowing Claire to hold a preferred toy helps her to relax while waiting.

After drawing a cartoon, the teacher reviews the story with Claire repetitively, especially immediately prior to group time. This story can be varied over time to teach new routines within the same group time.

SOCIAL MAPPING

Social Mapping (Curtis & Dunn, 1999) is a strategy used to review social situations, events, field trips, family reunions, and so on, in a concrete visual way. A social map clearly illustrates the contributions of all the people involved. Although social maps

Figure 4 How Cognitive Picture Rehearsal Can Teach Skills

are not limited to cartoons, cartooning can be an effective way to present the information including the use of stick figures.

The process begins by writing what Gray has called a fear-reducing story (1994). This is a story made up of descriptive sentences about the upcoming event. The story might mention *who* the child will be sitting next to on the bus or car ride, *what* the child is hoping or anticipating about the event, and what the teacher, peer or parent is hoping or looking forward to. This sets the stage for a more relaxing event, while it highlights some of the ways another person may influence the social outing.

After the event, the person with ASD fills out a worksheet designed to prompt thoughts about the trip and, ultimately, formulate his or her contribution to the social map. Each person involved with the trip fills out a worksheet of their own and brings it to the group meeting or family gathering after the trip. The person organizing the event should bring a large sheet of paper or poster board, markers, and glue. Each person takes a turn and shares what he or she recalled on the worksheet, using it as a visual guide. The social map is created using stick figures labeled with each person's name and details of each person's input based on the meeting. Photographs, particularly photos of the person with ASD having fun with a peer or family member, can add interest to the map. The end product is a visual representation of a social event that displays pieces of information from everyone's perspective. The map can be hung in the classroom or at home to be reviewed and studied over time, not unlike a photo album of someone's family vacation.

Figure 5 Social Map Worksheet

Worksheet: Science Museum, Friday, May 13, 2005

Your name: _____

Your partner's name: _____

On the way to the museum I was thinking about _____

One thing about the museum I thought was cool is _____

One thing my partner thought was cool is _____

A word to describe my favorite exhibit would be _____

For lunch I brought _____

I would like to go to the science museum again. Yes   No

An example might be Mrs. Smith taking her third-grade class to the local museum. Prior to the trip, she writes a brief story about what the children will see at the museum. She knows her student with ASD is concerned with buses, so she includes the fact that they will be taking a large bus (and includes the bus company name). She assigns each student to a travel partner and states this in the story. She writes that she is very excited about the dinosaur exhibit and about eating lunch at the park. She asks for input prior to writing the story so that she can include some other perspectives. Mrs. Smith carefully corrects any unrealistic hopes and clarifies any rules that would be helpful to remember. The story is then sent home with each student to be shared with parents, read, and reread.

After the museum trip, Mrs. Smith hands out the social map worksheet (Figure 5) and assists her students in filling it out. She has the partners work together to help each other by prompting memories.

When the worksheets are completed, Mrs. Smith gathers her class into a group and creates a social map using the information from the worksheets. She puts thoughts in the thinking bubbles based on the worksheets and adds pictures to increase understanding and motivation (see Figure 6).

Like all good teaching strategies, cartooning is best done proactively. Creating time to draw and review cartoons throughout the day is beneficial. However, cartoons can also be drawn in a crisis situation when verbal processing is not productive. By drawing what is going on using talking bubbles and thinking bubbles, you can eliminate the need to talk out loud. The vocabulary used in cartooning is less abstract and more direct than language typically used in social situations. A wonderful example of how this can assist in comprehension comes from my friend, Emily. Emily had a tendency to say what was on her mind, whether it hurt someone's feelings or not. Cartooning was used to help her understand that even though she might think these things, the words should stay in her thinking bubble and not get into her talking bubble. Emily announced to her mother that she got it, that the best way to not hurt others' feelings was to "not pop your think bubble!"

Figure 6 Classroom Social Map

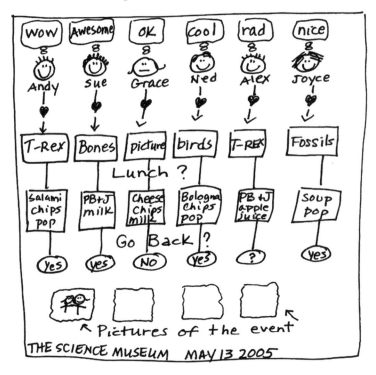

REFERENCES

Attwood, T. (1998). *The links between social stories, comic strip conversations and the cognitive models of autism and Asperger syndrome.* Retrieved on October 17, 2005, from www.tonyattwood.com.

Baron-Cohen, S. (1995). *Mindblindness: An essay on autism and theory of mind.* Cambridge, MA: MIT Press.

Baron-Cohen, S., & Howlin, P. (1993). The theory of mind deficit in autism: Some questions for teaching and diagnosis. In S. Baron-Cohen, H. Tager-Flushberg, & D. Cohen's (Eds.), *In understanding other minds perspectives from autism* (pp. 466–480). Oxford: Oxford University Press.

Curtis, M., & Dunn, K. (1999, Spring). Social mapping. *The Morning News* (pp. 7–8). Jenison, MI: Jenison Public Schools.

Gray, C. (1994). *Comic strip conversations.* Arlington, TX: Future Horizons.

Groden, J., & LeVasseur, P. (1995). Cognitive picture rehearsal: A System to teach self-control. In K. Quill, *In teaching children with autism* (pp. 287–306). New York: Delmar Publishers.

Klin, A., & Volkmar, F. (1993). Social development in autism: Historical and clinical perspectives. In S. Baron-Cohen, H. Tager-Flushberg, & D. Cohen (Eds.), *In understanding other minds' perspectives from autism* (pp. 40–55). Oxford: Oxford University Press.

KARI DUNN BURON

CASEIN-FREE

Milk contains three major components: lactose (which is milk's sugar), caseins (which are mild proteins), and fat. When a person needs a casein-free diet, that person needs to avoid milk because of the proteins within the milk. Although this seems rather simple, one needs to become extremely mindful of reading product ingredients. Hidden milk ingredients include whey, sodium caseinate, sodium lactylate, protein, high protein, and protein enriched products. Some families of children with ASD have decided to try a gluten-free/casein-free diet as they believe the gluten and casein may adversely affect their child's neurological processes. Some parents report that removing gluten and casein from their child's diet results in increased attention as well as reduced tantrums.

FURTHER INFORMATION
www.gfcfdiet.com: This Web site has resources for parents of children with ASD who wish to implement a gluten-free/casein-free diet.

MAYA ISRAEL

CATATONIA

Catatonia is a condition marked by changes in muscle tone or activity associated with a large number of mental and physical illnesses. There are two distinct sets of symptoms that are characteristic of this condition. In catatonic stupor, the individual experiences a deficit of motor (movement) activity that can render him/her motionless. Catatonic stupor is marked by immobility and a behavior known as *cerea flexibilitas* (waxy flexibility) in which the individual can be made to assume bizarre (and sometimes painful) postures that they will maintain for extended periods of time. The individual may become dehydrated and malnourished because food and liquids are refused. Catatonic excitement, or excessive movement, is associated with violent behavior directed toward oneself or others. The individual is extremely hyperactive, although the activity seems to have no purpose. A variety of symptoms are associated with catatonia. Among the more common are echopraxia (imitation of the gestures of others) and echolalia (parrot-like repetition of words spoken by others). Other signs and symptoms include violence directed toward oneself, the assumption of inappropriate posture, selective mutism, negativism, facial grimaces, and animal-like noises. Recognition of catatonia is made on the basis of specific movement symptoms. These include odd ways of walking such as walking on tiptoes or ritualistic pacing, and rarely, hopping and skipping. Repetitive odd movements of the fingers or hands, as well as imitating the speech or movements of others, also may indicate that catatonia is present.

JEANNE HOLVERSTOTT

CAT SCAN

Computed axial tomography (CAT scan or CT scan) is a radiological study that essentially takes a rapid series of x-ray pictures from many angles, while the person is lying flat on a table. The images are then run through a computer, which generates a series of three dimensional views or "slices" that can show organs and soft tissues as well as bones. These studies may be done with or without contrast dye to enhance the image of the specific organs or body systems.

BRUCE BASSITY

CENTRAL AUDITORY PROCESSING DISORDER (CAPD)

Central auditory processing disorder (CAPD) is a dysfunction of the coordination between the ears and the brain but is not a hearing impairment. There are many possible causes for CAPD including head trauma, lead poisoning, and frequent and severe ear infections. Additionally, sometimes the causes of CAPD cannot be determined.

The symptoms of CAPD can vary greatly, but often include the following: (a) sensitivity to loud sounds; (b) difficulty with reading, writing, spelling, or speech and language; (c) difficulty comprehending abstract information; (d) difficulty with organization; and (e) difficulty following conversations.

A child displaying the symptoms of CAPD may be misdiagnosed as ADHD due to the commonality of symptoms. In addition, CAPD can occur in conjunction with other disabilities making the diagnosis of CAPD difficult. The only way of obtaining a diagnosis of CAPD is through an audiologist who performs central auditory processing tests to determine if there is a problem. Once a child is diagnosed with CAPD, the child is referred to a speech pathologist.

The main areas of difficulty for children with CAPD are: (a) auditory attention problems (not remembering directions, materials, and so on); (b) auditory discrimination problems (difficulty hearing the difference between words that sound similar); (c) auditory figure-ground problems (difficulty maintaining attention where there is background noise); and (d) auditory cohesion problems (difficulty drawing conclusions, understanding math problems, following complex directions).

There are several things teachers and parents can do to help children with CAPD. Because all children with CAPD have unique strengths and areas of difficulty, there is no generic list of accommodations that can help all children with CAPD. However, the following is a list of suggestions that may be helpful.

When required to complete important tasks, reduce background noise as much as possible. For example, when studying, provide a quiet study area. When taking tests, provide an area away from loud noises (e.g., not near the cafeteria!).

Help the child recognize that he or she must look at and attend to the person talking.

Ask the child to repeat important directions to make sure they have understood them completely. Make sure the child understands the directions by asking specifics required in the assignment.

Develop a system of organization for school materials, schedule of events, and other areas that are difficult for the child to keep organized.

Maintain a positive attitude and do not blame the child for displaying the previously mentioned difficulties.

FURTHER INFORMATION

Friel-Patti, S. (1999). Clinical decision-making in the assessment and intervention of central auditory processing disorders. *Language, Speech, and Hearing Services, 30*(4), 345–352.

Rosen, S. (2005). A riddle in a mystery inside an enigma: Defining central auditory processing disorder. *American Journal of Audiology, 14*(2), 139–142.

MAYA ISRAEL

CENTRAL COHERENCE

Central coherence refers to the tendency to process information in a global way by integrating and connecting all sources of information to elaborate higher levels of meanings. Persons who process information in typical ways show a tendency to use the context to make sense of the events. However, persons within the autism spectrum tend to process only parts or details of the information, disregarding the context or failing to process the information as a whole. The consequences of a poor central coherence, for example, are the inability to see connections among themes and experiences, generalizing and applying new knowledge to different situations, or inflexibility in their points of view.

FURTHER INFORMATION

Briskman, J., Happe, F., & Frith, U. (2001) Exploring the cognitive phenotype of autism: Weak central coherence in parents and siblings of children with autism: II. Real life skills and preferences. *Journal of Child Psychiatry, 42,* 309–316.

Cumine, V., Leach, L., & Stevenson, G. (1998). *Asperger Syndrome, a practical guide for teachers.* London: David Fulton Publishers.

Frith, U. (2003). *Autism explaining the enigma.* Oxford: Blackwell Publishing.

Happ, F. (1999). Autism: Cognitive deficit or cognitive style? *Trends in Cognitive Sciences, 3,* 216–222.

Jolliffe, T., & Baron-Cohen, S. (2001). A test of central coherence theory: Can adults with high-functioning autism or Asperger syndrome integrate fragments of an object? *Cognitive Neuropsychiatry, 6,* 193–216.

SUSANA BERNAD-RIPOLL

CERTIFIED BEHAVIOR ANALYST. *See* Board Certified Behavior Analyst

CHAINING

Chaining requires that a task be divided into several smaller steps. The steps are then taught in order, either reverse or forward. As each step is mastered, a new step is added onto the "chain." This is a similar process to task analysis, but steps are always taught in the context of the whole task. In reverse chaining, the last step is taught first, and the previous steps are completed by another individual or are prompted. Once able to complete the last step independently and on a consistent basis, the individual is then taught the second-to-last step, and the process continues.

KATIE BASSITY

CHECKLIST FOR AUTISM IN TODDLERS (CHAT)

The Checklist for Autism in Toddlers (CHAT; Baron-Cohen et al., 1996; Baird et al., 2000) is a screen for autism given at around 18 months of age. The CHAT is administered by parents or a primary health care worker, and consists of nine short questions asked of the parent about the child's behavior, and five short observational tasks. Research indicated that if a child failed the CHAT it was 97 percent likely that they had autism spectrum disorders (ASD). However, the CHAT in its original format missed many cases of Asperger syndrome and subtler ASDs, and research is now underway to revise the instrument into the Q-CHAT (Quantitative Checklist for Autism in Toddlers). Other adaptations include the M-CHAT (**Modified Checklist for Autism in Toddlers**).

REFERENCES

Baird, G., Charman, T., Baron-Cohen, S., Cox, A., Swettenham, J., Wheelwright, S., & Drew, A. (2000). A screening instrument for autism at 18 months of age: A six year follow up study. *Journal of the American Academy of Child and Adolescent Psychiatry, 39,* 694–702.

Baron-Cohen, S., Cox, A., Baird, G., Swettenham, J., Nightingale, N., Morgan, K., Drew, A., & Charman, T. (1996). Psychological markers in the detection of autism in infancy in a large population. *British Journal of Psychiatry, 168,* 158–163.

FIONA J. SCOTT

CHECKLIST FOR OCCUPATIONAL THERAPY

The Checklist for Occupational Therapy (OTA-Watertown, 1997) is a series of four checklists—infant, preschool, school-age, and adolescent-adult—providing information about certain behaviors and whether they are seen frequently or not. The items look at behaviors that can be related to **sensory processing** difficulties (movement, sound, sight, self-regulation, touch), although the categories of behaviors change across the age ranges. The infant-through-school-age checklists ask whether a behavior occurs frequently or not, whereas the adolescent-adult checklist can be rated on a 1–5 scale with 1 being never and 5 being always. The instrument can be completed by teachers, day care providers, **occupational therapists**, or **physical therapists** without specific prior training.

REFERENCE

Occupational Therapy Association [OTA]-Watertown, (1997). *Checklist for occupational therapy*. Watertown, MA: OTA-Watertown. Retrieved September 17, 2006, from http://www.otawatertown.com/sensintdys.html.

LISA ROBBINS

CHELATION

Chelation is a highly controversial medical procedure that involves the use of chelating agents, which include DMSA (dimercaptosuccinic acid), DMPS (2,3-dimercapto-1-propanesulfonic acid), and ALA (alpha lipoic acid) to remove **heavy metals** such as **mercury**, iron, arsenic, and lead from the body. Chelation is often administered by intravenous infusions or by swallowing oral pills.

FURTHER INFORMATION

Autism Research Institute: media@autismresearchinstitute.com.
National Autistic Society: www.nas.org.uk.

KATHERINE E. COOK

CHILD BEHAVIOR CHECKLIST FOR AGES 1½ TO 5

The Child Behavior Checklist for Ages 1½ to 5 years is the most widely used general behavioral scale for assessing children. The Child Behavior Checklist is a test consisting of 99 items designed to assess a child's behavior and social competency, as reported by the parents. It provides descriptions of problems and disabilities as well as what concerns parents most about their child and the best things about the child. The tool requests that parents rate their child on a scale of not true, sometimes true, or true on a variety of social issues. Administration time ranges from 10 to 20 minutes (Hart & Lahey, 1999).

REFERENCE

Hart, E. & Lahey, B. (1999). General child behavior rating scales. In D. Shaffer, C. Lucas, & J. Richters (Eds.), *Diagnostic assessment in child and adolescent psychopathology* (pp. 65–87). New York: Guilford Press.

AMY BIXLER COFFIN

CHILDHOOD ASPERGER SYNDROME TEST (CAST)

The Childhood Asperger Syndrome Test (CAST; Scott, Baron-Cohen, Bolton, & Brayne, 2002; Williams et al., 2005; Williams et al., 2006) is a 37-item parental report questionnaire for children ages 4 to 11 years, asking for simple yes/no information as to whether the child shows certain social or communicative behaviors that are thought to be associated with Asperger syndrome or broad autism spectrum disorder (ASD). Unlike many other screening tests, the CAST has been validated for use with a non-clinical sample and can therefore be used as a screen for ASD prior to referral into services. Research indicates the CAST has a sensitivity of 100 percent (it can detect every case of ASD), with a specificity of 97 percent (it tends towards being overinclusive, misidentifying 3 percent as having possible ASD). Research indicates that those who are misidentified typically have some other difficulty with language or social skills.

REFERENCES

Scott, F. J., Baron-Cohen, S., Bolton, P., & Brayne, C. (2002). The CAST (Childhood Asperger Syndrome Test): Preliminary development of a UK screen for mainstream primary school age children. *Autism, 6,* 9–31.

Williams, J., Allison, C., Scott, F. J., Stott, C., Bolton, P., Baron-Cohen, S., & Brayne, C. (2006). The Childhood Asperger Syndrome Test (CAST): Test-retest reliability. *Autism, 10,* 415–427.

Williams, J., Scott, F. J., Stott, C., Allison, C., Bolton, P., Baron-Cohen, S., & Brayne, C. (2005). The CAST (Childhood Asperger Syndrome Test): Test accuracy. *Autism, 9,* 45–68.

FIONA J. SCOTT

CHILDHOOD AUTISM RATING SCALE (CARS)

The Childhood Autism Rating Scale (CARS) is a standardized instrument designed to assist in the diagnosis of autism. The rating scale can be used with children as young as 2 years of age. Each of 15 items covers a specific characteristic, ability, or behavior that includes relationships with people, imitation, affect, use of body, relation to nonhuman objects, adaptation to environmental change, visual responsiveness, auditory responsiveness, near-receptor responsiveness, anxiety reaction, verbal communication, nonverbal communication, activity level, intellectual functioning, and the clinician's general impression. These items are rated by the specialist using a 7-point system based on the degree to which the child's behavior deviates from that of a typical child in the same age group. A total score is computed by summing the individual ratings on each of the 15 items. Children who score above a predefined level are categorized as having autism. Based on these scores, identified children are further classified into categories ranging from mild and moderate to severe.

See also standardization.

FURTHER INFORMATION

DiLalla, D., & Rogers, S. J. (1994) Domains of the childhood autism rating scale: Relevance for diagnosis and treatment. *Journal of Autism and Developmental Disorders, 24,* 115–128.

Rellini, E., Tortolani, D., Trillo, S., Carbone, S., & Montecchi, F. (2004) Childhood Autism Rating Scale (CARS) and Autism Behavior Checklist (ABC): Correspondence and conflicts with DSM-IV criteria in diagnosis of autism. *Journal of Autism and Developmental-Disorders, 34,* 703–708.

Schopler, E., Reichler, R., DeVellis, R. F., & Daly, K. (1980). Toward objective classification of childhood autism: Childhood Autism Rating Scale (CARS). *Journal of Autism and Developmental Disorders, 10,* 91–103.

Schopler, E., Reichler, R. J., & Renner, B. R. (1988). *The Childhood Autism Rating Scale (CARS).* Los Angeles: Western Psychological Services.

SUSANA BERNAD-RIPOLL

CHILDHOOD DISINTEGRATIVE DISORDER

Childhood disintegrative disorder (CDD) is a rare disorder with distinctive clinical features, often has a poor prognosis, and is sometimes associated with encephalopathy. The *Diagnostic and Statistical Manual of Mental Disorders* (DSM-IV-TR; APA, 2000) specifies that following at least 2 years of normal development as manifested by age-appropriate verbal and nonverbal communication, social relationships, and play and adaptive skills there is a clinically significant loss of skills in at least two of the following areas: (a) expressive or receptive language, (b) social skills or adaptive behavior, (c) bowel or bladder control, (d) play, and (e) motor skills. In addition, there must be abnormalities of functioning in at least two of the following areas: (a) qualitative impairment in social interaction (e.g., impairment in nonverbal behaviors, failure to develop peer relationships, lack of social or emotional reciprocity); (b) qualitative impairments in communication (e.g., delay or lack of spoken language, inability to initiate or sustain conversation, stereotyped and repetitive use of language, lack of varied make-believe play); and (c) restricted, repetitive, and stereotyped patterns of behavior, interests, and activities, including motor stereotypes and mannerisms.

It is clear from the previous description that there is a substantial degree of overlap in presentation between CDD and autism spectrum disorders. The distinct difference is that in autism spectrum disorders a child may not develop appropriate skills, whereas in CDD there was clearly normal level of skill followed by loss of that previously acquired skill.

However, Heller (1908), who first reported on the condition, also noted that children presented with anxiety and affective symptomatology such as moody, negativistic behaviors, and other professionals have since emphasized deterioration in self-help skills (Volkmar, 1992, 1994). These characteristics are not emphasized in the DSM-IV-TR (2000) description.

The etiology of the condition is not yet clear, although there has been some association noted with neurological disorders (Evans-Jones and Rosenbloom, 1978), and with known medical conditions such as measles encephalitis. Heller (1908) did not include any known conditions as being associated with CDD, and in terms of a diagnosis specific neurological diseases should be ruled out. Those that should be excluded include **tuberous sclerosis complex** (Creak, 1963), neurolipidoses (Malamud, 1959), metachromatic leukodystrophy (Corbett, Harris, Taylor, & Trimble, 1977), and subacute sclerosing panencephalitis (Rivinus, Jamison, & Graham, 1975).

Prognosis of the condition is generally poor. Volkmar (1992) followed up on 76 cases over a period of 1 to 22 years, and reported that a minority showed minimal improvements while three quarters showed a static course of presentation, with overall functioning in the moderate to severe range of **mental retardation**. All the children required special education and commonly received services in **residential facilities**.

REFERENCES

American Psychiatric Association. (2000). *Diagnostic and statistical manual of mental disorders* (4th ed., text rev.). Washington, DC: Author.

Corbett, J., Harris, R., Taylor, E., & Trimble, M. (1977). Progressive disintegrative psychosis of childhood. *Journal of Child Psychology and Psychiatry, 18,* 211–219.

Creak, E. M. (1963). Childhood psychosis: A review of 100 cases. *British Journal of Psychiatry, 109,* 84–89.

Evans-Jones, L. G. & Rosenbloom, L. (1978). Disintegrative psychosis in childhood. *Developmental Medicine and Child Neurology, 20,* 462–470.

Heller, T. (1908). Dementia infantalis. *Zeitschrift fur die Erforschung und Behandlung des Jugenlichen Schwachsinns [Journal for Research and Treatment of Juvenile Feeblemindedness],* 2, 141–165.

Malamud, N. (1959). Heller's disease and childhood schizophrenia. *American Journal of Psychiatry, 116,* 215–218.

Rivinus, T. M., Jamison, D. L., & Graham, P. J. (1975). Childhood organic neurological disease presenting as psychiatric disorder. *Archives of Disease in Childhood, 50,* 115–119.

Volkmar, F. R. (1992). Childhood disintegrative disorder: Issues for DSM-IV. *Journal of Autism and Developmental Disorders, 22,* 625–642.

Volkmar, F. R. (1994). Childhood disintegrative disorder. *Child and Adolescent Psychiatric Clinics of North America, 3,* 119–129.

FIONA J. SCOTT

CHILDREN'S ATTRIBUTIONAL STYLE QUESTIONNAIRE (CASQ)

The Children's Attributional Style Questionnaire (CASQ: Seligman et al., 1984) is designed to assess attributional style in children ages 8–13. The 48 items are divided equally between positive ("You get an A on a test") and negative events ("You break a glass"). Respondents select between two possible causes for the statement, and each option represents the presence or absence of an attribution dimension (e.g., internal or external cause). Attributions for each dimension are computed by calculating the number of internal, stable, or global responses.

FURTHER INFORMATION

Abramson, L. Y., Alloy, L. B., Kaslow, N. J., Peterson, C., Seligman, M. E., & Tanenbaum, R. L. (1984). Attributional style and depressive symptoms among children. *Journal of Abnormal Psychology, 93*(2), 235 –238.

JEANNE HOLVERSTOTT

CHILDREN'S CATEGORY TEST (CCT)

Children's Category Test (CCT; Boll, 1993) is an individually administered instrument designed to assess nonverbal learning and memory, concept formation, and problem-solving abilities in children ages 5–16 years. It provides information on the child's ability to change problem-solving strategies, to develop alternative solutions, and to benefit from experience. This constellation of mental processes is highly related to fluid intelligence, or those abilities that involve problem solving with novel material. Because of its nonverbal nature, the child's reasoning ability can be assessed independently of his/her expressive language skill level. Thus, the CCT is less educationally dependent than verbal reasoning measures. In addition, the CCT directly assesses the cognitive processes required for successful academic achievement by measuring the child's ability to learn, to solve problems, and to develop, test, and modify hypotheses. The CCT may be used to determine whether a child is able to perform these learning-based processes despite the existence of learning disorders, verbal or motor deficits, neurological deficits, or emotional handicaps. Because of its nonverbal, untimed, and nonmotor format, the CCT can be used to assess a wide range of children for whom other, more traditional, **psychometric** procedures are inappropriate.

REFERENCE

Boll, T. (1993). *The Children's Category Test.* San Antonio, TX: PsychCorp.

JEANNE HOLVERSTOTT

CHILDREN'S DEPRESSION INVENTORY (CDI)

The Children's Depression Inventory (CDI; Kovacs, 1992) is a self-report test that assists in the assessment of the cognitive, affective, and behavioral signs of depression in children and adolescents 6 to 17 years old. This assessment takes approximately 15 minutes to complete with the respondent selecting the statement that best describes his or her feelings for the past 2 weeks for 27 different items. The CDI contains six scales commonly associated with depression (Negative Mood, Interpersonal Difficulties, Negative Self-Esteem, Ineffectiveness, and Anhedonia); and it is designed for a variety of situations, including schools, child guidance clinics, pediatric practices, and child psychiatric settings.

REFERENCE

Kovacs, M. (1992). *The Children's Depression Inventory*. North Tonawanda, NY: Multi-Health Systems, Inc.

JEANNE HOLVERSTOTT

CHRONOLOGICAL AGE

Chronological age refers to the number of days or years a child has lived since birth. To determine an individual's chronological age, subtract his or her birth date from a specific date. For example, Jacob was born on June 25, 2005. His chronological age should be five-and-half years (or 66 months) on December 25, 2010. Chronological age is frequently used in **psychometrics** as a standard against which certain variables, such as behavior and intelligence, are measured. Chronological age is also sometimes used to compare an individual with a normative sample of others of the same chronological age.

KAI-CHIEN TIEN

CIRCLE OF FRIENDS

Circle of Friends or Circle of Support (Falvey, Forest, Pearpoint, & Rosenberg, 1997) is a program for children who have difficulties making friends. The object is to make sure the child is included in activities and feels a part of a group. A facilitator is required and could be a parent, counselor, or teacher. A *social map* is prepared for the child with the child's help. This map of circles lists the social contacts of the child. See Figure 7 for an example of a social map.

In the center of the social map is the child. In the first circle are the people who are the closest to the child such as family (Intimate). In the second circle are friends (Friendship). The third circle represents people who may participate in the child's life such as doctors, teachers, and counselors (Participation). The fourth circle contains people who may interact with the child in passing such as policemen, firemen, and neighbors (Exchange). Often the Friendship circle has few people.

Once it is determined who is in each of the rings a meeting is held for the entire class. The system is explained to the class by one or two classmates who have volunteered to be mapped. This map is drawn on the board. Most classmates will have several friends in the Friendship circle.

Then the map is drawn for the child with disabilities. Volunteers are asked to be in the child's Friendship circle. These children then act as mentors for the child. These classmates make sure they greet the child, walk to class with him, or be friendly or helpful in other ways. There are weekly meetings (usually 15–20 minutes) in which the mentors talk about what the good things were that happened that week, and then they discuss behaviors that may have caused problems and suggest ways to correct them.

The child also participates and tells what he or she liked and didn't like for that week. The goal is a situation in which everyone learns and friendships develop. This is a program that can be written into a child's **Individualized Education Program**.

REFERENCE

Falvey, M. A., Forest, M., Pearpoint, J. M., & Rosenberg, R. L. (1997). *All my life's a circle: Using the tools, circles, maps, and paths.* Ontario: Inclusion Press.

TERRI COOPER SWANSON

CLASSROOM READING INVENTORY

Classroom Reading Inventory (CRI; Silvaroli, 2000) was designed to be used by teachers of all experience levels to test reading comprehension, word-recognition abilities, inferential and critical reading skills, and thinking abilities. The CRI includes a pretest and a posttest.

REFERENCE

Silvaroli, N. J. (2000). *Classroom Reading Inventory.* Dubuque, IA: Brown and Benchmark Publishers.

JEANNE HOLVERSTOTT

CLINICAL ASSESSMENT (EDUCATIONAL)

Clinical assessments are tests that are administered on an individual basis by a trained professional or specialist. These measures typically assess general intellectual ability, specific cognitive abilities, scholastic aptitude, and oral language development.

THERESA L. EARLES-VOLLRATH

CLINICAL ASSESSMENT (MEDICAL)

Clinical assessment refers to assessment of a medical, psychiatric, or psychological problem by a qualified health professional based on examination/observation, interview, and possibly testing of the individual with the problem (along with family members) in order to arrive at a diagnosis. Clinicians draw on prior knowledge, training, and experience to form a diagnostic impression that may be tentative pending further testing, observation, or trial treatment. Treatment recommendations or a treatment plan are given as part of a clinical assessment.

BRUCE BASSITY

Figure 7 Circle of Friends

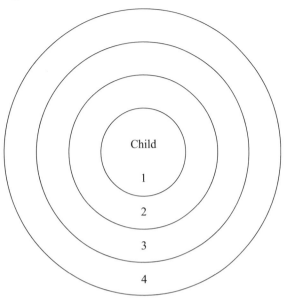

First Circle: Intimacy
Second Circle: Friendship
Third Circle: Participation
Fourth Circle: Exchange

CLINICAL EVALUATION OF LANGUAGE FUNDAMENTALS–PRESCHOOL

Clinical Evaluation of Language Fundamentals–Preschool (CELF-P; Wiig, Secord, & Semel, 1992) is an individually administered, norm-referenced test developed to identify, diagnose, and use in follow-up evaluation of language and communication disorders in preschool children ages 3 to 6. Administering the CELF-P takes approximately 30–45 minutes. A variety of subtests provide in-depth assessment of a child's language skills as well as a preliteracy scale and phonological awareness subtest. Additionally, a pragmatics profile helps to describe the child's language use at school or at home.

See also norm-referenced assessment.

REFERENCE

Wiig, E. H., Secord, W., & Semel, E. (1992). *Clinical Evaluation of Language Fundamentals–Preschool.* San Antonio, TX: PsychCorp.

JEANNE HOLVERSTOTT

CLINICAL OPINION

Clinical opinion is established through the evaluation and assessment of an individual and is often required for eligibility requirements for services. Clinical opinion may be established by professionals such as medical or health service providers.

TERRI COOPER SWANSON

CLINICAL PRACTICE GUIDELINES

Clinical practice guidelines are a standardized approach to the diagnosis and treatment of a specific diagnostic entity, which is often developed or adopted by health professional organizations or government agencies. Typically, these guidelines are supported by outcome-based research. These guidelines are modified over time to reflect new findings and improvements.

BRUCE BASSITY

CLINICAL SIGNIFICANCE

Many researchers use statistical significance to determine the efficacy of a research project. Statistical significance relies on the use of statistical tests to determine whether or not the results meet an accepted criterion level. Clinical significance does not rely on statistical tests to determine effectiveness; rather; it relies on the true effects of the intervention on the individual or on any other problem identified as a relevant priority in the field. Clinical significance refers to a judgment about whether the intervention made a real and important difference in the lives of the individuals who participated in the research and/or whether the results will be useful or applicable to the population in general.

THERESA L. EARLES-VOLLRATH

CLINICAL SOCIAL WORKER

A clinical social worker is a licensed practitioner who helps individuals, families, or communities improve or restore their competence in social functioning. Social workers must understand the dynamic interaction of social, economic, and cultural institutions. They assist people in managing everyday life stresses in addition to helping them overcome more traumatic events.

STEVE CHAMBERLAIN

CLINICAL TRIAL

A clinical trial is a research method used to determine the effectiveness and safety of a new intervention (e.g., drug, device, therapy, or other intervention). A trial typically involves the use of the new intervention with one group of people, while others receive placebo treatment with short- and long-term outcomes monitored. Clinical trials usually include four phases. Phase I trials involve a small number of participants (e.g., 20–80) to assess the safety and side effects of an intervention. Once the initial safety of the therapy has been confirmed in Phase I trials, Phase II trials are performed on larger groups (e.g., 100–300) and are designed to assess clinical efficacy of the therapy as well as to continue Phase I assessments in a larger group of volunteers and patients. Phase III studies are randomized, controlled trials on large patient groups (1,000–3,000 or more) and are aimed at being the definitive assessment of the efficacy of the new intervention, especially in comparison with currently available alternatives. Phase IV trials, which follow Food and Drug Administration approval, involve the post-launch safety surveillance and ongoing technical support of an intervention.

JEANNE HOLVERSTOTT

CLOSTRIDIUM TETANI

Clostridium tetani is the organism that causes tetanus (Mylonakis, 2006). Tetanus is extremely fatal in humans. Mortality rates are from 13 to 52 percent. Because the disease is so fatal, widespread immunizations have taken place in the United States. The tetanus organism is found in infected manure, dirt, clothing, skin, and in 10 to 25 percent of human gastrointestinal tracts (Mylonakis, 2006).

Most cases of tetanus result from small puncture wounds or cuts, which become infected with the *Clostridium tetani* spores. The resulting toxin is what causes the painful spasms, rigidity of voluntary muscles, the "lockjaw" symptom, and eventual death.

REFERENCE

Mylonakis, E. (July 18, 2006). *Tetanus*. Retrieved September 22, 2006, from www.emedicine.com.

LYNN DUDEK

COGNITIVE BEHAVIOR MODIFICATION

Cognitive Behavior Modification (CBM) is a technique that allows an individual with exceptionality to function independently in his or her daily life (Quinn, Swaggart, & Myles, 1994). It has been widely used in a variety of settings with individuals addressing issues of aggression, anxiety, panic disorders, substance abuse, **schizophrenia**, bipolar disorder, borderline personality, depression, limited self-control, poor social problem solving, and related problems (Kendall, 1993; Larson & Lochman, 2002; Leahy & Beck, 1988; Mayer, Lochman, & Acker, 2005). More recently, this technique has also been applied successfully with individuals with autism who exhibit a range of skills (Quinn, Swaggart, & Myles, 1994).

CBM unites cognitive theory with **behavior modification** (Mahoney, 1974). In other words, CBM is a combination of cognitive and behavioral learning principles to shape and encourage desired behaviors. To be more specific, Hughes (2000) defined that CBM refers to a diverse assemblage of theoretical and applied orientations that share three underlying assumptions: (a) an individual's behavior is mediated by cognitive events (i.e., thoughts, images, expectations, and beliefs); (b) a change in mediating events results in a change in behavior; and (c) an individual is an active participant in his or her learning. The third assumption recognizes the reciprocal relationships among an individual's thoughts, behavior, and his or her environment and views the individual as a positive participant of environmental influence.

Mayer, Lochman, and Acker (2005), in a very broad and basic sense, considered the evolution of CBM as occurring in three stages over several decades. Concurrent with the work of early behaviorists, in which explicit and observable behaviors were considered the only acceptable data allowed in research, the early focus was on purely observable stimulus-response (S-R) phenomena. Later on, consideration of mediation processes in a stimulus-response model was seen in the work of Hull and Tolman. Organism-specific variables (O) became important, and the S-R psychology moved toward S-O-R psychology (Mahoney, 1974). A third stage of development assembled thinking, perception, motivation, and cognitive mediation processes, drawn from the research of Bolles, Bower, and Neisser (Kazdin, 1978). Sharpening the historical focus on these developments, Mayer et al. further argued that CBM can be seen as having emerged in the late 1950s, 1960s, and 1970s as a result of the following three factors. First, psychology in the 1970s had "gone cognitive," with particularly significant developments in modeling, self-instruction, and problem-solving protocols. Next, research in self-control had gone beyond traditional behavior therapy approaches to include a specific cognitive component. Third, the development of the comprehensive cognitive therapeutic procedures was completed and the cognitive-behavioral therapy, being recognized as a field, started to obtain its own right.

The strategy of CBM is known by a variety of other names, including self-management, self-monitoring, self-instruction, and metacognition (Quinn et al., 1994). Those names also reflect characteristic components of a CBM procedure identified by Lloyd (1980). CBM is a technique that teaches individuals to monitor their own behavior, pace, or performance, and delivers self-reinforcement at established increments of time. In addition, the strategy is designed to provide specific steps to facilitate appropriate cognitive processing during the completion of a task. Kneedler and Hallahan (1981; as cited in Wahlberg, 1998) stated, "CBM is not an external structure to manipulate behavior; rather, it concentrates on activating an individual to act as his or her won behavior agents" (p. 224). To be more specific, educationally speaking, in CBM, the teacher or supervisor strives for the activation of a student's cognitive processes in a behavior change system to alter his or her thinking as well as behavior. Thus far, the premise of CBM is that, as a prerequisite to behavior change, individuals must develop their ability to notice (a) how they feel, think and behave and (b) the impact their behavior has on others (Meichenbaum, 1980). The CBM approach emphasizes the modification of thinking as a means of changing feelings and behavior (Corey, 1991; Harris, 1988; Hughes, 1988).

An early demonstration of CBM was used by Meichenbaum and Goodman (1971) when they introduced cognitive approaches to behavior modification to a group of hyperactive children who demonstrated poor self-control (Wahlberg, 1998). Furthermore, Meichenbaum's work on self-instruction has contributed a foundational element to CBM (Craighead, 1982). Meichenbaum (1977) stated: "The focus of self-instruction training has been on the child's conscious self-regulatory ability" (p. 103). He proposed that self-instruction would support the development of the following skills: (a) controlling impulsive behavior; (b) attending to important events or cues; (c) focusing on specific goals; (d) coping with stressors; and (e) managing verbal and nonverbal behavior. In self-instruction, the individual is taught to regulate his or her behavior through self-talk. The individual is taught to ask and to answer covertly questions that guide his or her own performance. The questions are of four types: (a) the nature of the problem (What is it I have to do?); (b) plans, or self-instruction for solving the task (How should I do it?); (c) self-monitoring (Am I using my plan?); and (d) self-evaluation (How did I do?). Educationally, self-instruction is essentially students teaching themselves. With the help of teachers or other professionals, students can use "self-speech" to control behaviors. Meichenbaum outlined five steps in his self-instruction model to teach individuals to use self-speech as part of self-instruction.

Step 1: Demonstrate by Model
As a teacher, speak aloud about the steps you are going through to reach a solution to a problem or situation. For example, if the task is to make a peanut butter sandwich, talk through the steps while making the sandwich. "What do I need to make a peanut butter sandwich? I need peanut butter, two pieces of bread, and a knife. Okay, now I have to put some peanut butter on one piece of bread and spread it out with my spread knife easily and slowly. The next step is to put another piece of bread on top of it. Finished. I did it!"

Step 2: Modeling with Overt Adult Guidance
The student will begin to independently approach a problem or situation while saying the steps aloud. The teacher is there to help the student with what he or she is doing correctly and incorrectly.

Step 3: Modeling with Overt Self-Guidance
The student now approaches the problem without the teacher. The student is still saying the steps aloud.

Step 4: Modeling with Faded Self-Guidance
The only difference between this step and the previous step is that the child is now whispering the steps to himself or herself.

Step 5: Modeling with Covert Self-Guidance
At this point, the student can now approach the problem independently. The student is still thinking about the steps in his or her head (silent self-guidance).

A large amount of research has been done focusing on CBM in working with children and young adolescents (Walberg, 1998). CBM techniques have been shown to be effective ways to help children and young adolescents deal with a variety of functional difficulties (Kazdin, 1991; Wahlberg, 1998). Quinn et al. (1994) reviewed the literature on CBM for persons with autism from 1989 to 1994 and found that although the research is limited to a small number of investigations, the results are

Table 1. CBM Instructional Sequence for Traditional Autism

Steps	What to do?
1. Modeling	The teacher verbalizes aloud what he or she is doing while demonstrating the strategy steps of a task.
2. Put-through	Following modeling, the teacher puts the student through the process, providing prompts if necessary. This procedure is performed on a daily basis until the student performs the task with minimal prompting. The teacher collects data and monitors the process until the student is able to master the task at the pre-established criteria.
3. Self-recording	After following a signal or visual representation of a step, the student places a chip on a board, places a mark on a self-monitoring sheet, or otherwise records the occurrence of the target behavior.
4. Self-rewarding	After the picture sequence or after the self-monitoring has been completed, the student self-rewards from a menu of preferred reinforces.

positive: "All of the studies reviewed indicated that CBM is an effective strategy for helping to monitor social and vocational skills while teaching independence" (p. 2). In addition, it is also an effective strategy to promote academic and vocational skill acquisition by individuals with autism. Quinn et al. further proposed that one solution to the dilemma of attending difficulties exhibited by children with autism spectrum disorders (ASD) is to teach them to maintain a record of on-task behavior through the use of CBM; however, the premise is that children must possess the skills necessary to complete assigned work. Quinn et al. stated, "This procedure is most appropriate for students who have the skills necessary to independently perform a particular task but are unable to complete it due to attending difficulties" (p. 4). In terms of CBM implementation for individuals with autism, Quinn et al. outlined instructional sequences for individuals with traditional autism and individuals with high-functioning autism, respectively. The instructional sequences are delineated in Table 1 and Table 2.

Table 2. CBM Instructional Sequence for Traditional Autism

Steps	What to do?
1. Self-monitoring	The student listens to the audio/ape signal; when he or she hears a signal, the student self-question, "Am I paying attention?"
2. Self-recording	The student quickly assesses whether or not she or he was attending. If the student was attending, he or she circle "yes" on the self-monitoring sheet. If the student was off task, he or she circles "no" on the self-monitoring sheet.
3. Self-rewarding	The student provides a self-reward for on-task behavior by saying, "Good job." If the student was off task, he or she will silently prompt himself or herself by saying, "Get back to work." The student resumes work immediately.

REFERENCES

Corey, F. (1991). *Theory and practice of counseling and psychotherapy*. Belmont, CA: Brooks/Cole Publishing Company.

Craighead, W. E. (1982). A brief clinical history of cognitive-behavioral therapy with children. *School Psychology Review, 11*, 5–13.

Harris, K. R. (1988) Cognitive-behavior modification: Application with exceptional students. In E. L. Meyen, G. A. Vergason, & R. J. Whelan (Eds.), *Effective instructional strategies for exceptional children* (pp. 253–268). Denver: Love Publishing Company.

Hughes, J. N. (2000). Cognitive behavior therapy. In C. R. Reynolds & E. Feltcher-Janzen (Eds.), *Encyclopedia of special education: A reference for the education of the handicapped and other exceptional children and adults* (pp. 407–409). New York: J. Wiley & Sons.

Hughes, J. N. (1988). *Cognitive behavior therapy with children in schools*. New York: Pergamon Press.

Kazdin, A. E. (1978). *History of behavior modification: Experimental foundations of contemporary research*. Baltimore: University Park Press.

Kazdin, A. E. (1991). Effectiveness of psychotherapy with children and adolescents. *Journal of Consulting and Clinical Psychology, 89*, 785–798.

Kendall, P. C. (1993). Cognitive-behavioral therapies with youth: Guiding theory, current status, and emerging developments. *Journal of Consulting and Clinical Psychology, 61*, 235–247.

Larson, J., & Lochman, J. E. (2002). *Helping schoolchildren cope with anger: A cognitive behavior intervention*. New York: Guilford Press.

Leahy, R. L., & Beck, A. T. (1988). Cognitive therapy of depression and mania. In A. Gorgotas & R. Cancro (Eds.), *Depression and mania* (pp. 214–267). New York: Elsevier.

Lloyd, J. W. (1980). Academic instruction and cognitive behavior modification: The need for attack strategy training. *Exceptional Education Quarterly, 1*, 53–63.

Mahoney, M. J. (1974). *Cognition and behavior modification*. Cambridge, MA: Ballinger.

Mayer, M., Lochman, J., & Acker, R. V. (2005). Introduction to the special issue: Cognitive-behavior interventions with students with EBD. *Behavioral Disorders, 30*, 197–212.

Meichenbaum, D. (1977). *Cognitive-behavioral modification: An integrated approach*. New York: Plenum.

Meichenbaum, D. (1980). Cognitive-behavior modification: A promise yet unfulfilled. *Exceptional Education Quarterly, 1*, 83–88.

Meichenbaum, D., & Godman, J. (1971). Training impulsive children to talk to themselves: A means of developing self-control. *Journal of Abnormal Psychology, 77*, 115–126.

Quinn, C., Swaggart, B. L., & Myles, B. S. (1994). Implementing cognitive behavior management programs for persons with autism. *Focus on Autistic Behavior, 9*(4), 1–13.

Wahlberg, T. (1998). Cognitive-behavioral modification for children and young adolescents with special problems. *Advances in Special Education, 11*, 223–253.

KAI-CHIEN TIEN

COGNITIVE LEARNING STRATEGIES

Cognitive learning strategies are principles or rules that help students solve problems or complete learning activities independently (Friend & Bursuck, 2006) by guiding the ways they acquire, store, retrieve, and use information (Alley & Deshler, 1979; Deshler & Lenz, 1989). In short, cognitive learning strategies teach students how to modify their thinking and problem-solving skills, and how to learn and problem solve effectively (Alley & Deshler, 1979; Bock, 2000, 2005, 2006; Deshler & Schumaker, 1993; Salend, 2005).

A cognitive learning strategy consists of a series of specific steps that must be completed in the order specified. An acronym is often used to help students remember the

81

strategy steps (Bender, 2004). For instance, in the reading comprehension strategy, POSSE (Englert & Mariage, 1991), the acronym POSSE represents the strategy steps as follows:

P *Predict* ideas.
O *Organize* the ideas.
S *Search* for the structure.
S *Summarize* the main idea.
E *Evaluate* your understanding.

Thus, when students use POSSE, they first *predict* the ideas that will be discussed in the reading passage. They then use a **graphic organizer** to *organize* these ideas. Students then *search* for the structure of the reading assignment. After reading the assignment, students *summarize* the main idea from the reading. Finally, students *evaluate* their understanding of the reading assignment.

Research investigating cognitive learning strategies has demonstrated that they work very well with students who present strategy production deficiencies due either to developmental immaturity or executive dysfunction (Bender, 2004; Bock, 2000, 2005, 2006; Boudah, Lenz, Bulgren, Schumaker, & Deshler, 2000; Schumaker & Deshler, 1992). This research also supports use of cognitive learning strategies across all subject content areas (e.g., reading comprehension, reading fluency, writing, spelling, mathematics) and many academic activities (e.g., completing multiple-choice tests, taking notes; Bender, 2004; Ellis, Deshler, Lenz, Schumaker, & Clark, 1991).

Research has identified eight steps teachers should follow when providing learning strategy instruction (Bender, 2004; Ellis et al., 1991). The strategy instruction steps are as follows:

Step 1: Pretest and commitment
Step 2: Describe the strategy
Step 3: Model the strategy
Step 4: Verbal strategy rehearsal
Step 5: Controlled practice and feedback
Step 6: Grade-appropriate practice and feedback
Step 7: Posttest and communication to generalize
Step 8: Generalize the strategy

In Step 1, teachers pretest the students to identify students who do not have effective learning strategies and solicit commitment from these students to participate in learning strategy instruction. In Step 2, teachers describe the learning strategy. In Step 3, teachers model use of the strategy. In doing so, teachers also share their thinking behaviors. This helps students learn how the learning strategy guides the teachers' thinking. In Step 4, teachers guide students in verbally rehearsing the strategy. In this step, students also begin to memorize the strategy steps and acronym. Teachers then provide practice and feedback using practice materials developed specifically for Step 5. Once students demonstrate mastery of strategy use on the controlled practice materials, teachers provide practice and feedback using grade-appropriate materials. These materials often come directly from current class assignments (e.g., the daily reading assignment). Once students demonstrate mastery of strategy use on the grade-appropriate materials, teachers go on to Step 7, posttest and communication to generalize. The posttest evaluates students' strategy recall and application to grade-appropriate materials. During this instructional step, teachers also discuss the need to generalize this strategy to all class assignments. The final instructional step involves helping the students generalize strategy use to all relevant content areas. This often involves teaching classroom teachers the learning strategy and asking them to remind students to use the strategy when giving assignment instructions.

Most students with autism spectrum disorders (ASD) present signs of executive dysfunction (i.e., problems keeping several tasks going at the same time and switching between them, problems making high-level decisions to resolve conflicting responses, problems overriding automatic behavior, and problems inhibiting inappropriate impulsive actions; Ozonoff & Griffith, 2000; Russell, 1997). Executive dysfunction leads to strategy production dysfunction. Cognitive learning strategy instruction is one way to teach these students how to use effective meta-cognitive (or learning) strategies. However, the unique information processing skills of students with ASD (Bock, 2005, 2006; Ozonoff & Griffith, 2000; Russell, 1997) require several strategy modifications:

Figure 8 Story Graphic Organizer

SODA Strategy

Stop:
1. Where should I go to observe?
2. What is the room arrangement?
3. What is the routine or schedule?

Observe:
1. What is/are _____ doing?
2. What is/are _____ saying?
3. What happens when _____ say and do these things?

Deliberate:
1. What would I like to do?
2. What would I like to say?
3. How will _____ feel when I do and say these things?
4. How will _____ act when I do and say these things?
5. Why will _____ act this way?

Act:
When I go to _____ I plan to:
(a)
(b)
(c)
(d)

Modification 1: Visual supports
Modification 2: Learning strategy story
Modification 3: Strategy teaching script

Since many students with ASD are visual learners, strategies should include both acronyms and visual icons representing each strategy step (see Figure 8). A graphic organizer should also be used to clearly delineate each of the strategy steps. Many students with ASD are not able to understand others' thoughts and actions. Consequently, watching the teacher model strategy use may not be beneficial for them. Instead, teachers should create a learning strategy story that provides a "thinking model" from the student's perspective that is derived from the lived experience of the student who will learn the strategy. For instance, if a student has difficulties participating in the activity period, the learning strategy story should describe activity period and how to use the strategy to participate in activity period. Finally, teachers should develop a specific teaching script—a specific set of questions and responses teachers will use to teach SODA to students with ASD.

The cognitive learning strategy in Table 3 includes a strategy graphic organizer, strategy story, and strategy teaching script. SODA was used to help a student

Table 3. Making Sense of Activity Period

(Stop, Observe, Deliberate, Act)

Directions: Read the following story silently. When you are finished, raise your hand to let your teacher know you are ready to discuss the story.

Sometimes when I go to activity period I get into trouble and am sent to the principal's office. Ms. Jones, my activity period teacher, tells me that I should stay in the principal's office until I am "… willing to get along with the other students." This confuses me because I am *always willing* to get along with the other students. During activity period I talk with all the other students. I talk about NASA, space, and space travel. Sometimes they stop playing their game and ask me a question about space travel. Sometimes they tell me to leave them alone. Sometimes they ask me to go away. I leave when they ask me to leave. I go to another student and talk about space travel. I think I am getting along with the other students during activity period, but then Ms. Jones sends me to the principal's office. When I go back to activity period, I'm going to use SODA to help me figure this out.

When I enter my homeroom for activity period, I will Stop. I will then ask myself, "Where should I go to observe?" (*I will sit at my desk to observe.*) I will ask myself, "What is the room arrangement?" (*I will notice if there is any change in the room arrangement.*) Finally, I will ask myself, "What is the routine?" (*I will look at the board in the front of the room to see what games or activities Ms. Jones has planned for today.*)

I will then Observe. While observing I will ask myself, "What are Ms. Jones and the other students doing?" (*I will watch Ms. Jones and the other students to see what they are doing. Ms. Jones may be showing us what games we will play today. The students may be deciding who they want to play with and what game they want to play. The students may be reading the game directions.*) I will then ask myself, "What are Ms. Jones and the other students saying?" (*I will listen to Ms. Jones and the other students to hear what they are saying. Ms. Jones may be asking who wants to play "Clue." The students may be saying what they want to play. The students may be talking about other things, like the basketball game or their favorite music group.*) I will also ask myself, "What happens when Ms. Jones and the other students say and do these things?" (*Ms. Jones may smile and thank the students who form groups and begin playing their game right away. The students may smile and laugh as they play their games.*)

I will then Deliberate about my observations. To help me deliberate, I will ask myself, "What would I like to do?" (*I now realize that we go to activity period to play games. I would like to play a game with Joe.*) I ask myself, "What would I like to say?" (*I now realize that we can visit as we play games. Joe likes to visit about NASA, space, and space travel. I would like to visit with Joe about NASA, space, and space travel as we play a game.*) I will ask myself, "How will Ms. Jones and the other students feel when I do and say these things?" (*They will feel happy.*) I will ask myself, "How will Ms. Jones and the other students act when I do and say these things?" (*They will let me join a group and play a game. They will not tell me to leave them alone. I will not be sent to the principal's office.*) And finally, I will ask myself, "Why will Ms. Jones and the other students act this way?" (*They want to play games and visit during activity period. They want me to do this, too. That's why they won't tell me to go away.*)

After I've completed my deliberations, I will decide how I will Act during activity period. *I can now see that when I walk around the room talking to the other students about NASA, space, and space travel during activity period that they cannot play games or visit with each other. This makes them mad. Then they ask me to go away and leave them alone. Then Ms. Jones sends me to the principal's office. If I play a game and visit about things that interest the other students, they will feel happy and want me to stay and play the game with them. And I won't be sent to the principal's office.* When I go to activity period I plan to:

walk up to Joe and ask what game he wants to play today;
tell Joe that I want to play that game too and ask if I can play the game with him;
listen to Joe and his friends talk about cars they like during the game;

talk about cars I like during the game;
talk about how space travel has led to improvement in these cars over recent decades; and
help Joe put the game away at the end of the period.

Strategy teaching script.

Teacher directions: Complete this teaching script immediately after the student has read the strategy story. Bring the SODA graphic organizer and a blank sheet of paper to cover it up. (You will gradually uncover sections of the **graphic organizer** as directed below.)

Teacher: You just read a story about your participation in activity period. What was the name of the strategy that you used to help you figure out what to do during activity period?

Student: SODA.

Teacher: That's right! (If the answer was correct.) Now tell me what the letters S, O, D, and A represent. [Teacher uncovers the SODA icons on the left side of the SODA graphic organizer.]

OR

The strategy was called SODA. (If the answer was incorrect.) Now tell me what the letters S, O, D, and A represent.

Student: S represents "stop." O represents "observe." D represents "deliberate." A represents "act."

Teacher: Exactly! [Teacher uncovers the SODA icons on the left side of the SODA graphic organizer.]

When you go to homeroom for activity period, you must stop, observe, deliberate, and then act. While stopped, what three questions must you ask yourself?

Student: Where should I go to observe? What is the room arrangement? What is the routine or schedule?

Teacher: Right again! [Teacher uncovers the "stop" self-questions on the left side of the SODA graphic organizer.] When going to activity period, you must stop and ask yourself: Where should I go to observe? *I will sit at my desk to observe.* What is the room arrangement? *I will notice if there is any change in the room arrangement.* What is the routine or schedule? *I will look at the board in the front of the room to see what games or activities Ms. Jones has planned for today.*

OR

Correct any questions the student missed.

This teaching script follows the same pattern through all four sections of the SODA graphic organizer.

---

understand how to participate in activity period, lunch, and cooperative learning during English class. The teaching story and script were developed for activity period. Additional stories and teaching scripts were developed for lunch and cooperative learning.

Strategy story.

Teacher directions: Introduce the student to this activity by saying, "SODA is a strategy some people use to figure out what to do and say when they are confused. The following short story shows how you can use SODA to figure out what to do and say when you go to activity period. Please read the story silently and raise your hand when you are finished so we can talk about it."

REFERENCES

Alley, G., & Deshler, D. (1979). *Teaching the learning disabled adolescent: Strategies and methods.* Denver: Love.

Bender, W. (2004). *Learning disabilities: Characteristics, identification, and teaching strategies* (5th ed.). Boston: Allyn & Bacon.

Bock, M. (2000). *The impact of social behavioral learning strategy training on the social interaction skills of eight students with Asperger syndrome.* Unpublished manuscript, University of North Dakota.

Bock, M. (2005). *SODA: Learning strategy intervention for a child with Asperger syndrome.* Manuscript submitted for publication.

Bock, M. (2006). *SODA strategy instruction: Demystifying social interactions for students with Asperger syndrome.* Manuscript in preparation, University of North Dakota.

Boudah, D., Lenz, B., Bulgren, J., Schumaker, J., & Deshler, D. (2000). Don't water down! Enhance content learning through the unit organizer routine. *Teaching Exceptional Children, 32*(3), 48–57.

Deshler, D., & Lenz, B. (1989). The strategies instructional approach. *International Journal of Disability, Development, and Education, 6*(3), 203–244.

Deshler, D., & Schumaker, J. (1993). Strategy mastery by at-risk students: Not a simple matter. *Elementary School Journal, 94,* 153–157.

Ellis, E., Deshler, D., Lenz, B., Schumaker, J., & Clark, F. (1991). An instructional model for teaching learning strategies. *Focus on Exceptional Children, 24*(1), 1–14.

Englert, C., & Mariage, T. (1991). Making students partners in the comprehension process: Organizing the reading "POSSE." *Learning Disability Quarterly, 14,* 123–138.

Friend, M., & Bursuck, W. (2006). *Including students with special needs: A practical guide for classroom teachers* (4th ed.). Boston: Allyn & Bacon.

Ozonoff, S., & Griffith, E. (2000). Neuropsychological function and the external validity of Asperger's syndrome. In A. Klin, F. R. Volkmar, & S. S. Sparrow (Eds.), *Asperger's syndrome* (pp. 72–96). New York: Guilford.

Russell, J. (Ed.). (1997). *Autism as an executive disorder.* Oxford: Oxford University Press.

Salend, S. (2005). *Creating inclusive classrooms: Effective and reflective practices for all students* (5th ed.). Upper Saddle River, NJ: Merrill/Prentice Hall.

Schumaker, J., & Deshler, D. (1992). Validation of learning strategy interventions for students with learning disabilities: Results of a programmatic research effort. In B. Y. L. Wong (Ed.), *Contemporary intervention research in learning disabilities* (pp. 22–46). New York: Springer-Verlag.

MARJORIE A. BOCK

COGNITIVE PROCESSES

The ability to think about a task including intellectual abilities, such as memory and the ability to solve problems and make judgments based on past experiences and the context of the situation.

KATHERINE E. COOK

COLLABORATIVE TEAM

Collaboration is a necessary practice in special education, where education professionals work together to assess and educate students with disability. Collaborative teams can occur through coordination of services, consultation among professionals, and teaming during service provision.

KATHERINE E. COOK

COMIC STRIP CONVERSATIONS. *See* Cartooning

COMMUNICATION AND SYMBOLIC BEHAVIOR SCALES (CSBS)

The Communication and Symbolic Behavior Scales (CSBS; Wetherby & Prizant, 2002) is a norm-referenced, standardized instrument used to assess infants, toddlers, and preschoolers at risk for communication delays and impairments. This assessment is used during natural play routines and other adult-child interactions. The 22 five-point rating scales survey children's language skills as well as their symbolic development, which are demonstrated by the children's gestures, facial expressions, and play behaviors. The CSBS should be administered by a speech-language pathologist, early interventionist, psychologist, or other professional trained to assess developmentally young children. The assessment takes approximately 50–75 minutes to administer with the parents or caregivers completing a Caregiver Questionnaire, which provides background information that serves as a baseline against which to evaluate a child's performance. The early childhood professional then takes a direct sampling of the child's communicative behaviors in structured and unstructured play situations in the child's natural environment.

REFERENCE

Wetherby, A., & Prizant, B. M. (2002). *Communication and Symbolic Behavior Scales.* Baltimore: Brookes Publishing Co.

JEANNE HOLVERSTOTT

COMMUNICATION AND SYMBOLIC BEHAVIOR SCALES DEVELOPMENTAL PROFILES (CSBS DP)

Communication and Symbolic Behavior Scales Developmental Profiles (CSBS DP; Wetherby and Prizant, 2002) is a norm-referenced screening and evaluation tool designed to help determine the communicative competence (use of eye gaze, gestures, sounds, words, understanding, and play) of children with a functional communication age between 6 months and 24 months (chronological age from about 6 months to 6 years).

The tool is administered by a certified speech-language pathologist, early interventionist, psychologist, pediatrician, or other professional trained to assess developmentally young children. The CSBS DP may be used as a starting point for **Individualized Family Service Plan** (IFSP) planning, as an outcome measure to help determine the efficacy of intervention, and as a guide to indicate areas that need further assessment. The CSBS DP contains three components. The Infant-Toddler Checklist, for use with children from 6 to 24 months of age, can be used independently or with the other components of the CSBS DP. It is the first step in routine screening to decide if a developmental evaluation is needed. A parent or a primary caregiver who nurtures the child on a daily basis can complete the Checklist's 24 multiple-choice questions in approximately 5 to 10 minutes. Clinicians may also present the questions in an interview format. If the scores resulting from the Checklist indicate concern, the child is further evaluated with the Caregiver Questionnaire and a Behavior Sample of the child interacting with the clinician and caregiver is taken.

REFERENCE

Wetherby, A. M., & Prizant, B. M. (2002). *Communication and Symbolic Behavior Scales Developmental Profile.* Baltimore: Brookes Publishing Co.

JEANNE HOLVERSTOTT

COMMUNICATION BOARD

A communication board is an **assistive technology device** and a **visual strategy** that promotes expressive communication. Depending upon the individual's need the communication board may use letters, words, commonly needed phrases, line drawings, or photographs.

A communication board is typically used with individuals with limited verbal ability. This may mean that the individual does not have the ability to verbalize or may have difficulty finding the right words when in stressful situations. For the young child a communication board may be used so that they can make simple requests such as asking for their favorite toy or letting their teacher know their need to go to the bathroom. For the adult with Asperger syndrome or high-functioning autism who drives a car, they may have difficulty expressing themselves if they were to get pulled over by the police. To assist with their communication they could have a communication board in their car that included information related to their disability, who they are, and where they live.

Communication boards can be simple to complex and take a variety of forms. They can be used in any setting, with any aged person and with a variety of abilities. They are designed to help the individual be successful in getting their wants, needs, and ideas across.

See also augmentative and alternative communication.

TERRI COOPER SWANSON

CO-MORBID/CO-OCCURRING

Co-morbidity refers to the existence of one (or more) disorders occurring simultaneously with a primary disorder.

JEANNE HOLVERSTOTT

COMPREHENSIVE ASSESSMENT OF SPOKEN LANGUAGE

The Comprehensive Assessment of Spoken Language (CASL; Carrow-Woolfolk, 1999) is an individually and orally administered, oral language assessment battery for ages 3 through 21. The CASL takes approximately 30–45 minutes to administer the 15 tests that measure language processing skills (comprehension, expression, and retrieval) in four language structure categories: lexical/semantic, syntactic, supralinguistic, and pragmatic. One benefit to the CASL is that the need for reading and writing is replaced by verbal or nonverbal (pointing) responses. Therefore, the CASL battery is ideal for measuring delayed language, oral language disorders, dyslexia, and aphasia.

REFERENCE
Carrow-Woolfolk, E. (1999). *Comprehensive Assessment of Spoken Language.* Circle Pines, MN: American Guidance Services.

JEANNE HOLVERSTOTT

COMPREHENSIVE AUTISM PROGRAM PLANNING SYSTEM (CAPS)

The Comprehensive Autism Program Planning System (CAPS; Henry & Myles, 2007) is a process approach that is focused on designing and implementing a comprehensive intervention program specifically for individuals with autism spectrum disorders. This process is designed to promote the acquisition of core content, whether it is educational, vocational, or community based, and facilitate the individualized planning of interventions to meet the social, communication, sensory, and educational needs of

Figure 9 Comprehensive Autism Planning System (CAPS)

Child/Student:_____ Program Manager:_____ Date:_____

Time	Activity	Targeted skill short-term objective	Specially Designed Instruction	Data collection forms	Communication / Social Skills	Sensory Strategies	Instructional Materials	Generalization Plan

persons with ASD. A team of individuals, including parents, general and special education staff, support services (i.e., speech language pathologists, occupational therapists, physical therapists), and administration (i.e., local and regional), complete the CAPS planning matrix for an individual's "typical" day at school, home, or the workplace. This process begins with informal information gathering about factors directly related to the individual's program success, such as issues related to motivation, communication, sensory issues, and generalization (see Figure 9). These components inform the completion of the planning matrix, which can include the following categories: time, activity, target skill/short-term objective, specially designed instruction (materials need to aid instruction, i.e., a visual schedule), data collection, instructional materials, social and communication skills, sensory issues, and generalization. This individualized team planning approach aims to create consistency across time and setting, share information with interested parties, and organize an individual's program with many methodologies that target the core challenges faced by individuals with autism spectrum disorders.

REFERENCE

Henry, S., & Myles, B. (2007). *Comprehensive autism planning system.* Shawnee Mission, KS: Autism Asperger Publishing Company.

JEANNE HOLVERSTOTT

COMPUTED AXIAL TOMOGRAPHY. *See* CAT Scan

COMPUTED TOMOGRAPHY. *See* CAT Scan

CONCEPT FORMATION TEST FROM HALSTEAD-REITAN BATTERY. *See Halstead-Reitan Neuropsychological Test Battery*

CONCRETE LANGUAGE

Concrete language is characterized by using specific and observable terminology to describe a person, place, or thing. Specific words are chosen and used that make the communicative message visual, versus abstract language that utilizes vague and general vocabulary where the listener is responsible for their own interpretation of the message.

KATHERINE E. COOK

CONCURRENT VALIDITY

Concurrent validity refers to a parameter demonstrated when a test correlates positively with a previously validated measure. The two measures may be for the same construct, or for different, but presumably related constructs.

JEANNE HOLVERSTOTT

CONFIDENTIALITY

Confidentiality is the act of ensuring that information is accessible only to authorized individuals. According to the procedural safeguards created by the **Individuals with**

Disabilities Education Act (IDEA), there is a "right to confidentiality of personally identifiable information, including the right of parents to written notice of and written consent to the exchange of such information" [20 U.S.C. § 1439(639)]. In addition to IDEA, two other major pieces of legislation regulate third-party access to educational and medical records: the Family Educational Rights and Privacy Act (FERPA, 1975) and the Health Insurance Portability and Accountability act (HIPPA, 1996).

REFERENCES
Family Educational Rights and Privacy Act (FERPA) 20 U.S.C. § 1232 *et seq.*
Health Insurance Portability and Accountability Act (HIPPA).
Individuals with Disabilities Education Act (IDEA), 20 U.S.C. § 1401 *et seq.*

THERESA L. EARLES-VOLLRATH

CONSENT

Consent is the act of giving written permission by an individual who is fully informed on information relevant to the proposed activity. According to the **Individuals with Disabilities Education Act** (IDEA), written parental consent is required prior to the following: initial evaluation, placement of students in special education, change of placement, and release of records (IDEA, 20 U.S.C. § 1414(a) (1) (D)). Consent must be given voluntarily by parents who have sufficient information and who have the capacity to give consent. In addition, consent can be revoked at any time while the activity for which consent was given occurs.

REFERENCE
Individuals with Disabilities Education Act (IDEA), 20 U.S.C. § 1414(a) (1) (D).

FURTHER INFORMATION
Yell, M. L. (2006). *The law and special education* (2nd ed). Upper Saddle River, NJ: Prentice Hall.

THERESA L. EARLES-VOLLRATH

CONSEQUENCE

A consequence is what happens immediately after a behavior or response. A consequence may be intentional, unintentional, positive, or negative. Regardless, the consequence shapes the behavior that precedes it. For example, a student who disrupts math class and is consequently sent from the room may be escaping math class. In this case, the consequence is exactly what the student desires and only serves to strengthen the behavior, disrupting class. Therefore, it is important to be aware of the **function of behavior** before assigning a consequence.

KATIE BASSITY

CONSTIPATION

Constipation is a condition in which the passage of stool decreases in frequency and/or stools become hard, dry, and difficult to pass. Numerous factors can contribute including diet, lack of appropriate schedule, psychological problems, intestinal obstruction, and medications. There is a wide variety on "normal" frequency of bowel movement, ranging from 2–3 times a day to 1–2 times per week.

BRUCE BASSITY

CONTINGENCY

A contingency is the relationship between a behavior and its associated **consequences**. A contingency exists when an event is consistently presented, removed, or withheld following the occurrence of a specific behavior. Contingencies can occur naturally (Ferster, 1965), or they can be contrived (e.g., when a piece of food is given for an appropriate response).

REFERENCE

Ferster, C. B. (1965). Arbitrary and natural reinforcement. *Psychological Record, 17,* 341–347.

JEANNE HOLVERSTOTT

CONTINGENCY CONTRACTING

A contingency contract is an agreement between two individuals, usually a student and teacher or other adult. Also known as a behavior contract, it is usually written out and explicitly names a desired behavior that the student commits to in return for explicitly named reinforcement that the teacher or other adult will provide when the desired behavior occurs. A contingency contract is generally put in place to encourage a positive behavior in place of an existing undesired behavior.

KATIE BASSITY

CONTROL GROUP/CONTROL CONDITION

The control group (also called control condition or comparison group) is used to compare the different groups in an experimental research study. For example, in an investigation of a reading intervention, one group of children would receive the intervention that is being studied while the control group would not receive the intervention and would either receive an alternate treatment or no treatment at all. The purpose of the control group is to increase the strength by which researchers can claim that the intervention (the independent variable) caused the changes in subject behavior and that other factors were not involved.

FURTHER INFORMATION

Everitt, B. S. (2002). *The Cambridge dictionary of statistics* (2nd ed.). Cambridge: Cambridge University Press.
Salkind, N. J. (2005). *Exploring research* (6th ed.). Upper Saddle River, NJ: Prentice Hall.

PAUL G. LaCAVA

CORRECTIONAL FACILITY

A court appointed facility for juvenile offenders where education services are provided for an established time period set by the juvenile court system. Educational services are continued if the student had an **Individualized Education Program** (IEP) at the time of entrance into the juvenile system.

KATHERINE E. COOK

CRITERION-REFERENCED ASSESSMENT

A criterion-referenced assessment measures a student's mastery of specific content or skills. These assessments provide information regarding what a student knows related to a standard or criteria; in contrast, **norm-referenced assessments** measure how much one knows.

FURTHER INFORMATION

Pierangelo, R., & Giuliani, G. (1998). *Special educator's complete guide to 109 diagnostic tests: How to select and interpret tests, use results in IEPs, and remediate specific difficulties.* West Nyack, NY: Center for Applied Research in Education.

Taylor, R. L. (2006). *Assessment of exceptional students: Educational and psychological procedures* (7th ed.). Needham Heights, MA: Allyn and Bacon.

THERESA L. EARLES-VOLLRATH

CT SCAN. *See* CAT Scan

CURRICULUM

Curriculum is the subject matter that is to be taught by the teacher and mastered by the student. Curriculum is usually described in terms of its scope and sequence. One might examine the curriculum of a special school, for example, to determine whether it matches the **Individualized Education Program** of a student who had been recommended to receive services there.

KATHERINE E. COOK

CURRICULUM-BASED ASSESSMENT

Curriculum-Based Assessment (CBA) is an ongoing, alternative method of assessing student performance that compares the student's abilities with the curricular sequence he will be taught or the content that has been taught. An advantage of this assessment method is that the results relate directly to instructional objectives and materials.

FURTHER INFORMATION

Scheuermann, B. & Webber, J. (2002). *Autism: Teaching does make a difference.* Belmont, CA: Wadsworth/Thomson Learning.

THERESA L. EARLES-VOLLRATH

D

DAILY LIVING SKILLS

Daily living skills are those behaviors that are required for independence in the current environment and in adult life. Depending on age and ability level, daily living skills may include knowledge to: (a) purchase foods and prepare meals, (b) manage personal finances (counting money, making change, and using banking services independently), (c) care for personal and home needs (bathing independently, doing laundry, and cleaning the house), (d) navigate the community using various means of transportation (knowing where one lives, being able to make short trips, and using public transportation or driving a car), (e) understand health and safety issues (knowing who to contact in an emergency), (f) social interaction skills (interpersonal skills, self confidence, self-advocacy, communicating with others appropriately), and (g) decision making/problem solving. For many students identified with ASD, these skills may be included in school learning in order to ensure the individual achieves the greatest self-reliance and independence in adult life.

FURTHER INFORMATION
Brolin, D. (1997). *Life centered career education: A competency based approach* (4th ed.). Reston, VA: Council for Exceptional Children.

ANDREA M. BABKIE

DANCE THERAPY

Dance, or movement therapy, is the therapeutic use of movement and dance as a method to treat emotional, cognitive, social, and physical disorders (ADTA, 2006). Dance/movement therapy can be a tool for stress management, the prevention of physical and mental health problems, easing chronic pain, and enhancing the circulatory and respiratory systems. It can also benefit those with diagnoses including learning disabilities, visual or hearing impairments, or mental handicaps.

This type of therapy promotes improvement by creating bonds between clients, decreasing muscular tension, trusting personal impulses, and encouraging self-expression. In addition, this movement is physical and provides the benefits of exercise and improved health. One of the guiding ideas behind dance therapy is the connection between the mind and body and how this connection influences a person's well-being and mental functioning.

The designation of Dance Therapy Registered (DTR) is for individuals who are at the entry level, have a master's degree, and completed 700 hours of a supervised clinical internship. The Academy of Dance Therapists Registered (ADTR) is an advanced designation and is reserved for those individuals who have completed 3,640 hours of supervised clinical work as well as other supervision requirements by a dance therapist who has received the Academy of Dance Therapists Registered designation.

Dance/movement therapists can work with clients on an individual basis or in a group setting in general hospitals, psychiatric hospitals, developmental centers, mental health centers, schools, and rehabilitation centers. Referrals and/or recommendations may come from a primary care physician regardless of whether the dance/movement therapist is an independent provider or part of a treatment team.

REFERENCE

American Dance Therapy Association 2006. (n.d.). *Who we are*. Retrieved September 20, 2006, from www.adta.com.

LYNN DUDEK

DAS-NAGLIERI COGNITIVE ASSESSMENT SYSTEM (CAS)

Das-Naglieri Cognitive Assessment System (Naglieri, 1999) is a norm-referenced measure of intelligence based on the PASS theory of cognitive processing. PASS consists of four cognitive components (planning, attention, simultaneous, and successive processes) that form a complex and interdependent system. Planning refers to a set of decisions or strategies an individual adopts and modifies to solve a problem and to reach a goal. Planning tasks in the CAS require an individual to develop some approach of solving the task in an efficient and effective manner. Attention implies that the individual is alert. Alertness can be sustained for a period of time and is selective. Arousal, or alertness, is a prerequisite for learning and memory. Attention tasks in the CAS require the individual to selectively attend to one and ignore the other aspect of a two-dimensional stimulus. Simultaneous processing refers to the person's facility in relating and integrating discrete pieces of information. Simultaneous tasks in the CAS require the individual to interrelate the component parts of a particular item to arrive at the correct answer. The relationship between all the component parts must be incorporated into some complete pattern or idea. Successive processing refers to the person's ability to keep things in a particular order. Successive tasks in the CAS require the individual to either reproduce a particular sequence of events or answer some questions that require correct interpretation of the linearity of events. The CAS is appropriate for use with individuals between the ages of 5 and 18.

REFERENCE

Naglieri, J. (1999). *Essentials of CAS Assessment (Essentials of Psychological Assessment Series)*. New York: Wiley.

JEANNE HOLVERSTOTT

DATA

Data is a large class of practically important statements collected from each subject or the variables through measurements or observations. Those statements may comprise numbers, words, or images. Data on its own has no meaning. It only takes on meaning and becomes information when interpreted by some kind of data processing system. People or computers can find patterns in data to perceive information, and information can be used to enhance knowledge.

KAI-CHIEN TIEN

DEEP PRESSURE PROPRIOCEPTION TOUCH TECHNIQUE

Deep pressure proprioception touch technique is a method of intervention that provides sensory information to the joints and larger muscle groups in the body through firm touch and pressure. This information helps the individual organize his body and movements into more purposeful, adaptive responses.

KELLY M. PRESTIA

DEMENTIA INFANTALIS. *See* Childhood Disintegrative Disorder

DESENSITIZATION

Desensitization is a method to reduce or eliminate an individual's negative reaction to a substance or stimulus. In pharmacology, desensitization is the loss of responsiveness to the continuing or increasing dose of a drug. In psychology, desensitization (or graduated exposure therapy) is a process for mitigating the harmful effects of phobias or other disorders. It also occurs when an emotional response is repeatedly evoked in situations in which the action tendency that is associated with the emotion proves irrelevant or unnecessary. A common application of desensitization is the pairing of an aversive stimulus with a reinforcing stimulus with gradual, increased exposure to what is aversive. For example, an individual who fears snakes would begin by looking at a snake from afar and gradually working to hold the snake.

JEANNE HOLVERSTOTT

DESIRED BEHAVIOR. *See* Target Behavior

DETOXIFICATION

Detoxification is a practice that purportedly removes toxins from the body in order to improve functioning and/or reduce symptoms related to the presence of toxins (heavy metals, poisons). Detoxification is not currently supported by empirical research.

See also chelation; heavy metals; vaccinations.

JEANNE HOLVERSTOTT

DEVELOPMENTAL AGE

Developmental age is an index of development stated as the age of an individual and determined by specified standardized measurements such as motor and mental tests and body measurement. It is a measure of a child's development or maturation in different domains expressed in terms of age norm. In other words, developmental age is the physical, neurological, social, emotional, and intellectual growth changes that have occurred within a particular child. Those growth changes are unique to the child and make the child different from every other child. All children mature at slightly different rates. A child's developmental age may or may not correspond with his or her chronological age.

KAI-CHIEN TIEN

DEVELOPMENTAL DELAY

As defined by the Division of Early Childhood (DEC) in 1991, "developmental delay is a condition which presents a significant delay in the process of development. It does not refer to a condition in which a child is slightly or momentarily lagging in development." Without early or special interventions it is likely that educational performance at school age will be affected. Developmental delay can be diagnosed by the child's pediatrician through a series of tests or checklists.

REFERENCE

Division of Early Childhood. (1991). Retrieved October 17, 2006, from http://www.dec-sped.org/pdf/positionpapers/PositionStatement_DevDelay.pdf.

JAN L. KLEIN

DEVELOPMENTAL DISORDER

Developmental disorder is the term used to describe a diagnostic grouping of conditions seen from childhood and into adulthood. These include speech and language delay, reading delay, autism spectrum disorders, generalized learning disabilities, enuresis, and encopresis. They are a heterogeneous group that are characterized by abnormality or delay in the development of functions and abilities that normally are seen during childhood development or maturation. Disorders such as autism spectrum disorders (also known diagnostically as **pervasive developmental disorders**) are considered primarily as neurodevelopmental disorders with neurological or genetic factors influencing the cause, presentation, and progress of the disorder.

Other disorders that are usually grouped elsewhere are conduct disorder, oppositional-defiant disorder, and hyperactivity (grouped as disruptive behavior disorders), and anxiety disorders, phobias, depression, obsessive-compulsive disorder, and somatization (grouped as emotional disorders). However, the division between these groupings is somewhat spurious and due more to convenience than to any defined difference between the developmental status of the conditions. Indeed, all of the disorders reported in disruptive behaviors and emotional disorders can be seen in children and present during development, so are often also referred to as developmental.

In addition, there are other disorders seen in childhood that do not fit neatly into the aforementioned groupings: Tourette's syndrome, anorexia nervosa, early onset schizophrenia, attachment disorders, and so on. Thus developmental disorders do not cover the whole range of childhood psychiatric or mental health difficulties that are seen (Goodman & Scott, 2005, pp. 27–28).

In terms of the pervasive developmental disorders, those developmental disorders that incorporate autism, these are currently listed in the *Diagnostic and Statistical Manual of Mental Disorders* (DSM-IV-TR: APA, 2000) to include the following: **Autistic disorder, Asperger's disorder, Pervasive Developmental Disorder–Not Otherwise Specified, Rett's disorder**, and **Childhood Disintegrative Disorder**. The latter two conditions are different than the former three in that they are thought to be of different origin or etiology to autism disorders, but are included under the general term of pervasive developmental disorders due to the similarity in features, the desire to differentiate between similar presentations, and the fact that the difficulties seen are pervasive.

REFERENCES

American Psychiatric Association. (2000). *Diagnostic and statistical manual of mental disorders* (4th ed., text rev.). Washington, DC: Author.

Goodman, R., & Scott, S. (2005). *Child psychiatry* (2nd ed.). Oxford: Blackwell Publishing.

FIONA J. SCOTT

DEVELOPMENTAL INDIVIDUAL-DIFFERENCE RELATION-BASED INTERVENTION (DIR)

Developed by Stanley Greenspan and Serena Wieder, developmental individual difference relation-based intervention (DIR) is often referred to as **floor time**; however, the floor time component is only part of the approach. DIR is a framework for assessment and intervention for children with challenges related to social relatedness and communication. The general approach of the DIR model is to assist children in developing logical understanding of the world around them through a variety of interventions including floor time.

OVERVIEW OF THE DIR MODEL

Greenspan and Wieder believe that teaching children through the DIR model enables them to become independent thinkers. This is done through using emotional and motivating experiences to help the child master the building blocks of social skills, language, independence, learning specific concepts, and academics.

DIR focuses on several components as part of the intervention program. These include: (a) home programming, (b) school programming, (c) specific therapies, (d) biomedical interventions, and (e) family support. Additionally, according to Greenspan, home and school programs should consist of the three following learning experiences: (a) floor time sessions, (b) semi-structured problem-solving interactions, and (c) sensorimotor activities. These activities are incorporated in the development of the child's milestones.

Within the DIR model, autism is considered as a form of developmental delay (Greenspan & Wieder, 1998, 2003). For example, failure to attain the capabilities of joint attention (Reed, 2002) and social reciprocity (Conners & Multi-Health Systems Staff, 1995; Goldstein, Johnson, & Minshew, 2001; Heaton, Chelune, Talley, Kay, & Curtis, 1993; Korkman, Kirk, & Kemp, 1998; Minshew & Goldstein, 2001) are consistent across autism and pervasive developmental disorders. Other missed milestones in functional language and early motor capacities, along with planning, sequencing, and symbolic functioning required for pretend-play also indicate possible autism or a related condition (Greenspan & Wieder, 2003). Finally, modulation of sensory input is also highly correlated with autism and other pervasive developmental delays (Kientz & Dunn, 1997; Stone & Lemanek, 1990).

As with physical development, charting the social, emotional, cognitive, language, and motor skills according to typical developmental landmarks helps determine and address the developmental delays associated with pervasive developmental delays such as autism (Greenspan & Wieder, 2003).

Greenspan and Wieder (1998) identify six developmental milestones children with autism need to master in order to develop the necessary skills of communication, thinking, and coping with the world on a cognitive-emotional level. Due to the developmental nature of the stages, each milestone must be mastered before attempting to reach the next level.

Six Developmental Milestones

Milestone 1: Self-Regulation and Interest in the World

Success in this stage means the child is able to use his five outer (sight, touch, taste, smell, and hearing) and two inner (vestibular and proprioception) senses to gather information from the environment while self-regulating the strength and quality of the input for successful interaction with the environment. For some children, failure to master this stage demonstrates itself in becoming overwhelmed with sensory input resulting in irritable behavior or shutting down. Other children, due to lack of perceptible data from the environment, will take little interest in their environment and seem detached.

Milestone 2: Intimacy

Success in this stage means the child demonstrates interest in interacting in a warm, joyful, and loving manner with their peers as well as others. Failure to master this level of development—likely due to sensory processing difficulties—results in the environment becoming confusing, scary, or painful. Many children who experience difficulties at this stage prefer the company of older people because adults are more able to scaffold conversations and other interactions with them.

Milestone 3: Two-Way Communication

The initiation of interaction is considered as *opening* the circle of communication, whereas the response to another person's intent to interact is considered as *closing* the circle of communication. Success in this stage presents a child who feels secure in his interactions with others as a prerequisite for understanding that his communicative intent affects others' reactions and that he has an impact on the world. Two-way communication occurs with single gestures to initiate (open) and to respond to (close) circles of communication (Greenspan & Wieder, 1998). Failure to master this level of development results in a child that can be hard to engage, seems oblivious to the environment, or perhaps watches from the sidelines appearing that they would like to get involved. Difficulty in reading nonverbal and pragmatic information impinges on successful two-way communication, necessitating outside help in facilitating interaction and taking initiative.

Milestone 4: Complex Communication

The child who successfully navigates this level has mastered the basics of two-way communication and developed a vocabulary for expressing wishes. This child now conceptualizes behavioral sequences that he or she can use to convey wishes and intentions as well as reading them in others. Failure to reach and work through this developmental phase stems from issues of sensory integration leading to difficulties in motor planning, logical thought, and reading the behavior of others without direct (often intensive) instruction. As the complexity of two-way communication increases, the child becomes more overwhelmed and confused, resulting in defensive, irritable, or isolationist behaviors.

Milestone 5: Emotional Ideas—"The Ability to Create Ideas"

The child begins to engage in appropriate representational play at this stage (Greenspan & Wieder, 1998; Miller & Eller-Miller, 1989; 2000). The child now uses toy cars for pretend races, travel, accidents, and repairs rather than turning it upside down to spin the wheels. A baby doll will be fed and told "night night" when it is time to sleep. The child also begins to narrate these activities, and words now have meaning rather than being just symbols of objects, events, people, and ideas. The child can use words to explain thoughts and feelings, and to create stories. Emotional islands of expression are formed around these activities.

The child who is unable to master this milestone continues to have difficulties with intimate and two-way communication. While he or she often shows an interest in toys and can keep calm, however, communication occurs only when motivated. He or she may use one-word requests for wants and needs but will rarely use items for representative play or create a story.

Milestone 6: Emotional Thinking

A child who is at stage six is able to connect the islands of emotional expression and sequence several representative pretend-play events. For example, instead of playing with the toy cars and doll as explained previously as separate events, the two activities are now connected. For example, after the doll goes to sleep, mommy and daddy doll may bring her into the car for a drive to the ice cream store or a friend's house where the baby doll may wake up to play with friends or to eat. The child develops a greater understanding of self, how his or her actions affect another person, and vice versa. For example, the child can now say, "I am happy that you gave me cookies and milk," and can interact on higher levels of emotionality as verbal and spatial skills increase.

The child who is unable to reach this stage remains unable to link the emotional islands described earlier. The previous emotional milestones seem to have been achieved at times but often fall apart under stress and result in being unable to close circles of communication.

According to Greenspan and Wieder (1998), mastering these developmental milestones gives the child a foundation of "critical basic tools for communicating, thinking, and emotional coping" (p. 89) and decreases the negative impact the autism spectrum disorder has for the person's development. Stress is placed on the child mastering each developmental level before attempting to complete the next level as opposed to chronological age as a consideration.

REFERENCES

Conners, C. K., & Multi-Health Systems Staff. (1995). *Conners continuous performance test.* Toronto: MHS.

Goldstein, G., Johnson, C. R., & Minshew, N. J. (2001). Attentional processes in autism. *Journal of Autism & Developmental Disorders, 31*(4):433–440.

Greenspan, S., & Wieder, S. (1998). *The child with special needs: Encouraging intellectual and emotional growth.* Reading, MA: Addison Wesley.

Greenspan, S., & Wieder, S. (2003). Assessment and early identification. In E. Hollander (Ed.), *Autism spectrum disorders* (pp. 57–86). New York: Marcel Dekker, Inc.

Heaton, R. K., Chelune, G. J., Talley, J. L., Kay, G. G., & Curtis, G. (1993). *Wisconsin card sorting test (WCST) manual revised and expanded.* Odessa, FL: Psychological Assessment Resources.

Kientz, M. A., & Dunn, W. (1997). A comparison of the performance of children with and without autism on the Sensory Profile. *American Journal of Occupational Therapy, 51,* 530–537.

Korkman, A. S., Kirk, U., & Kemp, S. (1998). *A developmental neuropsychological assessment.* San Antonio, TX: The Psychological Corporation.

Miller, A., & Eller-Miller, E. (1989). *From ritual to repertoire: A cognitive-developmental systems approach with behavior-disordered children.* New York: Wiley-Interscience.

Miller, A., & Eller-Miller, E. (2000 November). The Miller method: A cognitive-developmental systems approach for children with body organization, social and communication issues. In S. Greenspan & S. Wieder (Eds.), *ICDL clinical practices guidelines: Revising the standards of practice for infants, toddlers and children with developmental challenges* (pp. 489–516). Bethesda, MD: The Interdisciplinary Council on Developmental and Learning Disorders.

Minshew, N. J., & Goldstein, G. (2001). The pattern of intact and impaired memory functions in autism. *Journal of Child Psychology and Psychiatry, 42,* 1095–1101.

Reed, T. (2002). Visual perspective taking as a measure of working memory in participants with autism. *Journal of Developmental and Physical Disabilities, 14*(1), 63–76.

Stone, W. L., & Lemanek, K. L. (1990). Parental report of social behaviors in autistic preschoolers. *Journal of Autism and Developmental Disorders, 20,* 513–522.

FURTHER INFORMATION

American Psychiatric Association. (2000). *Diagnostic and statistical manual of mental disorders* (4th. ed., text rev.). Washington, DC: Author.

Gutstein, S. (2000). *Autism Aspergers: Solving the relationship puzzle: A new developmental program that opens the door to lifelong social & emotional growth.* Arlington, TX: Future Horizons.

Gutstein, S. (2003). Can my baby learn to dance? In L. Willey (Ed.), *Asperger syndrome in adolescence: The ups, downs, and inbetweens* (pp. 98–128). London: Jessica Kingsley Publishers.

Spence, S. J. & Geschwind, D. H. (2003). Autism screening and neurodevelopmental assessment. In E. Hollander (Ed.), *Autism spectrum disorders* (pp. 39–56). New York: Marcel Dekker, Inc.

STEPHEN SHORE

DEVELOPMENTALLY APPROPRIATE PRACTICE

Professionals who adhere to developmental models such as those based on Piaget's theories often refer to their philosophy as developmentally appropriate practice (DAP). This practice is based on knowledge about what is typically expected of and experienced by children of different ages and developmental stages. As Katz (1995) states, "what should be learned and how it would best be learned depend on what we know of the learner's developmental status and our understanding of the relationships between early experience and subsequent developments" (p. 109). The philosophy and the guidelines for DAP are described in widely disseminated materials published by the National Association for the Education of Young Children (NAEYC; Bredekamp, 1987; Bredekamp & Copple, 1997).

REFERENCES

Bredekamp, S. (1987). *Developmentally appropriate practice in early childhood programs serving children from birth through age 8.* Washington, DC: National Association for the Education of Young Children.

Bredekamp, S., & Copple, C. (1997). *Developmentally appropriate practice in early childhood programs.* Washington, DC: National Association for the Education of Young Children.

Katz, L. (1995). *Talk with teachers of young children: A collection.* Norwood, NJ: Ablex.

KAI-CHIEN TIEN

DEVELOPMENTAL MILESTONES

Developmental milestones are a set of functional skills that most children can do at a certain age range as defined by the American Academy of Pediatrics. These milestones are used by qualified professionals to check developmental progress. These milestones can be broken down into the following areas: (a) motor skills; (b) sensory and thinking skills; and (c) language and social skills. During the first year, the milestones are usually assessed at 3, 6, and 12 months. Although each milestone has a corresponding age level, the actual age when a normally developing child reaches that milestone can vary.

REFERENCE

American Academy of Pediatrics. (n.d.). Retrieved October 17, 2006, from http://www.aap.org/healthtopics/stages.cfm.

JAN L. KLEIN

DEVELOPMENTAL PLAY ASSESSMENT INSTRUMENT (DPA)

The Developmental Play Assessment Instrument (DPA; Lifter, Sulzer-Azaroff, Anderson, & Cowdery, 1993) is designed as a curriculum-based assessment of children's play activities, providing an evaluation of the quality of a child's toy play skills in relation to those of typically developing children.

Play activities have been identified as critical to the development of language, motor skills, and social interaction in children with developmental disabilities. The DPA identifies a child's current level of performance in the play curriculum and then determines the steps necessary for that child to acquire more developmentally challenging play activities.

REFERENCE

Lifter, K. Sulzer-Azaroff, B., Anderson, S., & Cowdery, G. (1993). Teaching play activities to preschool children with disabilities: The importance of developmental considerations. *Journal of Early Intervention, 17*(2), 139–159.

JEANNE HOLVERSTOTT

DEVELOPMENTAL QUOTIENT

Used to express a developmental delay, the adaptive Developmental Quotient (DQ) is a ratio of the developmental (functional) age to the **chronological age** and is expressed as a **percentile**. The overall developmental score relates to performance in four domains: motor skills (e.g., balancing, sitting); language use; adaptive behavior (e.g., alertness, exploration); and personal-social skills (e.g., feeding, dressing). DQ can be calculated on the basis of standardized developmental tests suitable for young children, but DQ is also used for estimates of mental age based on the impressions of professionals (e.g., child psychologists, pediatricians, and teachers) as well as parents or other family members.

See also standardization tests.

JAN L. KLEIN

DEVELOPMENTAL SURVEILLANCE

Developmental surveillance is a flexible, continuous process whereby knowledgeable professionals perform skilled observations of children during the provision of health care. The components of developmental surveillance include: (a) eliciting and attending to parental concerns, (b) obtaining a relevant developmental history, (c) making accurate and informative observations of children, and (d) sharing opinions and concerns with other relevant professionals.

Pediatricians often use age-appropriate developmental checklists to record milestones during preventive care visits as part of developmental surveillance.

JAN L. KLEIN

DEVELOPMENTAL THERAPY

Developmental therapy (DT) is a program designed to enhance social functioning during interactions between people. Misunderstandings of social situations may lead to withdrawal, aggression, and lower self-esteem, especially in students with an autism spectrum disorder. This structured teaching program can be used for students from birth to age 16, with various disabilities. Developmental therapy matches teaching strategies to a student's needs, helps create an understanding of uneven or splinter skills, assists in revising program strategies, and then evaluates the progress.

Developmental therapy consists of five stages; each stage consists of four components. The components that DT addresses are: behavior, communication, socialization, and academics. The stages included in the program are as follows:

- Stage 1: Responding to the environment with pleasure
- Stage 2: Responding to the environment with success
- Stage 3: Successful group participation
- Stage 4: Investing in group process, with concern for others
- Stage 5: Using individual and group skills in new situations

Students in stage one may be impulsive, display no problem solving skills, have tantrums, aggressions, and/or display self-injurious behaviors when problems occur. This lack of ability to handle problems may be attached to anxiety, stemming from feelings of abandonment, helplessness, deprivation, and uncertainty.

The four components address several milestones during each stage—behavior, communication, socialization, and academics—used in developmental therapy. Behavioral milestones in stage one include indicating awareness of sensory stimuli, responding to stimuli, independently responding to play materials, spontaneously moving from area to area, and indicating recall of routine without assistance. In the area of communication, stage one's main goal is for the students to use words to gain their needs. Milestones in the communication component include producing sounds, attending to the person speaking, responding to a verbal stimuli with a motor behavior, responding to verbal cues, using recognizable word approximation or words to describe, label, or request, and producing recognizable single words or meaning sequencing of words. These communication milestones prepare a child for work toward the socialization goal of trusting and communicating with adults. To accomplish this, the student indicates an awareness of others, attends to other's behaviors, responds to an adult when his or her name is called, engages in organized and solitary play, interacts with an adult nonverbally or verbally to have needs met, demonstrates an understanding of a single verbal request or direction, and conveys a beginning awareness of self. The last component's goal, academics, requires the student to respond to the environment with intentional body movements and basic mental processes of memory, classification, and receptive language. Milestones in this area show spontaneous short-term memory for people and objects, spontaneously imitate simple, familiar actions of adults, show fine- and large-motor skills associated with an 18-month-old developmental level, and indicate an understanding of names of familiar objects, matching shapes of objects with corresponding space, identifying own body parts, and sorting two types of similar objects with slightly different attributes.

The overall goal of stage two, responding to the environment with success, is accomplished by addressing the concerns of the students. These concerns include pleasing adults, low confidence or self-esteem, limited awareness of cause and effect, ineffective responses to adults and peers, impulsive behaviors, and frustration directed toward adults. The students' motivation to gain adult approval and seek recognition allows the adults to address the four components in this stage.

The behavioral milestone for stage two focuses on participating in routines and activity with success. Teaching students to play with materials appropriately, wait without physical intervention by an adult, and participate in sitting and movement activities without intervention helps strengthen skills. During these activities, adults encourage the students to use words constructively, such as answering questions or requests with relevant words, indicating comprehension of others, spontaneously using simple word sequences, spontaneously using words to share information with adults and other children, and describing simple, tangible characteristics of oneself and others. Socially, the students in this stage work on initiating imaginative play and appropriate social movement towards peers and participating in sharing activities and interactive play with peers. Academically, the student develops self-help skills and motor coordination comparable to the level of a 5-year-old. The student also concentrates on language, mental processes of discrimination, sequencing, and numeration, up to the number 10.

While focusing on the skills needed to interact and participate appropriately in groups, the time Stage 3 students take to progress varies. The concern with looking good to others motivates students and recognition of fair play and a preoccupation with law and order makes the introduction of rules a smooth transition. Instructors teach and evaluate skills such as completing individual tasks independently, understanding the rules and reasons that regulate behavior, refraining from unacceptable behavior when others are losing control, and maintaining acceptable physical and verbal behavior in a group. The students need to show that they are able to spontaneously describe personal experiences and ideas, show positive and negative feelings appropriately, participate in group discussions, describe attributes of themselves and others, and recognize the feelings of other students. An improvement in the student's communication skills directly affects their socialization goal of finding satisfaction in group activities. Students share materials, take turns, imitate appropriate behavior of peers, lead or demonstrate a group activity, and participate in activities suggested by other students. These beginning level skills of Stage 3 help students develop a friendship with a peer and spontaneously seek out assistance from peers (social milestones serve as the end goal). Academically, Stage 3 students vary from being able to perform at the level of a 6-year-old to reading and writing simple sentences, using addition and subtraction involving time and money, using place value, regrouping, and multiplication to solve problems.

Real-life experiences and group activities are used with Stage 4 students to address the goal of investing in group processes and demonstrating concern for others. These students are concerned with meeting the expectations of others. When presented with a problem, they accept responsibility for themselves and vacillate between conforming to the peer group or standing apart. The behavioral milestones in Stage 4 address skills that enable the student to contribute to the group's success. Participating in new activities with control, implementing acceptable alternative behaviors, and accepting responsibility for their actions and attitudes are the skills taught to achieve the behavioral goal. Both communication and socialization goals target group communication and participating successfully as a group member. The student learns to express their feelings appropriately in a group and explain the cause-and-effect relationships between feelings and behaviors. Listening to group members, expressing awareness of other's actions, suggesting group activities, and problem solving all signal the student's accomplishment of the socialization milestones in Stage 4. Academics, the last component in Stage 4, covers skills needed for successful social group experiences, such as computing values for money up to 10 dollars, writing to communicate information, events, and feelings, and reading for pleasure and personal information.

The final stage, Stage 5, teaches skills students need in new situations. These skills help students respond to life experiences with constructive behaviors, use appropriate words to establish and enrich relationships, initiate and maintain effective interpersonal relationships independently, and utilize academic skills for personal enrichment. Behavior, communication, academics, and socialization milestones continue to be taught and addressed in this stage.

Overall, developmental therapy emphasizes structured activities that help students promote their social-emotional functioning. The activities that are incorporated into DT help students feel successful and produce social-emotional competence while promoting responsible behavior in students. Developmental therapy serves as a useful teaching method for students on the autism spectrum.

FURTHER INFORMATION
Wood, M. M. (1996). *Developmental therapy–developmental teaching: Fostering social-emotional competence in troubled children and youth* (3rd ed.). Austin, TX: Pro-Ed.

MELISSA L. TRAUTMAN

DIAGNOSTIC AND STATISTICAL MANUAL OF MENTAL DISORDERS– FOURTH EDITION–TEXT REVISED (DSM-IV-TR)

The *Diagnostic and Statistical Manual of Mental Disorders* (DSM), published by the American Psychiatric Association (APA), is a guidebook most commonly used by mental health professionals in the United States to diagnose mental disorders. The DSM uses medical concepts and terminology and classifies criteria-based disorders into distinct categories and subcategories. For example, **pervasive developmental disorder** includes **autistic disorder, Asperger's disorder, Rett's disorder, childhood disintegrative disorder**, and **pervasive developmental disorder–not otherwise specified**.

REFERENCE

American Psychiatric Association. (2000). *Diagnostic and statistical manual of mental disorders* (4th ed., text rev.). Washington, DC: Author.

JEANNE HOLVERSTOTT

DIET

Diet has been a focus for many families and professionals who attempt to help those with autism. Dietary interventions have been used to address several major concerns for those with autism spectrum disorders (ASD). For example, some individuals with autism have difficulties breaking down certain proteins such as gluten or casein. The **gluten-free** or **casein-free** diet has been one of the most used for those with ASD; this diet eliminates wheat, barley, oat, rye, and dairy products. Special diets have been used to treat infections from fungi such as *Candida*, a typically found yeast-producing disease in humans. This diet would reduce or eliminate certain sugars, carbohydrates, yeasts, and various foods prepared by curing or drying. Other well-known diets include the ketogenic and **Feingold diets**. Although there is limited and mixed supportive evidence for special diets, many have used this method, and much more research is needed in this area for parents and professionals to make important decisions.

See also diet therapy; gluten-free.

FURTHER INFORMATION

Simpson, R. L., de Boer-Ott, S. R., Griswold, D. E., Myles, B. S., Cook, K. T., Otten, K., et al. (2004). *Autism spectrum disorders: Interventions and treatments for children and youth*. Thousand Oaks, CA: Corwin Press.

PAUL G. LaCAVA

DIET THERAPY

The use of specific foods and special diets to treat diseases and conditions has existed for hundreds of years. Sailors used limes or vinegar to treat scurvy (for the vitamin C), and families treated thrush, an oral yeast overgrowth, with buttermilk. Today, diet therapy has been used to treat or lessen the effects of certain conditions from heart disease to autism. While there is no diet or medication that can cure autism, some believe that dietary changes may lessen the effects of autism spectrum disorder.

Current dietary interventions for the treatment of autism include the use of vitamins and minerals, **dimethylglycine** (DMG) supplements, **gluten/casein-free** foods, and secretin therapy. While some of these methods may show improvement in a child's behavior and/or language skills, well-controlled, consistent, empirically based research does not exist in sufficient amounts to warrant widespread use.

VITAMINS AND MINERALS

Through anecdotal reports, families have shared the benefits of using vitamin and mineral supplements in children on the autism spectrum. The rationale behind using vitamins and minerals is the idea that these children may have absorption problems and/or nutritional deficiencies due to dietary difficulties (ASA, 2006). Intestinal disorders can interfere with the proper absorption of some vitamins and minerals. This is what drives some to believe that children with autism may have deficiencies in vitamins A and several B complexes as well as minerals like magnesium.

Before beginning vitamin therapy, a physician and/or health care professional must examine the child. Throughout vitamin therapy the child's doctor should monitor blood levels, behaviors, and reactions as some vitamins may be toxic at certain levels.

DIMETHYLGLYCINE

Dimethylglycine (DMG) is an amino acid that is naturally found in plant and animal cells (and in foods like brown rice and liver). DMG is produced in the cells and aids in the metabolism of certain chemicals in the body. Claims have been made that it aids in the management of autism because it is an oxygenator of brain and body tissues (citation). This compound is also believed to augment immune responses. More human-based studies are needed to examine the effectiveness of this compound.

GLUTEN/CASEIN-FREE

This diet is the removal of all foods that contain gluten (the protein in wheat) and casein (the protein in milk). Some children with autism have difficulties breaking down certain proteins (GFCF Diet, 2006). By eliminating these foods, it is believed that the by-product of the breakdown of gluten and casein, an opiate-like compound, will be eliminated and thus improve the functioning of children with autism. As with any dietary manipulation, the child's physician must be consulted.

SECRETIN THERAPY

Secretin is a hormone that is found naturally in the body (ASA, n.d.). Over the past few years, infusions of secretin were believed to decrease the symptoms of autism. Since that time, research has shown that the use of secretin to treat autism is ineffective (Sturmey, 2005).

REFERENCES

Autism Society of America (ASA). (n.d.). Biomedical and dietary approaches. Retrieved September 20, 2006, from www.autism-society.org.

GFCF Diet. (2006). Introductory FAQs. Retrieved September 20, 2006, from www.gfcfdiet.com.

Sturmey, P. (2005). Secretin is an ineffective treatment for pervasive developmental disabilities: A review of 15 double-blind randomized controlled trials. *Research in Developmental Disabilities, 26*, 87–97.

LYNN DUDEK

DIFFERENTIAL ABILITY SCALES

The Differential Ability Scales (DAS; Elliott, 1990) is an individually administered battery of cognitive and achievement tests for children and adolescents ages 2 years, 6 months through 17 years, 11 months. Because the DAS covers such a wide age range, it is divided into three levels: Lower Preschool (ages 2 years, 6 months through 3 years, 5 months), Upper Preschool (ages 3 years, 6 months through 5 years, 11 months), and School-Age (6 years, 0 months through 17 years, 11 months). The DAS was designed to measure specific, definable abilities and to provide interpretable profiles of strengths and weaknesses. The DAS also contains three achievement tests, co-normed with the cognitive battery, which allows direct ability-achievement discrepancy analysis. The DAS is considered suitable for use in any setting in which the cognitive abilities of children and adolescents are to be evaluated, although many of the DAS subtests are not appropriate for students with severe sensory or motor disabilities. The DAS cognitive battery yields a composite score labeled General Conceptual Ability (GCA) that is defined as the general ability of an individual to perform complex mental processing that involves conceptualization and transformation. The DAS contains a total of 20 subtests grouped into core cognitive, diagnostic, or achievement tests. The core cognitive subtests are those used to compute the GCA and cluster scores, while the diagnostic subtests are those considered important and useful in the interpretation of an individual's strengths and weaknesses, but which do not assess complex mental processing well.

See also normalization.

REFERENCE

Elliott, C. D. (1990). *Differential Ability Scales*. San Antonio, TX: PsychCorp.

JEANNE HOLVERSTOTT

DIFFERENTIAL DIAGNOSIS

Differential diagnosis is a list of any and all conditions that might be the cause of the particular signs and symptoms under investigation. By comparing signs and symptoms of similar diseases/conditions, the possibilities can be narrowed down and more specific diagnostic testing or possible treatments can be instituted.

BRUCE BASSITY

DIFFERENTIAL REINFORCEMENT

Differential reinforcement occurs when a target behavior is reinforced while another behavior is not, or a target behavior is reinforced under certain conditions but not others, which increases positive behavior and decreases inappropriate behavior (Alberto & Troutman, 1999). The following are the five types of differential reinforcement:

1. Differential reinforcement of other behavior (DRO): reinforcement given when after a predetermined period of time the target behavior has not occurred (Reynolds, 1961). The focus is on a behavior never occurring as opposed to one occurring and then being reinforced.
2. Differential reinforcement of incompatible behavior (DRI) is the reinforcement of a behavior occurring at a time when it is impossible for the target behavior to occur (Deitz & Repp, 1983). For example, if a child is reinforced for having hands in his lap when the behavior of concern is doodling, having his hands in his lap would be an incompatible behavior to be reinforced. Having hands in your lap and doodling cannot occur at the same time.
3. Differential reinforcement of alternative behavior (DRA): reinforces an appropriate and functional alternative to the inappropriate behavior (Alberto & Troutman, 1999). The two behaviors are not incompatible. For example, a student may be reinforced for using appropriate words to express emotion instead of using aggressive acts. The appropriate words and aggression are not incompatible, but the words are an alternative behavior to the aggression.
4. Differential reinforcement of low rate of behavior (DRL): reinforces target behavior when it is present at a low rate (Cooper, Heron, & Heward, 1987).

5. Differential reinforcement of high rate of behavior (DRH): reinforces target behavior when it is present at higher rates (Cooper, Heron, & Heward, 1987).

REFERENCES

Alberto, P. A., & Troutman, A. C. (1999). *Applied behavior analysis for teachers*. Upper Saddle River, NJ: Merrill, 279–289.

Cooper, J. O., Heron, T. E., & Heward, W. L. (1987). *Applied behavior analysis*. Upper Saddle River, NJ: Prentice Hall.

Deitz, D. E., & Repp, A. C. (1983). Reducing behavior through reinforcement. *Exceptional Education Quarterly, 3*, 34–46.

Reynolds, G. S. (1961). Behavioral contrast. *Journal of the Experimental Analysis of Behavior, 4*, 57–71.

JESSICA KATE PETERS AND TARA MIHOK

DIMETHYLGLYCINE (DMG)

Dimethylglycine (DMG) is a non-protein amino acid found naturally in animal and plant cells. It is the main component of calcium pangamate, also called pangamic acid, and best known as vitamin B15. DMG is legally classified as a food, and it is available in many health food stores without a prescription. The history of DMG began in 1965 when two Russian investigators, M. G. Blumena and T. L. Belyakova, published a report showing considerable improvement in the speech of 12 of a group of 15 mentally handicapped children who had not been able to use speech to communicate (Rimland, 1990). The children had been treated with a substance variously known as calcium pangamate. In addition to enriched vocabulary, the children began to use simple sentences, their general mental state improved, and there was better concentration and interest in toys and games. An American psychiatrist used DMG on children with autism produced similar results. Concurrently, B-15 entered the United States market, with manufacturers claiming to have replicated the Russian formula. The Food and Drug Administration was forced to intervene, outlawing B-15 and permitting the sale of DMG as a food, not as a drug or vitamin. While anecdotal evidence exists supporting the benefits of DMG for children with autism, there is no clear empirical research supporting such claims.

See also diet therapy.

REFERENCE

Rimland, B. (1990). Dimethylglycine (DMG), a nontoxic metabolite, and autism. *Autism Research Review International, 4*(2), 3.

JEANNE HOLVERSTOTT

DIR/FLOOR TIME. *See* Developmental Individual-Difference Relation-Based Intervention

DIRECT INSTRUCTION

Direct instruction is used to describe a lesson where the teacher has control. The steps of a direct instruction include: (a) the teacher giving a lecture, (b) the teacher guiding the students through a complex problem with the problem broken down into simple steps, (c) the students are given, one by one, the simple steps to carry out on their own, and (d) the students are given one or many simple problems to accomplish on their own.

The primary goal of direct instruction is to increase student achievement through carefully focused instruction. Clear instruction eliminates misinterpretations and can greatly improve and accelerate training. It provides a model of instruction that emphasizes the use of carefully planned lessons designed around a specific knowledge base and a well-defined set of skills for each subject.

JAN L. KLEIN

DIRECT OBSERVATION

Part of the **assessment** process, direct observation is a common method of collecting information by formally observing an individual, several persons, or even a group. In direct observation, one may observe specific behaviors (such as the number of times a student raises his hand in class) or overall general behavior.

PAUL G. LACAVA

DISABILITY

A disability refers to restrictions or lack of ability to perform an activity within a range that is considered typical. A disability can be temporary or permanent and typically produces difficulties when attempting to function in society. For a person with autism, disability may refer to impaired development in communication, social interaction, and behavior.

JAN L. KLEIN

DISCRETE TRIAL TRAINING (BRIEF DEFINITION)

Discrete trial training is a behavioral method stemming from the field of **applied behavior analysis** (ABA) and is commonly used in the field of autism. The teaching method includes several key steps. First, the teacher gives the student an instruction. Many times this instruction will be given during **direct instruction**, but can also be given during other routines or **incidental teaching**. The child is then expected to respond to the teacher who then follows the response by giving corrective feedback and/or reinforcement for correct or approximated responses. Each sequence of steps is considered to be one discrete trial. This type of instruction is only one method within the field of **applied behavior analysis** (Anderson, Taras, & Cannon, 1996).

REFERENCE
Anderson, S. R., Taras, M., & Cannon, B. O. (1996). Teaching new skills to young children with autism. In C. Maurice, G. Green, & S. L. Luce (Eds.), *Behavioral intervention for young children with autism* (pp. 181–194). Austin, TX: Pro-Ed.

TARA MIHOK

DISCRETE TRIAL TRAINING (EXTENDED DEFINITION)

Discrete trial training (DTT) is a highly structured teaching method that involves carefully manipulated sequences of **antecedents** and **consequences** in order to elicit a target behavior. Therapists primarily use DTT with children with autism or other developmental disabilities; however, DTT can be used with other children as well. DTT requires the teacher to break down skills into small and specific instructional steps. Educators teach each part in isolation until the child masters the skill, and then the educator adds the next step. The steps are taught through repeated trials. Each trial has a clear beginning and a clear end, hence the term *discrete*. At the onset of teaching a new skill, the teacher uses an errorless teaching approach heavily prompting the student to avoid incorrect responding. The level of prompting decreases the student being able to respond independently. If the response is incorrect, an error correction procedure involving prompting will occur. DTT should and typically does occur in a designated "work area" free of distractions (e.g., a table or space where student and teacher sit directly across from one another).

The skills that can be taught using DTT include: compliance, attending, language, imitation, preacademic/academic, motor, self-help, and beginning play and social skills. The components of a discrete trial include: antecedent/instruction (SD-discriminative stimulus), behavior/response (R), consequence (SR-reinforcing stimulus), and the intertrial interval (ITI). Again, a prompt (SP-prompting stimulus) will also be present when teaching a new skill (errorless teaching) or in an error correction procedure. The discrete trial has also been referred to as a three-term contingency for the three main components: antecedent, behavior, consequence (or ABC).

THE ANTECEDENT/INSTRUCTION (SD–DISCRIMINATIVE STIMULUS)

The antecedent initiates a discrete trial. Most antecedents are verbal in nature and need to be delivered with an authoritative instructional voice. Initially, antecedents should be simple (e.g., "throw away") due to language difficulties. Later, when a student acquires more language skills, they can become more complex (e.g., "Throw away your plate and put your cup in the sink"). The antecedent may also be nonverbal (e.g., holding up a card for the student to read and follow directions). It is important to avoid pairing the child's name with the antecedent. When this is done, the child associates his name as part of the sequence of the trial. A child responds to his name but it should be set apart from other instructions. It is equally important to avoid repeating an antecedent without providing a consequence. By repeating an antecedent, we actually train a child to wait until he hears an instruction for the third or fourth time before he responds. If more than one person works with a particular student, it is imperative that a consistent format and planned wait time is used. This consistency must be maintained across all team members, and any changes to either should be a team decision.

THE RESPONSE/BEHAVIOR (R)

Consistent criteria must be used to determine an appropriate response. Extraneous behaviors (e.g., self-stimulatory behaviors) should not be present at the time of the response. The time that lapses between the delivery of the antecedent and the child's response should not extend 3–5 seconds. Otherwise, a child learns that a delayed response is acceptable and provides time for off-task behaviors to occur. A non-response is considered incorrect and may occur for several reasons. The student may not be ready, may not know the correct response, or finds the response aversive. The predetermined criteria for mastering a step must be met before adding the next step. Changes in the criteria need to be agreed upon by all team members.

THE CONSEQUENCE (SR–REINFORCING STIMULUS)

The consequence consists of a reward for correct responses to strengthen a desirable behavior or an informational "no" and the removal of a reward to weaken an undesirable behavior. Positive reinforcement occurs when something preferred is delivered to the child (e.g., edibles). On the other hand, negative reinforcement occurs when something unpleasant to the child is removed (e.g., "escape"). It is imperative that the consequence immediately follows the response in order for the child to correctly associate the direction and behavior. Conducting a reinforcement inventory on a regular basis allows a teacher to determine the most highly preferred reinforcers (primary) versus less preferred reinforcers (secondary). A reinforcer should always be paired with social reinforcement in order to train "praise" as a reinforcer in itself. Particular attention should be paid to not satiate any one reinforcer. Vary the reinforcement provided, conduct regular reinforcement inventories, and limit the use of the reinforcer outside of the work session. Provide high levels of reinforcement while introducing and shaping (accepting closer and closer approximations) a response and then fade reinforcement to a more intermittent schedule. Using a **token economy** reinforcement system (e.g., blocks in a cup or a penny board) teaches delayed gratification. With this system, more trials can be completed before a reinforcement break is given, maximizing therapy times.

THE INTERTRIAL INTERVAL (ITI)

The intertrial interval is simply a brief pause between trials. It should be just long enough to signal the end of one trial (consequence provided) and the beginning of the next (antecedent given). It must be short enough to avoid eliciting avoidance or undesirable behaviors. Often times, a teacher utilizes brief time to record data and reset the teaching items needed for the next trial.

THE PROMPT (SP–PROMPTING STIMULUS)

A team decision determines the sequence of prompting used to teach a specific skill. In order to avoid prompt dependency, prompt least to most (e.g., model, visual, position, verbal, physical). When teaching independent functioning skills, it is important to prompt physically rather than verbally. Otherwise, children with autism tend to associate verbal prompts as part of the skill sequence and become dependent on the verbal cue. Pay particular attention that you are not inadvertently prompting a child with your body language. Systematic fading of prompts is also necessary to avoid prompt dependency. For example, fade a physical hand over hand prompt to a prompt at the wrist, then the elbow, then the shoulder, and then an independent response. Prompted trials should always be followed by unprompted trials to ensure independent responses. Once a child has mastered a skill, reduce the reinforcement for prompted trials (e.g., offer a secondary reinforcer) and provide primary reinforcers for independent responses only.

Putting It All Together

The order of the discrete trial can thus be represented as:

SD → R → SR → ITI
(SP)
-or-
A → B → C → ITI
Antecedent Behavior Consequence Intertrial Interval

Generalization

Due to the highly structured nature of DTT, it is imperative that a teacher programs or plans for **generalization** of skills. Generalization must occur across individuals, materials, environments, and antecedents as language skills increase. When teaching items are mastered and moved to maintenance-level programs, they are typically introduced into target generalization programs in one or more of the previous areas depending on the child and the skill. For example, when a label is mastered expressively, the original teaching picture can be put in a **maintenance** program while the "label" is moved to generalization programs (e.g., materials—different pictures of the same item) that would eventually include all four areas listed herein.

Further Information

Leaf, R., & McEachin, J. (1999). *A work in progress: Behavior management strategies and a curriculum for intensive behavioral treatment of autism.* New York: DRL Books.

Lovaas, O. I. (1981). *Teaching developmentally disabled children: The me book.* Baltimore: University Park Press.

Lovaas, O. I. (2003). *Teaching individuals with developmental delays: Basic intervention techniques.* Austin, TX: Pro-Ed.

Maurice, C., Green, G., Luce, S. C. (1996). *Behavioral intervention for young children with autism: A manual for parents and professionals.* Austin, TX: Pro-Ed.

Simpson, R. L., & Myles, B. S. (1998). *Educating children and youth with autism: Strategies for effective practice.* Austin, TX: Pro-Ed.

Sundberg, M. L., & Partington, J. W. (1998). *Teaching language to children with autism or other developmental disabilities.* Pleasant Hill, CA: Behavior Analyst, Inc.

MICHELE MULLENDORE

DISCRIMINATION

Discrimination is the act of making distinctions between stimuli on the basis of a particular category (i.e., race, color, shape, gender). Behavior analytic approaches focus heavily on the development and reinforcement of making correct discriminations. More generally, discrimination is critical in the development of language (pronoun usage) and social competence (social cues).

See also differential reinforcement.

JEANNE HOLVERSTOTT

DISCRIMINATIVE STIMULUS

In the field of **applied behavior analysis**, the discriminative stimulus is usually referred to as the SD. The SD is an **antecedent** trigger that signals that a specific behavior will be either reinforced or punished based upon past experiences. The SD can be signals such as words, gestures, or sounds that cue the person that reinforcement will occur if the stimulus is followed by correct behavior (Lovaas, 2003). Discrimination between stimuli is often learned by a behavior being reinforced following one trigger and being punished in the presence of another (Driscoll, 2005). For example, in teaching a child to sit down, the phrase "Sit down" can be a discriminative stimulus to the child, assuming that he or she follows the instruction with the knowledge that reinforcement will follow. For other children, the bell ringing at the end of the day is the discriminative stimulus for them to leave the classroom to go home (assuming that leaving school is reinforcing to the child).

See also punishment; reinforcer.

REFERENCES
Driscoll, M. P. (2005). *Psychology of learning for instruction* (3rd ed.). Boston: Pearson Education, Inc.
Lovaas, O. I. (2003). *Teaching individuals with developmental delays: Basic intervention techniques.* Austin, TX: Pro-Ed.

TARA MIHOK AND ANDREA HOPF

DISINTEGRATIVE PSYCHOSIS. *See* Childhood Disintegrative Disorder

DISTRIBUTED PRACTICE

Distributed practice is a strategy in which the student exerts or distributes effort over time rather than concentrating effort within a short period. Frequent distributed practice helps students maintain and develop concepts and skills that were previously introduced in a sequence and gives the students the time needed to find appropriate and meaningful ways of integrating information from a variety of sources. Distributed practice does more than simply increase the amount learned; it frequently shifts the learner's attention away from the verbatim details of the material being studied to its deeper conceptual structure.

JAN L. KLEIN

DOPAMINE

Dopamine is a substance that is synthesized by the adrenal glands (located on top of the kidneys). It has several functions in the body including regulation of circulation and blood pressure and as a **neurotransmitter** in the brain. It is an immediate precursor to the formation of norepinephrine.

BRUCE BASSITY

DOUBLE BLIND

Double blind is a type of experimental research design where both the researchers and the participants do not know who is receiving the treatment. For example, in a medication investigation, neither the researcher nor the participants know who is receiving the drug under investigation or who is receiving the *placebo*. The purpose of the double-blind study is to increase the strength of claims by researchers that the intervention (the independent variable) caused the change in behavior for participants who received the treatment and that other factors were not an issue.

See also experimental design.

FURTHER INFORMATION

Everitt, B. S. (2002). *The Cambridge dictionary of statistics* (2nd ed.). Cambridge: Cambridge University Press.

Salkind, N. J. (2005). *Exploring research* (6th ed.). Upper Saddle River, NJ: Prentice Hall.

PAUL G. LaCAVA

DOUBLE INTERVIEW

The double interview is an informal assessment technique to explore one's capacity to shift perspective and the focus of one's language from talking about one's self to talking about another person. The first task in the double interview is for the assessing clinician to interview the client by asking specific questions to the client about the client (e.g., What are your hobbies? Do you have any siblings? What do you like/dislike about school? etc.). As the client answers, the assessor is to consider not only the client's ability to narrate a solid response to provide the assessor with a range of novel information, but the assessor is also evaluating the student's nonverbal aspects of communication (e.g., eye contact, body language, tone of voice, etc.). It is expected that the client should be near his or her communicative best when talking about him- or herself. The assessor is careful to only ask questions and to only provide brief responses to show interest in the client, or to ask follow-up questions to gain access to more information about the client.

Once the assessor has completed their interview with the client, they exclaim, "Wow, I just learned a lot about you (They can then state specifics of what they have learned) by interviewing you. But I realize that you don't know very much about me, so I thought it would only be fair if I let you interview me." The interviewer then reviews with the client that an interview consists of asking questions to the person who is being interviewed about that person. The assessor can also try and make the task easier on the client by providing pictures that give some information about the assessor by showing the client pictures of the assessor's family, etc. After providing this extra support, they then say, "OK, this is a good time to interview me." The assessor then waits and observes, writing down any response or question that the client provides. At this point it is very common for the client to have a much more difficult time generating language. It is often very difficult for the clients to ask any questions, and they may say, "I can't do this!" Given that this task requires the client to shift perspective and focus on the assessor, the client struggles given that this is one aspect of social thinking that is a great challenge for him or her. It is not uncommon for the client to start to explain that he or she "can never do this" and they "never know what to say to people." Preliminary research, done at the University of Kansas by Miller (2004) and Zweber (2004) demonstrated that the double interview helps to differentiate our clients with social cognitive deficits from their peers at age 8 years old and beyond.

REFERENCES

Miller, A. C. (2004). *Double interview task: Assessing the social communication of children with Asperger syndrome.* Unpublished Masters Thesis. University of Kansas.

Zweber, K. J. (2004). *Double interview: Assessing the social communication of adolescents with Asperger syndrome.* Unpublished Masters Thesis. University of Kansas.

FURTHER INFORMATION
Winner, M. (2002). *Thinking about you thinking about me.* San Jose, CA: Michelle Garcia Winner.

MICHELLE GARCIA WINNER AND JAMIE RIVETTS

DSM-IV. *See Diagnostic and Statistical Manual of Mental Disorders*–Fourth Edition–Text Revised

DUE PROCESS

Due process is a procedure guaranteed by federal law for families and school professionals for resolving disputes regarding special education services that cannot be resolved through mediation.

FURTHER INFORMATION
U.S. Department of Education. (2004). *Procedural safeguards: Due process hearings.* www.ed.gov/policy/speced/guid/idea/tb-safeguards-3.pdf.

KATHERINE E. COOK

DURRELL ANALYSIS OF READING DIFFICULTY (DARD)

The Durrell Analysis of Reading Difficulty (DARD; Durrell & Catterson, 1980) is an individually administered assessment for children ages pre-kindergarten and older designed to assess the reading abilities in the following skill areas: oral and silent reading, listening comprehension, word recognition and analysis, listening vocabulary, sounds in isolation, spelling and phonic spelling, visual memory of words, identification of sounds in words, prereading phonics abilities, syntax matching, identifying letter names in spoken words, phoneme awareness, letter names and letter writing, and copying.

REFERENCE
Durrell, D. D., & Catterson, J. H. (1980). *Durrell Analysis of Reading Difficulty.* San Antonio, TX: PsychCorp.

JEANNE HOLVERSTOTT

DYSBIOSIS

Symbiosis is the medical term for the balance between a person's intestinal tract and good bacteria. Good bacteria within the intestinal tract is responsible for **detoxification**, production of vitamins, and protection from unfriendly organisms. Dysbiosis is the opposite of symbiosis and is the medical term for an imbalance in the gastrointestinal tract. There are three main causes of dysbiosis: parasites, fungus overgrowth, and poor **diet**. Characteristics can be acute (diarrhea, nausea, abdominal pain, cramps) or chronic (loose stool, **constipation**, bloating, gas, food cravings, allergies, fibromyalgia, rheumatoid arthritis, and chronic fatigue syndrome).

KATHERINE E. COOK

DYSPHASIA

Dysphasia is a speech disorder characterized by impairments in expressive speech, writing, and impairments in comprehension of spoken and written language. Although individuals with dysphasia typically do not have impaired intellect, they are often viewed as mentally impaired. Aphasia is a severe form of dysphasia. This disorder arises from damage to the left side of the brain, which is responsible for speech and language.

KATHERINE E. COOK

E

EARLY COPING INVENTORY

The Early Coping Inventory (ECI; Zeitlin, Williamson, & Szczepanski, 1988) is an observation instrument used for assessing the coping-related behavior of children who function developmentally from 4 to 36 months. The 48 items in this inventory are divided into three categories. **Sensorimotor** organization behaviors are those skills used to regulate psychophysiological functions as well as to integrate sensory and motor process. Reactive behaviors are actions used to respond to the demands of physical and social environments. Self-initiated behaviors are autonomously generated, self-directed actions used to meet personal needs and to interact with objects and people. Professionals as well as nonprofessionals who are knowledgeable in infant development may administer and score the inventory. If observers are not familiar with the child, they should observe the child at least three times in different situations. Analysis of a child's scores on this instrument provides information about level of coping, style, and specific strengths and weaknesses. The findings can then be used to create educational and therapeutic interventions. In addition, the ECI can be used to involve parents in its use as a means of increasing knowledge of the child and communication with staff. The ECI can also be used to support staff development and training to increase observation skills, expand their domain of concern, facilitate teamwork, and measure child progress.

REFERENCE

Zeitlin, S., Williamson, G. G., & Szczepanski, M. (1988). *Early coping inventory*. Bensenville, IL: Scholastic Testing Service, Inc.

JEANNE HOLVERSTOTT

EARLY INTERVENTION

Early intervention is the purposeful application of resources with the aim of developing or improving interactions between an individual and the environment (Hooper & Umansky, 2004). It applies to children from birth to school age that are discovered to be at risk, have disabilities, or other special needs that may affect their development. Early intervention may be center-based, home-based, hospital-based, or a combination.

See also homebound/hospital bound program.

REFERENCE

Hooper, S. R., & Umansky, W. (2004). *Young children with special needs.* Upper Saddle River, NJ: Pearson Education, Inc.

KAI-CHIEN TIEN

ECHOIC/VERBAL BEHAVIOR

Echoic behavior is when a child uses verbal imitation. For example, in **verbal behavior** the child would use echoic behavior to request a desired item. The echoic behavior would be repeated and eventually the child would learn that the word has the specific function of getting his or her need met.

TERRI COOPER SWANSON

ECHOLALIA: IMMEDIATE, DELAYED, MITIGATED

Echolalia is the repeated use of words or phrases used by others. There are three different forms of echolalia: immediate, delayed, and mitigated. Immediate echolalia refers to words or phrases that are repeated immediately or very soon after the model of the utterances was first heard. Delayed echolalia refers to the echo of words or phrases after a lapse of time. Some children repeat one or numerous phrases from video clips; this is a form of delayed echolalia. The third form of echolalia is referred to as mitigated where the speaker clearly is repeating a phrase, but it is not an exact repetition. Historically echolalia was viewed to be noncommunicative. However, in recent years practitioners have realized that echolalia often serves a communicative function for the individual. For example, after hearing his mother one evening at dinner repeatedly ask with a tone of frustration if William wanted ketchup on his fish sticks (fisherboys), William starting using the phrase, "Do you want ketchup on your fisherboys?" to indicate that he was frustrated. Until William was taught a more appropriate and understood phrase he used, "Do you want ketchup on you fisherboys?" in any setting and situation where he felt anxious or frustrated.

KATHERINE E. COOK

ECOLOGICAL INVENTORY

This highly individualized assessment analyzes all aspects (i.e., leisure, domestic, school, community, vocational) of the learner's current and future environments. The student's abilities are then compared to the assessed demands of each of the target environments and a list of skills is identified for use as instructional priorities.

FURTHER INFORMATION

Brown, L., Branston, M. B., Hamre-Nietupski, S., Pumpian, I., Certo, N., & Gruenewald, L. (1979). A strategy for developing chronological-age-appropriate and functional curricular content for severely handicapped adolescents and young adults. *Journal of Special Education, 13,* 81–90.

Snell, M. E., & Brown, F. (2006). *Instruction of students with severe disabilities* (8th ed.). Upper Saddle River, NJ: Prentice Hall.

Westling, D. L., & Fox, L. (2004). *Teaching students with severe disabilities* (3rd ed.). Upper Saddle River, NJ: Prentice Hall.

THERESA L. EARLES-VOLLRATH

EDUCATIONAL PLACEMENT

There are different types of educational placement for children with autism. Depending on the child's need, his **Individualized Education Program** may be carried out in general education, in special education, at home, in an institution, or in other settings. In all cases, the parents have the right to be a member of the group that decides the educational placement of the child.

See also homebound/hospital bound program.

KAI-CHIEN TIEN

EISENBERG, LEON

Leon Eisenberg received his medical degree from the University of Pennsylvania (1946) and took his internship at the Mount Sinai Hospital in New York City. He took a fellowship in child psychiatry at the Johns Hopkins Hospital in Baltimore, Maryland, under the direction of Professor **Leo Kanner** (1954). Eisenberg worked closely with Kanner during this fellowship, and they became colleagues, publishing research together on autism. In 1967, he moved to Harvard as chief of psychiatry where he became chair of the Department of Social Medicine and Health Policy in 1980. In 1993, Dr. Eisenberg reached emeritus status at Harvard Medical School and continues to work full time. Eisenberg has published more than 250 articles in refereed journals, 130 book chapters, and 9 edited books.

FURTHER INFORMATION

Harvard Medical School Department of Social Medicine. (n.d.). Faculty: Leon Eisenberg. Retrieved on November 24, 2006 from www.hms.harvard.edu/dsm/WorkFiles/html/people/faculty/LeonEisenberg.html.

Kanner L., & Eisenberg, L. (1956). Early infantile autism. *American Journal of Orthopsychiatry*, 26, 55–65.

TERRI COOPER SWANSON

ELECTROENCEPHALOGRAM

An electroencephalogram (EEG) measures the electric activity in the brain. The electrical brain activity is measured by placing electrodes onto the scalp of the patient.

FURTHER INFORMATION

Tuchman, R. F., & Rapin, I. (1997). Regression in pervasive developmental disorders: Seizures and epileptiform electroencephalogram correlates. *Pediatrics*, 99(4), 560–567.

TERRI COOPER SWANSON

ELIGIBILITY

Eligibility is the process where the **Individualized Education Program** (IEP) team evaluates formal and **informal assessment** results to determine if a student qualifies for special education services. If a student meets eligibility, an IEP is written and implemented.

KATHERINE E. COOK

ELIMINATION DIET AND FOOD SENSITIVITIES

This medically supervised diet is used to identify food sensitivities and allergies. While food intake levels are maintained, the variety of foods consumed is restricted to the least reactive foods (those foods that cause the least digestive problems for the majority of people) such as rice and potatoes. Additional foods are gradually and systematically added according to the plan specified by the health care provider. The patient or caregiver keeps a daily food diary noting the foods eaten and any responses. After time, the physician may suggest a challenge, which is a medically supervised reintroduction of a suspected problem food to determine whether or not a food sensitivity exists. The duration of the diet varies by the sensitivity of the patient and by the success or lack of success detecting which food or foods are the causes of the patient's sensitivities. Elimination diet should not be confused with the **Gluten-free/Casein-free** Elimination Diet or the *Candida* Elimination Diet.

FURTHER INFORMATION

Hurt Jones, Marjorie (2001). *The allergy self-help cookbook: Over 325 natural foods recipes, free of all common food allergens: Wheat-free, milk-free, egg-free, corn-free, sugar-free, yeast-free.* New York: Rodale Books.

Le Breton, M., & Kessick, R. (2001). *Diet and intervention in autism: Implementing a gluten free and casein free diet: A guide for parents.* London: Jessica Kingsley Publishers.

Tidwell, J. (2006). Food allergies/intolerances. Retrieved August 18, 2006, from About health and fitness Web site: http://allergies.about.com/cs/foods/a/blfood.htm.

MYRNA J. ROCK

EMBEDDED FIGURES TEST (EFT)

An embedded figures test presents an individual with a simple (target) shape in isolation and then asks this person to find this same shape in a larger, more complex configuration. Research (Witkin, Dyk, Faterson, Goodenough, & Karp, 1962; Baron-Cohen & Hammer, 1997) has illustrated that males are significantly faster than females at locating the embedded figure.

REFERENCES

Baron-Cohen, S., & Hammer, J. (1997). Parents of children with Asperger syndrome: What is the cognitive phenotype? *Journal of Cognitive Neuroscience, 9,* 548–554.

Witkin, H. A., Dyk, R. B., Faterson, H. F., Goodenough, D. G., & Karp, S. A. (1962). *Personality through perception.* New York: Harper & Row.

JEANNE HOLVERSTOTT

EMBEDDED SKILLS

Embedded skills are present within naturally occurring activities and allow for opportunities to practice learning objectives. As such, they allow for new skills to be practiced in the presence of already learned or ongoing skills. For example, to practice letter recognition, a child would be allowed to select only movie titles with a particular letter present.

JEANNE HOLVERSTOTT

EMOTIONAL SUPPORT

Emotional support is assistance obtained through relationships, either professional or familial. Psychologists, social workers, counselors, and medical doctors are mental health professionals often enlisted by individuals to provide therapeutic support. Friendships and partnerships with family, friends, and caregivers can also serve as a source of emotional support.

JEANNE HOLVERSTOTT

EMPIRICAL EVIDENCE. *See* Empiricism

EMPIRICISM

Empiricism is a Western concept that espouses knowledge can be derived through careful observation and cataloging of phenomena and extrapolating laws or principles from these observations. Empiricism's origins in the West in its most developed form are in the philosophy of Aristotle, whose theories on intellectual inquiry first introduced the process of experiment or a controlled, replicable experience. The process of replication enables others to build a knowledge base by testing for the truths of the laws and theories. The resultant knowledge areas are then grouped to further designate experimental sciences, such as physics and medicine. Empirical evidence of the observed behaviors of individuals with autism further expands the understanding and knowledge of the disorder.

See also experimental design.

MELANIE D. HARMS

ENCOPRESIS

Encopresis is the involuntary passage of stool taking place over at least 6 months in duration and in an individual over the age of 4 years. This is often a result of chronic **constipation** or retaining of stools.

BRUCE BASSITY

ENGAGEMENT

Engagement is the amount of time that children spend involved with the environment (adults, peers, or materials) in a way that is appropriate given their age, abilities, and surroundings.

See also age appropriate; chronological age; mental age.

JAN L. KLEIN

ENURESIS

Enuresis is the involuntary discharge of urine after the age when voluntary bladder control is usually established, typically around 5 years of age. Nocturnal (night time) enuresis is the most common form in children, present in approximately 10 percent of 5-year-olds and 1 percent of 15-year-olds. Enuresis may be due to bladder control never being established or a regression in bladder control.

BRUCE BASSITY

ENVIRONMENT

Does the natural environment (water, air, earth) contain toxins that may contribute to autism? Moreover, do other man-made substances in the environment contain materials that may contribute to autism? These questions have been some of the most controversial within the field of autism into the mid-2000s. The role of the environment in the cause of autism has been a question addressed for many decades. Recently, the role of the environment has been questioned as a potential source for the huge increases in the prevalence of autism.

Historically, autism was considered an emotional disorder caused by ineffective parenting. That is, the social environment was deficient between child and parent and thus autism was the outcome. This was proven wrong after decades of research and autism became known as a neurobiological/developmental disorder.

Although the conceptualization of autism has changed over time, the question of what may contribute to the etiology of this disability still remains. Some believe that autism is caused by genetics alone. Others believe that their child became autistic when exposed to some environmental toxin. In the 2000s, it is common to believe that a combination of a genetic predisposition to autism as well as some environmental insult causes autism. The severity of the disability would therefore depend on the number of genes affected in the individual as well as the type of environmental insult that occurs.

Some environmental toxins that have been questioned in the development of autism include **heavy metals** such as **mercury**, chemicals, pesticides, pre- and postnatal viruses, flame retardant materials, and food additives. There have been reports of individual cases of autism spectrum disorders (ASD) being associated with various prenatal infections and environmental toxins. This includes maternal use of alcohol and cocaine, as well as infection by cytomegalovirus.

In the 1990s and into the 2000s, the claim that the MMR **vaccination** and mercury were possible culprits causally connected to autism became a critical research concern. Some believed that the huge increase in autism over the previous years was causally related to either the MMR vaccination in young children or in the mercury that was part of the preservative thimerosal that was in many childhood vaccines. It was claimed that children who had weak immune systems, or those who were already predisposed to having autism, were placed at risk with the ongoing accumulation of mercury in these vaccinations. It was claimed that their systems could no longer process and expel the mercury poisoning and thus autism developed.

As of 2007, this remains highly controversial. However, the preponderance of the evidence from government and other medical/scientific studies suggests that neither the MMR vaccination nor the use of mercury/thimerosal were causally connected to the increase in autism. Much research is still needed in this critically important area, and it is not yet known if there is a connection between autism and vaccinations or mercury for some subsets of particularly vulnerable individual children. At this point, however, conclusive evidence has not been presented to confirm which environmental factors contribute to autism.

FURTHER INFORMATION

Centers for Disease Control and Prevention. (2004). *FAQs about MMR vaccine and autism.* Retrieved March 30, 2005, from http://www.cdc.gov/nip/vacsafe/concerns/autism/autism-mmr.htm.

Kennedy, R. (February 2005). Deadly immunity [Electronic version]. *Rolling Stone*, Retrieved August 18, 2005, from http://www.rollingstone.com/politics/story/_/id/7395411?rnd=11243888 56090&has-player=true&version=6.0.11.847.

Kirby, D. (2005). *Evidence of harm: Mercury in vaccines and the autism epidemic: A medical controversy*. New York: St. Martin's Press.

National Broadcasting Company. (Executive Producer). (February 23, 2005). *The Today Show* [Television Broadcast]. New York: National Broadcasting Company.

Rutter, M. (2005). Etiology of autism: Findings and questions. *Journal of Intellectual Disability Research, 49*, 231–238.

PAUL G. LACAVA

ENVIRONMENTAL STRESSORS

Environmental stressors refer to a variety of internal and external events that could interfere with an individual being successful in the immediate future, and as such, need to be monitored and acted on as quickly as possible. Such stressors may include: (a) prejudice toward someone who is perceived as "different" and the effect that might have on the person, such as negative self-concept, anxiety, and expectation of failure; (b) restricted social and vocational opportunities; (c) inadequate social supports; (d) life changes such as a new teacher, a new job, living arrangements, family losses, and other life changes; (e) the inability to process sensory information and "make sense" of the world; and (f) victimization, including social and sexual abuse. These stressors need to be considered seriously when working with individuals with ASD as lack of immediate action to reduce or assist the individual's handling of these stressors can have a long-term impact on the person's ability to develop life skills and develop the skills necessary to manage their world.

ANDREA M. BABKIE

EPIDEMIOLOGY

Epidemiology is the study of outbreaks of disease. Scientific analysis is used by epidemiologists to understand how diseases start, how they are spread, and how they can be prevented. There are several possible causes of autism including: (a) genetics, (b) **vaccinations**, (c) environment, and (d) **diet**. At this time there are no research supported cures or solutions to prevent autism spectrum disorders.

See also environment.

TERRI COOPER SWANSON

ERROR CORRECTION

Error correction is the process or procedure followed when a student gives an incorrect response. Methods of error correction include, but are not limited to, **overcorrection, time-out**, and a **no-no-prompt procedure**. Because some students with autism spectrum disorders are highly sensitive to error correction, there is often an attempt to use "neutral" forms of error correction such as offering no verbal reaction to a student's incorrect response and instead intentionally looking away from the student for a few seconds.

See also applied behavior analysis.

KATIE BASSITY

ESCAPE TRAINING

Escape training is similar to negative reinforcement. When a student does not enjoy an activity or situation, he may be allowed to escape it after completing a certain portion of the work or activity. In this way, the student learns that some work must be completed, but that once the work is completed, he will be allowed to move to a more enjoyable activity.

KATIE BASSITY

ESTABLISHING OPERATION

An establishing operation, as described by Michael (1982) is "any change in the environment which alters the effectiveness of some object or event as reinforcement and simultaneously alters the momentary frequency of the behavior that has been followed by that reinforcement" (pp. 150–151). Establishing operations may either increase the effectiveness of the **reinforcer** (due to deprivation) or decrease the effectiveness of the reinforcer (due to satiation; Alberto & Troutman, 1999). These environmental, social, or physiological events affect the motivation of an individual and thus affect the behavior that is influenced by the reinforcers (Michael, 1993). Because a person's desire for food is greater when he or she is hungry, behavior that is reinforced by food may be strengthened before a meal. On the contrary, edible reinforcement may be less effective after a meal, weakening a behavior linked to that reinforcement. Establishing operations have also been referred to as setting events or motivating operations (Laraway, Snycerski, Michael, & Poling, 2003).

REFERENCES
Alberto, P. A., & Troutman, A. C. (1999). *Applied behavior analysis for teachers* (p. 230). Upper Saddle River, NJ: Merrill.
Laraway, S., Snycerski, S., Michael, J., & Poling, A. (2003). Motivating operations and terms to describe them: Some further refinements. *Journal of Applied Behavior Analysis, 36*, 407–414.
Michael, J. (1982). Discriminating between discriminative and motivational functions of stimuli. *Journal of the Experimental Analysis of Behavior, 37*(1), 149–155.
Michael, J. (1993). Establishing operations. *The Behavior Analyst, 16*, 191–206.

FURTHER INFORMATION
Michael, J. (2000). Implications and refinements of the establishing operation concept. *Journal of Applied Behavior Analysis, 33*, 401–410.

TARA MIHOK AND JESSICA KATE PETERS

EVALUATING ACQUIRED SKILLS IN COMMUNICATION–REVISED (EASIC-R)

Evaluating Acquired Skills in Communication–Revised (EASIC-R; Riley, 1991) is an inventory that was developed to measure spoken language, both receptive and expressive, of children with autism ages 3 months to 8 years. The EASIC-R has also been used successfully with individuals who have developmental language delays. The tool assesses semantics, syntax, morphology, and pragmatics communication skills at five levels: Pre-Language, Receptive 1, Expressive 1, Receptive 2, and Expressive 2. Results can be displayed on the Skills Profile to show changes that have occurred from one testing session to another. In addition, results can be portrayed on the

Developmental Age Chart. The child's communication skills are arranged in easy to difficult order along with the age ranges at which children normally acquire each of the described skills. Administration time ranges from 15 to 30 minutes.

REFERENCE
Riley, A. M. (1991). *Evaluating Acquired Skills in Communication–Revised*. San Antonio, TX: Harcourt Assessment.

AMY BIXLER COFFIN

EVALUATION REPORT

An evaluation report provides a detailed, written summary of the information gained through the **assessment** process. There are no standardized formats for evaluation reports, however most reports contain many of the following sections: identifying data, reason for referral, background history, observations, tests administered, test results, test-by-test analysis, conclusions, and a summary table.

See also standardization.

FURTHER INFORMATION
Overton, T. (2003). *Assessing learners with special needs: An applied approach*. Upper Saddle River, NJ: Merrill/Prentice Hall.

THERESA L. EARLES-VOLLRATH

EVIDENCE BASED

The term *evidence based* was first used in the field of medicine (Cutspec, 2004) and has since been used to describe a variety of professions. The evidence-based approaches have advantages and disadvantages, but the variety of these approaches provides an implication that the term *evidence based* is not enough in itself to describe what a given profession provides. In the field of education, there is the potential for an evidence-based approach combined with knowledge and practice in an attempt to move from individualistic approaches and designing original research as the foundation on which to assess best practices for educators.

REFERENCE
Cutspec, P. A. (2004). Origins of evidence-based approaches to best practice: Evidence-based medicine. In P. A. Cutspec & A. L. Watson (Eds.), *Interlock: Identifying, synthesizing, validating, and disseminating evidence-based practices. Draft version two* (Ch. 2). Asheville, NC: Orelena Hawks Puckett Institute.

KAI-CHIEN TIEN

EXECUTIVE FUNCTIONS

Executive functions are higher-order cognitive skills and include inhibitory control, planning, organization, self-regulation, and problem solving. The development of executive functions parallels the neurodevelopment of the prefrontal regions of the brain, which are largely responsible for the neural networks that direct attention, perceptions of time and order, emotion, and response as well as the retention and utilization of memory. Deficits in the area of executive functions are evidenced by noncompliance, limited or neglect for the consequences of past actions, exaggerated or nonexistent emotional expression, difficulty with concepts such as time and money, and other difficulties related to social situations and organization.

MELANIE D. HARMS

EXPERIMENTAL DESIGN

Experimental design is a blueprint of a procedure that enables the researcher to test his hypothesis by reaching valid conclusions about relationships between independent and dependent variables. It refers to the conceptual framework within which the experiment is conducted.

JEANNE HOLVERSTOTT

EXPRESSIVE LANGUAGE

Expressive language is the use of language to express a thought, idea, or feeling. Typically expressive language is thought to indicate spoken language, but it also includes thoughts, ideas, or feelings that are expressed through written communication.

KATHERINE E. COOK

EXTENDED SCHOOL YEAR (ESY)

Extended School Year (ESY) refers to the special education and related services beyond the normal school year that are provided to a child with a disability. ESY may include the provision of summer schooling or other summer programming, the continued provision of services during vacation periods, or any other number of options. According to the **Individuals with Disabilities Education Act** (IDEA), every student with a disability must be considered for ESY services as part of the development of their **Individualized Education Program** (IEP; IDEA, 2004).

Eligibility for ESY is based on a variety of factors that are considered during the meetings to develop and review a student's IEP. The most appropriate method for determining eligibility for ESY is direct, ongoing assessment of IEP objectives as they relate to the regression and recoupment a child experiences (Browder, 1987; Browder & Lentz, 1985). Typically, to determine ESY eligibility, a team asks itself how much a student would suffer a regression in skills if his or her educational services were interrupted for a period of time and how much time would be required for the student to then regain the lost skills. Other factors that the child's team may look at include severity of the disability, degree of regression and necessary recoupment time, the ability of the parents to provide services at home, the student's vocational needs, the ability of the student to interact with nondisabled peers, and whether the student is at a crucial or "breakthrough" moment in his or her learning.

Examples of children with disabilities for whom ESY is especially important might include children who: (a) lose skills or behaviors relevant to their IEP goals and objectives while school is out, (b) have difficulty catching up, (c) have not yet fully learned and generalized an important skill or behavior and need help learning and practicing that skill in the formal educational setting, (d) have a disability that makes them vulnerable to interruptions in the educational program and who are at risk of withdrawing from the learning process, or (e) have a degenerative condition and need ESY to prevent or delay loss of skills or behaviors.

ESY can be provided in a variety of ways depending on the needs of the individual child. A school may provide all-day schooling during the summer months, other vacation periods, or only the related services that are necessary to avoid serious regression during vacation periods. Services may be provided in a traditional classroom setting, at the student's home, at recreational centers such as summer camps or community centers, or at any other location that is deemed appropriate to the needs of the student. Finally, services can also be provided one on one or in a group setting.

REFERENCES

Browder, D. (1987). *Assessment of individuals with severe handicaps: An applied behavioral approach to life skills assessment.* Baltimore: Brookes Publishing Co.

Browder, D., & Lentz, F. E. (1985). Extended school year services: From litigation to assessment and evaluation. *School Psychology Review, 14,* 188–195. EJ317622.

Individuals with Disabilities Education Improvement Act, 2004, Public Law 108-446. Retrieved November 27, 2004, from http://www.ed.gov/policy/speced/guid/idea/idea2004.html.

JAN L. KLEIN

EXTINCTION

Extinction occurs when a behavior that has a history of being reinforced with positive or negative reinforcement stops being followed by reinforcement. Once extinction begins, the likelihood is that there will be an increase in the rate of the behavior and possibly an increase in the intensity of the behavior; a decrease in the rate of the behavior should then follow. Spontaneous recovery, or the occasional display of the behavior after a period of the behavior's absence, may occur (Cooper, Heron, & Heward, 1987). Extinction can also be a termination of sensory reinforcement, specifically, such as the reinforcement gained by some when they eat non-edible items or smell items not intended to be smelled.

See also reinforcer.

REFERENCE

Cooper, Heron, & Heward (1987). *Applied behavior analysis.* Upper Saddle River, NJ: Prentice Hall.

TARA MIHOK

EYE GAZE

Eye gaze is the act of directing one's eyes toward a designated **stimulus**. This may be observed as an individual facing one way and his eyes glancing in another, providing the individual with the opportunity to process visual and auditory information at a pace appropriate to the individual. Because it is not uncommon for individuals on the autism spectrum to describe eye contact as painful, eye gaze serves as a replacement for eye contact. If an individual with autism demonstrates the ability to answer questions and perform actions that involve eye contact, they may be compensating with the use of eye gaze.

MELANIE D. HARMS

F

FACE RECOGNITION

Face recognition is a neural process that takes part in the ventral temporal cortex otherwise termed as the *fusiform face area* (FFA). Objects are processed in the internal gyri and based on its features, such as size, texture, color, and more. The perception of the face is processed part in features (eyes, nose, mouth, etc.) and part as a whole (one object) rather than individual features. Researchers (Boucher & Lewis, 1992; Braverman, Fein, Lucci, & Waterhouse, 1989; Hauck, Fein, Maltby, Waterhouse,& Geinstein 1998; Kline, Sparrow, de Bildt, Cicchetti, Cohen, & Volkmar, 1999; Ozonoff, Pennington, & Rogers, 1990) identify that individuals with autism and Asperger syndrome tend to activate a feature-based strategy when presented with face recognition tasks, meaning they identify a face by a feature rather than its whole presentation. The fact that individuals with autism are presenting primarily feature-based strategies to process faces lends to a deficit in processing individuals' facial affect relative to emotional response. The inability to read the face as a whole causes individuals with autism to miss social cues and must be considered when teaching social skills.

REFERENCES

Boucher, J., & Lewis, V. (1992). Unfamiliar face recognition in relatively able autistic children. *Journal of Child Psychology and Psychiatry, 33*, 843–459.

Braverman, M., Fein, D., Lucci, D., & Waterhouse, L. (1989). Affect comprehension in children with pervasive developmental disorders. *Journal of Autism and Developmental Disorders, 19*, 301–316.

Hauck, M., Fein, D., Maltby, N., Waterhouse, L., & Geinstein, C. (1998). Memory for faces in children with autism. *Child Neuropsychology, 4*, 187–198.

Kline, A., Sparrow, S. S., de Bildt, A., Cicchetti, D. V., Cohen, D. J., & Volkmar, F. R. (1999). A normed study of face recognition in autism and related disorders. *Journal of Autism and Developmental Disorders, 29*, 499–508.

Ozonoff, S., Pennington, B. F., & Rogers, S. J. (1990). Are there emotion perception deficits in young autistic children? *Journal of Child Psychology and Psychiatry, 31*, 343–361.

MELANIE D. HARMS

FACILITATED COMMUNICATION (FC)

Facilitated communication (FC) refers to a form of **augmentative and alternative communication** (AAC) that involves providing physical as well as instructional and emotional support to aid individuals with autism and other developmental disabilities to communicate by pointing. The method was first described by Crossley and McDonald (1980) as a method that could be used with people with cerebral palsy. Crossley subsequently began to use facilitated communication with individuals with autism in the 1980s (Biklen, 1990; Blackman, 1999).

Candidates for FC are said to include individuals who have limited or no speech or whose speech is highly disordered (e.g., echolalic) and who have unreliable pointing skills (Crossley, 1994). Crossley refers to the method as facilitated communication training (FCT), emphasizing the importance of developing the ability to ultimately communicate without physical support. Accounts of the same methodology are reported in the literature from Japan (Wakabayashi, 1973), Sweden, and the United States (Oppenheim, 1974; Schawlow and Schawlow, 1985). The recent literature provides descriptions of individuals who have achieved independent typing (Mukhopadhyay, 2000; Rubin et al., 2001) after first receiving physical support for their initial pointing. The Academy Award-nominated film, written by an FC user, Rubin, illustrates physically independent typing (Wurzburg, 2004). Other individuals who first learned to type with facilitation have learned to speak the words they are typing before and as they type (Biklen, 2005; Broderick and Kasa-Hendrickson, 2001; Broderick and Kasa-Hendrickson, in review).

For people with severe speech impairments, alternative forms of communication may include use of gestures or body language, manual sign language, writing, or communication aids (e.g. headpointers, eye gaze technology on computing devices, yes/no communication boards, computers). Facilitated communication is an augmentative system for individuals whose disability affects motor performance, including effective, independent use of the hands. The method involves a communication partner (facilitator) who may aid the person in achieving useful hand function. Initially, this may mean helping the person to isolate the index finger and/or to slow the person's pointing down by providing backward pressure under the wrist or forearm. Over time, the goal is to fade the physical support. Crossley writes,

> The facilitator uses his or her hand(s) to support or inhibit the aid user. The immediate aim is to allow the aid user to make choices and to communicate in a way that had been previously impossible. Practice, using a communication aid such as a picture board, speech synthesizer, or keyboard in a functional manner, is encouraged to increase the user's physical skills and self-confidence and reduce dependency. As the student's skills and confidence increase the amount of facilitation is reduced. (Crossley, 1994, p. 3)

The facilitated communication method involves a variety of supports, including verbal encouragement, monitoring the person's eye contact with the target, sequencing of activities, practice sessions as well as other strategies (see Biklen, 1993, pp. 20–23).

The theoretical explanation for facilitation is that individuals with developmental disabilities, including autism, often have not only motor difficulties but also developmental dyspraxia. Dyspraxia is a neurological condition characterized by difficulty in reliably producing voluntary actions. That is, the person may be able to do something, for example, say a particular word or fetch a toy, but may not be able to do it on command. The person may be able to carry out an action automatically or spontaneously, but not intentionally. Early descriptions of dyspraxia appear in the professional practice literature (e.g., Oppenheim, 1974) as well as in the neurological literature (Maurer and Damasio, 1982). The broader topic of motor disturbance and autism has been summarized by Leary and Hill (1996). Borthwick and Crossley (1999) suggest that difficulties with physical performance, including communication, be decoupled from assessments of intellectual capacity.

Facilitated communication has been called a controversial technique because, as most practitioners and researchers agree, it has been shown that a facilitator's physical touch of the typist's hand or arm may influence the person's pointing, thus affecting the message. A number of studies document the problem of influence and/or difficulties in verifying authorship in facilitated communication (Bebko, Perry, & Bryson, 1996; Bomba, O'Donnell, Markowitz, & Holmes, 1996; Cabay, 1994; Crews et al., 1995; Eberlin, McConnachie, Ibel, & Volpe, 1993; Klewe, 1993; Montee, Miltenberger, & Wittrock, 1995; Moore, Donovan, Hudson, Dykstra, & Lawrence, 1993; Regal, Rooney, & Wandas, 1994; Shane & Kearns, 1994; Smith & Belcher, 1993; Szempruch & Jacobson, 1993; Wheeler, Jacobson, Paglieri, & Schwartz, 1993). The study by Wheeler and his colleagues is often cited as the classic case where researchers were able to demonstrate that some facilitators unknowingly influence facilitated typing and also that some FC users had difficulty in demonstrating their thinking competence and communication skills when tested through an apparently simple message-passing experiment.

Subsequent research on message-passing reveals contradictory evidence, however; that is, several studies have demonstrated that under controlled conditions, over multiple sessions of testing, many individuals were able to demonstrate uninfluenced authorship (Cardinal, Hanson, & Wakeham, 1996; Sheehan & Matuozzi, 1996; Weiss, Wagner, & Bauman, 1996). Similarly and more recently, other studies, using a range of test situations as well as linguistic analysis and documentation of physical, independent-of-facilitator typing offer evidence demonstrating authorship (Broderick & Kasa-Hendrickson, 2001; Calculator & Singer, 1992; Emerson, Grayson, & Griffiths, 2001; Janzen-Wilde, Duchan & Higginbotham, 1995; Niemi & Kärnä-Lin, 2002; Rubin et al., 2001; and Zanobini & Scopesi, 2001).

In light of the controversy surrounding FC, researchers and practitioners alike have wanted to establish means by which to confirm the FC user's authorship. The most obvious protection against influence is physically independent typing and/or speaking before and while typing. Beukelman and Mirenda (1998) write, "in regard to a small group of people around the world who began communicating through FC (facilitated communication) and are now able to type either independently or with minimal, hand-on-shoulder support ... there can be no doubt that, for them, (facilitated communication) 'worked,' in that it opened the door to communication for the first time.... For them, the controversy has ended" (p. 327). Several individuals have reached the point where they can type without physical support (Blackman, 1999; Rubin et al., 2001). At the same time, there is an emerging literature relating typing to speech (Biklen & Burke, 2006; Broderick & Kasa-Hendrickson, 2001; Broderick & Kasa-Hendrickson, in review). Four documentary films feature people who have learned to communicate without physical support (Kasa-Hendrickson, Broderick, and Biklen, 2002; Mabrey, 2003; Terrill, 2000; Wurzburg, 2004).

Given that progress toward and achievement of physically independent typing and/or development of functional and dialogical speech can take several years or may not appear at all, standards have been developed to guide practitioners in the use of facilitation. For example, in an article written for school personnel, Duchan and her colleagues suggested a series of steps for using any controversial methods of communication, including facilitated communication (Duchan, Calculator, Sonnenmeier, Diehl, & Cumley, 2001). Among the procedures they identify is informed consent.

REFERENCES

Bebko, J., Perry, A., & Bryson, S. (1996). Multiple method validation study of facilitated communication: Individual differences and subgroup results. *Journal of Autism and Developmental Disabilities, 26*, 43–58.

Beukelman, D., & Mirenda, P. (1998). *Augmentative and alternative communication: Management of severe communication disorders in children and adults.* Baltimore: Brookes Publishing Co.

Biklen, D. (1990). Communication unbound: Autism and praxis. *Harvard Educational Review. 60*, 291–314.

Biklen, D. (1993). *Communication unbound: How facilitated communication is challenging traditional views of autism and ability/disability.* New York: Teachers College Press.

Biklen, D. (2005). *Autism and the myth of the person alone.* New York: NYU Press.

Biklen, D., & Burke, J. (2006). Presuming competence. *Equity and Excellence in Education, 39*, 1–10.

Blackman, L. (1999) *Lucy's story: Autism & other adventures.* Redcliffe, Queensland, Australia: Book in Hand.

Bomba, C., O'Donnell, L., Markowitz, C., & Holmes, D. (1996). Evaluating the impact of facilitated communication on the communicative competence of fourteen students with autism. *Journal of Autism and Developmental Disorders, 26*, 43–58.

Borthwick, C., & Crossley, R. (1999). Language and Retardation. *Psychology, 10*(38). Retrieved July 13, 2004, from http://psycprints.ecs.soton.ac.uk/archive/00000673/.

Broderick, A., & Kasa-Hendrickson, C. (2001). "Say just one word at first": The emergence of reliable speech in a student labelled with autism. *Journal of the Association for Persons with Severe Handicaps, 26*, 13–24.

Broderick, A., & Kasa-Hendrickson, C. (in review). I am so much more real than retarded: Deconstructing assumptions about speech and its relationship to competency. *Equity and Excellence in Education.*

Cabay, M. (1994). A controlled evaluation of facilitated communication with four autistic children. *Journal of Autism and Developmental Disorders, 24*, 517–527.

Calculator, S., & Singer, K. (1992). Preliminary validation of facilitated communication. *Topics in Language Disorders, 12*, ix.

Cardinal D. N., Hanson, D., & Wakeham, J. (1996). An investigation of authorship in facilitated communication. *Mental Retardation, 34*, 231–242.

Crews, W., Sanders, E., Hensley, L., Johnson, Y., Bonaventura, S., & Rhodes, R. (1995). An evaluation of facilitated communication in a group of nonverbal individuals with mental retardation. *Journal of Autism and Developmental Disorders, 25*, 205–213.

Crossley, R. (1994). *Facilitated communication training.* New York: Teachers College Press.

Crossley, R., & McDonald, A. (1980). *Annie's coming out.* New York: Penguin Books.

Duchan, J., Calculator, S., Sonnenmeier, R., Diehl, S., & Cumley, G. (2001) A framework for managing controversial practices. *Language Speech and Hearing Services in Schools, 32*, 133–141.

Eberlin, M., McConnachie, G., Ibel, S., & Volpe, L. (1993). "Facilitated communication": A failure to replicate the phenomenon. *Journal of Autism and Developmental Disorders, 23*, 507–529.

Emerson, A., Grayson, A., & Griffiths, A. (2001). Can't or won't? Evidence relating to authorship in facilitated communication. *International Journal of Language and Communication Disorders, 36 Suppl.*, 98–103.

Janzen-Wilde, M., Duchan, J., & Higginbotham, D. (1995). Successful use of facilitated communication with an oral child. *Journal of Speech and Hearing Research, 38*, 658–676.

Kasa-Hendrickson, C., Broderick, A., & Biklen, D. (Producers). (2002). *Inside the edge.* (Documentary Film). Syracuse, NY: Syracuse University.

Klewe, L. (1993). An empirical evaluation of spelling boards as a means of communication for the multihandicapped. *Journal of Autism and Developmental Disorders, 23*, 559–566.

Leary, M. R., & Hill, D. A. (1996). Moving on: Autism and movement disturbance. *Mental Retardation, 34*(1), 39–53.

Mabrey, V. (Producer/Director). (2003). *Breaking the silence.* [Documentary]. U.S., *60 Minutes II.* New York: CBS News, CBS Broadcasting, Inc.

Maurer, R., & Damasio, A. R. (1982). Childhood autism from the point of view of behavioral neurology. *Journal of Autism and Developmental Disorders, 12*(2), 195–205.

Montee, B., Miltenberger, R., & Wittrock, D. (1995). An experimental analysis of facilitated communication. *Journal of Applied Behaviour Analysis, 28*, 189–200.

Moore, S, Donovan, B., Hudson, A., Dykstra, J., & Lawrence, J. (1993). Brief report; Evaluation of eight case studies of facilitated communication. *Journal of Autism and Developmental Disorders, 23*, 541–552.

Mukhopadhyay, T. R. (2000). *Beyond the silence: My life, the world and autism.* London: National Autistic Society.

Niemi, J., & Kärnä-Lin, E. (2002). Grammar and lexicon in facilitated communication: A linguistic authorship analysis of a Finnish case. *Mental Retardation 40*, 347–357.

Oppenheim, R. (1974). *Effective teaching methods for autistic children.* Springfield, IL: Charles Thomas.

Regal, R., Rooney, J., & Wandas, T. (1994). Facilitated communication: An experimental evaluation. *Journal of Autism and Developmental Disorders, 24*, 345–355.

Rubin, S., Biklen, D., Kasa-Hendrickson, C., Kluth, P., Cardinal, D., & Broderick, A. (2001). Independence, participation, and the meaning of intellectual ability. *Disability & Society, 16*, 415–429.

Schawlow, A. T., & Schawlow A. L. (1985). The endless search for help. In M. R. Brady & P. Gunther (Eds.), *Integrating moderately and severely handicapped learners: Strategies that work* (pp. 5–15). Springfield, IL: Charles Thomas.

Shane, H., & Kearns, K. (1994). An examination of the role of the facilitator in "facilitated communication." *American Journal of Speech-Language Pathology, September*, 48–54.

Sheehan, C., & Matuozzi, R. (1996). Investigation of the validity of facilitated communication through the disclosure of unknown information. *Mental Retardation, 34*, 94–107.

Smith, M., & Belcher, R. (1993). Brief report: facilitated communication with adults with autism. *Journal of Autism and Developmental Disorders, 23*, 175.

Szempruch, J., & Jacobson, J. (1993). Evaluating facilitated communications of people with developmental disabilities. *Research in Developmental Disabilities, 14*, 253–264.

Terrill, C. (Producer/Director). (2000). *Inside story: Tito's story.* [Documentary]. England: BBC.

Wakabayashi, S. (1973). A case of infantile autism who became able to communicate by writing. *Psychiatria et Neurologia Japonica, 75*, 339–357.

Weiss, M., Wagner, S., & Bauman, M. (1996). A validated case study of facilitated communication. *Mental Retardation, 34*, 220–230.

Wheeler, D., Jacobson, J., Paglieri, R., & Schwartz, A. (1993). An experimental assessment of facilitated communication. *Mental Retardation, 31*, 49–60.

Wurzburg, G. (Producer/Director) (2004). *Autism is a world* [Documentary Film]. Atlanta: CNN.

Zanobini, M., & Scopesi, A. (2001). La comunicazione facilitata in un bambino autistico, *Psicologia Clinica dello Sviluppo, 5*, 395–421.

DOUGLAS BIKLEN

FACILITY-BASED EMPLOYMENT

Facility-based employment is a good choice for individuals who have more severely challenged job skills or who require intensive levels of supervision to complete the required tasks of their job. This type of employment is often found at **vocational rehabilitation** agencies or private nonprofit community organizations whose services include supported employment arrangements. Because employment is not competitively based for participants in the program, the benefits of such an environment would be successful socialization, active participation in work activities, and intensive support for all types of skill deficits. Eligibility assessments include IQ, work readiness, and general functioning level. Availability of these programs may be limited because of funding and low attrition rates unless the program operates for specific periods of time or sessions in order to accommodate a larger volume of participants. Since many of these programs have been operating in some cases for decades, they should be investigated carefully before committing to participation at any facility. Be sure to look for a program that is comprehensive and nurturing with a skilled staff that insists on a positive environment.

SHERRY MOYER

FADING

In order to increase **generalization** to a natural setting, fading of unnatural antecedent stimuli should take place. Fading is used as a part of a technique called transfer of **stimulus control**. The teacher presents the unnatural antecedent stimulus (or teaching stimulus) paired with the natural stimulus to replace the teaching stimulus with the stimulus in the natural environment. The teaching stimulus should be gradually faded, allowing the natural stimulus to control the person's behavior. The stimulus may be faded physically, spatially, audibly, and visually (Cooper, Heron, & Heward, 1987). For example, a teacher could use fading when teaching a student that when the bell rings, they are to leave the classroom. At first, the teacher may need to physically prompt the student to move when the bell rings. This physical prompt, in the absence of the bell ringing, is the student's stimulus for his behavior of getting up and moving out of the classroom. In the presence of the bell, the full physical prompt with two hands can be faded to a light pull on the arm and then to a touch on the arm. The end is that the student responds to the natural stimulus of the bell without any physical prompting.

See also antecedent; stimuli.

REFERENCE

Cooper, J. O., Heron, T. E., & Heward, W. L. (1987). *Applied behavior analysis*. Upper Saddle River, NJ: Prentice Hall.

TARA MIHOK

FALSE-BELIEF PARADIGM

The False-Belief Paradigm is a task designed to assess **theory of mind** (ToM) development. Theory of mind describes an area of research that focuses on a child's ability to understand mental concepts such as belief, desire, the difference between appearance and reality, and the existence of other minds. The classic false-belief paradigm presents a child with two dolls, two boxes (one red and one green), and a marble, all of which are in a single miniature scene. One doll puts the marble in the green box, so that it is hidden, and then departs. While the first doll is gone, the second doll removes the marble from the green box and puts it in the red box. The first doll then returns, and the child is asked: "Where will the first doll look for the marble?" Children younger than four typically reply that the doll will look in the red box, the actual location of the marble. They are unable to understand that the doll might have a false belief, one that does not correspond to reality. After the age of four, children begin to give the correct response: the doll will look in the green box, where it had last seen the marble. Individuals with autism of all ages have difficulty with the false-belief paradigm due to difficulties with understanding and reading the emotions and thoughts of others.

JEANNE HOLVERSTOTT

FAMILY ASSESSMENT INTERVIEW

The family assessment interview is part of the family assessment process (FAP) designed to match families with the appropriate services for their children and empower the families based on their individual strengths. Upon referral, a family assessment specialist meets with the members of the family for an initial interview and to conduct the necessary assessments. During this meeting, the specialist conducts a family assessment interview in order to facilitate an exchange of feelings and experiences, examine family challenges from multiple perspectives, and enhance communication between caretakers and youths. Depending on the needs of the family (i.e., mediation, crisis management), the specialist will compile this information and refer the family to the appropriate service provider (i.e., community-based service, mental health evaluation, **mediation**, designated assessment service, or other applicable service).

JEANNE HOLVERSTOTT

FAMILY EDUCATIONAL RIGHTS AND PRIVACY ACT (FERPA)

The Family Educational Rights and Privacy Act, also known as FERPA, is a federal law created in 1974 to protect students' educational records. The **Individuals with Disabilities Education Act** (IDEA, 1997) and the **Section 504 of the Rehabilitation Act of 1973** also address these areas (FERPA, 1974). The law applies to all educational institutions that receive funding from the United States Department of Education, including public schools, colleges, and universities, as well as many private schools that also receive some form of funding. Institutions may have their funding removed if they fail to follow FERPA regulations (FERPA, 1974).

FERPA was created for three specific reasons. First, schools were denying parent requests to access records while government agencies and prospective employers were allowed to see the records. Second, information contained in school records was not always factual, education-based, or objective. Third, access to student records varied greatly from state to state and was based on common law practices, case law, and local policies (Copenhaver, 2002).

FERPA designates the requirements for keeping educational records. Personal identifiable records must be kept confidential. All schools or educational entities are required by FERPA to follow the same basic guidelines. Districts must adopt a written policy designating the rules for obtaining and keeping educational records and following procedures that meet FERPA standards. Permanent files should be maintained on all students (Copenhaver, 2002). Students with special education services should have three separate files, one file for student information such as immunizations and discipline referrals, one for **Individualized Education Programs** (IEP) and other special educations forms, and a file for the special education teacher that holds student information. Schools must keep a logbook of who accesses the files. Only school personnel whose titles are given access by the district's educational records policy may see the records. These may include administrators, therapists, teachers, medical staff, social workers, school law enforcement, a parent serving official school duty, and board members (FERPA, 1974).

FERPA gives parents the right to review their child's education records. Education records relate directly to a student, contain personal information, and may include information recorded in a variety of formats including handwritten, tape, film, or print (Copenhaver, 2002). When requested, a school district must disclose the types of records they keep (FERPA, 1974). The institution must make the documents available within 45 days of receiving the request or within the school district's set limits. However, schools are not required to provide copies. Noncustodial parents may have access to the files unless that right has been removed due to state order, court order, or other legally binding document (FERPA, 1974). When the student is 18 or attends college, these rights transfer to them. At this point of transfer, students are referred to as "eligible students" (Holbum, 2003).

Parents or eligible students can request that a school amend records they believe to be incorrect (Holbum, 2003). If the school district does not amend the records, parents or eligible students may request a hearing. If the hearing is unsuccessful, parents or eligible students may place a statement explaining their views of the situation into the permanent education records. The statement from parents or eligible students must be included with the records it pertains to at each disclosure or time the file is viewed.

Parents or eligible students who believe that an institution is not correctly applying FERPA have the right to file a complaint with The U.S. Department of Education. Complaints should be directed to the Family Policy Compliance Office of the Department of Education.

Schools may release information regarding students when they are given written consent by the parent or eligible student. Exceptions are release within the public school system, release of directory information as outlined by their district policy, or in emergency or health-related situations. Parents and students must be notified each year of their rights pertaining to education records under FERPA. Parents should be provided information on what will be disclosed in directory information and have the opportunity to choose not to participate on a yearly basis. The law does not specify how the parents will be notified. Personal notes made by staff members and maintained by that person and not shared with others are exempt from parental disclosure. These personal journals are not required to be shared with parents or eligible students under FERPA requirements. These records do not include health and treatment information for persons age 18 and over that are maintained by health care professionals (Copenhaver, 2002). Also, records cannot be released to Medicaid for benefit claims without parental consent (Ahern, 2002).

There are specific requirements that must be fulfilled before disclosing information that is not available under the exceptions of the law such as "directory" information. A parent or a student who has become eligible must provide a written and signed consent form before personal information can be released. The form must state what documents are to be disclosed, why the documents are being disclosed, and who specifically the documents are being disclosed to. The institution will provide a copy of the information disclosed if the eligible student or parent requests it (FERPA, 1974).

The goal of The Family Education Rights and Privacy Act (1974) is to protect the confidentiality of students and families while providing information as appropriate. Interpretation of law may affect how school districts in various areas approach the law. This may in turn reflect how much information is released. Often districts are overcautious in their release of information (Center for Mental Health in Schools, 2002). Even with the variance of interpretation between education institutions, the outcome is still realized; education records are protected and privacy is maintained.

REFERENCES

Ahern, E. (2002). *Medicaid: Parent consent issues. Quick turn around (QTA)*. Alexandria, VA: National Association of State Directors of Special Education.

Center for Mental Health in Schools. (2002). *Confidentiality: A center quick training aid*. University of California–Los Angeles (UCLA).

Copenhaver, J. (2002). *Primer for Maintaining Accurate Special Education Records and Meeting Confidentiality Requirements when Serving Children with Disabilities—Family Educational Rights and Privacy Act (FERPA)*. Utah State University.

The Family Educational Rights and Privacy Act of 1974 (FERPA). Public Law No. 93-380 (20 U.S.C. § 1232g; 34 CFR Part 99).

Holbum, T. (2003). College student records: Legal issues, privacy, and security concerns. (ERIC Document Reproduction Service ED 480467).

Individuals with Disabilities Education Act Reauthorization of 1997. Public Law No. 105–17 (1997).

FURTHER INFORMATION

Brookshire, R., & Klotz, J. (2002). *Selected Teachers' Perceptions of Special Education Laws*. Paper presented at the annual conference of the Mid-South Educational Research Association. Chattanooga, Tennessee.

Doyle, S. L. (2002). *FERPA: What exactly is an educational record?* (ERIC Document Reproduction Service ED 473342).

O'Donnell, M. L. (2003). FERPA: Only a piece of the privacy puzzle. *Student Rights Journal of College and University Law*, 29(3) 679–717.

VALERIE JANKE REXIN

FAST FORWORD

Fast ForWord is an intervention for children with language, memory and processing problems. The intervention involves speech sound discrimination exercises, a two-tone sequencing exercise and receptive language exercises. Novel to their intervention was the application of neuroscience research on brain plasticity and auditory processing problems stemming from over 20 years of neuroscience research.

The exercises were designed to build the cognitive skills essential for learning language and learning to read: memory, attention, processing, and sequencing. Although many of the tasks they introduced were similar to those used conventionally by speech and language pathologists to treat language and processing disorders, the Tallal/

Merzenich intervention was different because the speech stimuli in the exercises were acoustically enhanced to conform to the perceptual needs of children with auditory processing problems. Further, children were asked to practice the exercises 2 hours a day, 5 days a week, for 4 to 6 weeks. This intense training protocol stemmed from research by Merzenich et al. (1996) showing that four characteristics of training maximize brain reorganization: (a) frequency of stimuli presentation, (b) adaptability, (c) simultaneous stimulation of several cognitive domains, and (d) timely motivation.

After the initial field trial of the intervention with almost 500 children, the intervention was named Fast ForWord. Today there are nine Fast ForWord products, all based on the same neuroscience research. The original intervention is now called Fast ForWord Language. The additional Fast ForWord products are designed around the same neuroscience principles to build the same cognitive skills of memory, attention, processing, and sequencing, but in the context of reading.

The results of the national field trial instituted to test the efficacy of the new intervention revealed that the average language gain nationwide was almost two standard deviations (representing a year and one-half growth in language skills) in most cases, achieved after 4 weeks of training. Among the children who participated in the national field trial were many who had diagnoses of autism spectrum disorders (ASD). Although many of the children with ASD had more severe language and processing issues than the average Fast ForWord participant, they made almost the same gains overall as the children for whom the intervention had been designed—namely, those with specific language impairment (Tallal et al., 1997).

What Is a Neuroscience-Based Perspective and How Does It Help in Intervention with Autism Spectrum Disorders?

Researchers have speculated for years that ASD must have something to do with brain processing differences. However, despite many studies of the brains of individuals with ASD, there has been little consensus as to the ways in which the brain might be organized differently in these individuals. Bauman and Kemper (1994) studied brain cells of persons with autism who have died of natural causes, noting that while there are abnormalities in the brain cells in some of the older parts of the brain that regulate movement and emotion, brain cells important for thought and language (cells in the outer brain parts, the cortex) appeared normal. Herbert and her associates worked to confirm the hypothesis that children on the autism spectrum may have intact cortical brain cells important for thought, language, and reasoning, but those cells may be organized differently, specifically in the way they communicate with each may pose a problem. Brain cells in the cortex have connecting fibers that are "wrapped" with an insulating sheet called myelin. Myelin is important because it allows brain cells to "talk" to each other using very efficient connections. According to Herbert, Ziegler, Makris, et al. (2004) and Herbert, Ziegler, Deutsch, et al. (2004), myelin begins to insulate brain cell connections at very specific times during the development of the brain. These researchers have found that in children with developmental language disorders and children with Asperger syndrome, the neuron pathways may get "wrapped" too soon or in unusual ways. This may cause the brain to become "hardwired" while the brain is still immature and not well organized. Herbert hypothesizes that this could interfere with the child's ability to process language and learn other higher cognitive tasks easily. Her research using MRI scans suggests that the brains of children with Asperger syndrome and developmental language disorders have the same number of cortical brain cells as those of children who do not exhibit autism spectrum disorders, but the connections between the brain cells are less efficiently organized.

Although research by Herbert, Ziegler, Makris, et al. (2004) and Herbert, Ziegler, Deutsch, et al. (2004) needs to be verified by other studies before firm conclusions may be drawn, it appears that if children with ASD demonstrate immature or inefficient connections, those are malleable in the human brain. Neuroscientists have demonstrated that intensive interventions can reroute brain connections, even in adults. The ability to Fast ForWord Language to normalize brain organization has been investigated in two studies (Temple et al., 2000; Temple et al., 2003). This research with children and adults with dyslexia, using MRI to create images of the brain working before and after Fast ForWord Language intervention, revealed neurological wiring changes in children and adults with dyslexia and associated auditory processing problems. Further, these investigations demonstrated that brain function could be normalized in 4 to 6 weeks.

How Do Fast ForWord Products Differ from Other Interventions for Children on the Autism Spectrum?

Because they were developed specifically for improving receptive language, memory, attention, processing, and sequencing the Fast ForWord products can augment other interventions for ASD that address behavioral and interaction patterns by filling in the auditory, language, and cognitive gaps that these children may experience. In a retrospective study of 100 children with ASD who used Fast ForWord Language, Melzer and Poglitsch (1999) reported that many therapists successfully implemented Fast ForWord Language in conjunction with sensori-integration modifications as part of an **Applied Behavior Analysis** (ABA) or naturalistic intervention programs. The authors noted that although there was substantial variability in the quantity and quality of gains realized as a result of Fast ForWord Language intervention, almost all of the children who complied with the intervention schedule showed enhanced attentional, receptive language, and expressive formulation skills. Children on the autism spectrum may require a significantly longer training period than children with other language or reading disorders, but the gains are significant.

References

Bauman, M. L., & Kemper, T. L. (1994). *The neurobiology of autism*. Baltimore: Johns Hopkins University Press.

Herbert, M. R., Ziegler, D. A., Makris, N., Filipek, P. A., Kemper, T. L., Normandin, J. J., et al. (2004). Localization of white matter volume increase in autism and developmental language disorder. *Annals of Neurology, 55,* 530–540.

Herbert, M. R., Ziegler, D. A., Deutsch, C. K., O'Brien, L. M., Kennedy, D. N., Filipek, P. A., et al. (2004). Brain asymmetries in autism and developmental language disorder: A nested whole-brain analysis. *Brain Advance Access,* November 24, 2004.

Melzer, M., & Poglitsch, G. (1999). *Use of Fast ForWord with children who have autism spectrum disorders*. Paper presented at the annual convention of the American Speech-Language Hearing Association, San Antonio, TX.

Merzenich, M. M., Jenkins, W. M., Johnston, P., Schreiner, C. E., Miller, S. L., & Tallal, P. (1996). Temporal processing deficits of language-learning impaired children ameliorated by training. *Science, 271,* 77–80.

Tallal, P., Saunders, G., Miller, S., Jenkins, W., Protopapas, A., & Merzenich, M. M. (1997). Rapid training-driven improvement in autistic and other PDD children. *Society for Neuroscience, 23*, 490–491.

Temple, E., Poldrack, R. A., Protopapas, A., Nagarajan, S., Salz, T., Tallal, P., et al. (2000). Disruption of the neural response to rapid acoustic stimuli in dyslexia: Evidence from functional MRI. *Proceedings of the National Academy of Sciences, 97*(25), 13907–13912.

Temple, E., Deutsch, G., Poldrack, R., Miller, S., Tallal, P., & Merzenich, M. (2003). Neural deficits in children with dyslexia ameliorated by behavioral remediation: Evidence from functional MRI. *Proceedings of the National Academy of Sciences, 100*(5), 2860–2865.

MARTHA S. BURNS AND PAULA TALLAL

FEINGOLD DIET

The Feingold diet was developed in 1973 by Benjamin Feingold, MD, a pediatric allergist, who proposed that salicylates, artificial colors, and artificial flavors caused hyperactivity in children. To treat or prevent this condition, Feingold suggested a diet that was free of such chemicals. Feingold also advised individuals to avoid certain over-the-counter and prescription drugs and to limit the purchases of mouthwash, toothpaste, cough drops, perfume, and various other nonfood products. There is no empirical evidence to support the efficacy of the Feingold diet.

JEANNE HOLVERSTOTT

FIGURATIVE LANGUAGE

Figurative language or speech contains specific words that are intended by the speaker to create interesting *images*. Figurative language provides a new way of looking at or understanding a message by making comparisons of different items to demonstrate the unique similarities. Figurative language is used to enhance the communicative meaning or message of the speaker.

KATHERINE E. COOK

FINE MOTOR SKILLS

Fine motor skills describe a movement that requires the use and coordination of the smaller muscles of the body. Examples of fine motor skills include writing, cutting with scissors, or buttoning a shirt.

KELLY M. PRESTIA

FLOOR TIME. *See* Developmental Individual-Difference Relation-Based Intervention

FLUENCY

Fluency is the normal rhythm and timing of words and phrases including variations in speed and pauses. A fluency disorder is defined as an interruption in the flow of spoken language by atypical rate, rhythm, and repetitions. Stuttering is the most common fluency disorder characterized by repetitions of consonant or vowel sounds as the speaker tries to express a thought, idea, or feeling.

KATHERINE E. COOK

FOOD INTOLERANCE/SENSITIVITIES. *See* Elimination Diet and Food Sensitivities

FOUR STEPS OF COMMUNICATION

Communication, verbal or nonverbal, is an ever-present complex process when relating to others. To help we realize how to begin the process of evaluating and treating persons who have difficulty sharing space with others/communicating effectively. The four steps of communication were developed by Winner (2002) to help understand how the communicative process unfolds. It is in this same order that we begin to address teaching social thinking skills to persons with near-normal to way-above-normal intelligence who also have social cognitive deficits. Most students with social cognitive deficits need to work on all four of these steps, meaning that we have to do far more with them than simply practice teaching them to participate in a conversation while sitting at a table.

Step 1: Thinking about Others and What They Are Thinking about Us

We THINK about who we are near or who we want to talk to or play with. We are aware people have little thoughts about all the people around them, and that we have those same types of thoughts. We even monitor our own behavior based on what we think other people might be thinking of us!

We consider what we know about the other person and what they like to do in order to keep the other person feeling like we are aware of them or thinking about them.

Step 2: Establishing a Physical Presence

When we desire to communicate or "hang out" with someone, while thinking about them, we have to establish a physical presence to show that person that we would like to talk to the person or just be with them. Our physical presence can include standing close enough to the person (often about an arm's length away), having our shoulders turned towards them, and keeping our body relaxed to move easily to include other people or to move away from a person as needed. Our physical presence usually communicates intent, which helps to kick off communication. For example, if you are thinking about me, and you want to hang out with me but you are standing about four feet away and looking around but wishing I would come to you, you have failed to establish a physical presence for me. I would not be able to "read your intention" to communicate with me.

Step 3: "Thinking with Your Eyes"

As we are thinking about the person we desire to communicate with and we establish physical presence, our intention to communicate is only explicitly clear once we have established eye-contact with the other person. This is the third step, since it is possible to engage in the previous two steps without using eye-contact, but communication or sharing space effectively is usually not functional without using our eyes, not only to show someone we are interested in talking, but to also watch the physical movements and facial expression of the others to determine their intentions, feelings, and needs, as well.

Step 4: Using Language to Relate to Others

While language is undisputedly central to all language-based communication, it is often not effective or functional if the first three steps are not in place. For example, if a student comes up to you to tell you all the details about the Titanic, and he or she talks endlessly without considering what you are thinking about and without establishing eye-contact, it may be interesting to listen to (if you are an adult), but this is not truly communication; it should better be described as "downloading" information. Language use in communication requires that language users constantly consider the thoughts, feelings, prior knowledge, experiences, intentions, and needs of the communicative partner. Each partner has to work to regulate their language to meet the needs of the listener while also conveying the message that helps them to add their own thoughts to the interaction. Effective language-based communication requires students to ask questions to others about other people, produce supportive responses, add their own thoughts by connecting their experiences or thoughts to what other people are saying, and so forth.

REFERENCE

Winner, M. (2002). *Thinking about you thinking about me.* San Jose, CA: Michelle Garcia Winner.

FURTHER INFORMATION

Winner, M. (2005). *Worksheets! For teaching social thinking and related skills.* San Jose, CA: Michelle Garcia Winner.

MICHELLE GARCIA WINNER AND JAMIE RIVETTS

FOUR STEPS OF PERSPECTIVE TAKING

Perspective taking should occur each time we share space with one or more people; it is as important when we are not talking to people as when we are engaged in an active discussion/conversation. One definition of perspective taking is the ability to read other people's thoughts, emotions, motives, intentions, belief systems, prior knowledge and experiences, and personality to gain insight into the communicative intent of the person conveying the message. Perspective taking is critical for people to work effectively together in groups; it is at this time that all people have to regulate their communication around their own needs as well as the needs of others.

The four steps of perspective taking were developed by Winner for us to better understand how a "thought" about another person quickly turns into behavioral regulation (2002). We can use the following four steps of perspective taking not only for us adults to better assess where a child may be struggling, but also as a teaching tool for older students with Asperger syndrome and like diagnoses, to help them understand more concretely the abstract process of perspective taking.

> **Step 1:** I think about you and you have a thought about me, when we are just sharing space (e.g., when sharing an elevator) or when we are talking or planning to talk.
> **Step 2:** I try to determine why you are near me. What is your motive/intention for being near me or thinking about me? Are we just in the same place at the same time by coincidence, or do you plan to harm or trick me?
> **Step 3:** Since I realize you are having a thought about me, I wonder what you are thinking about me.
> **Step 4:** As I try and figure out what you are thinking about me, I monitor and possibly regulate my behavior to keep you thinking about me the way I want you to think about me.

For example: When I am on an elevator by myself, I will often look in the mirror, fix my clothing, makeup, etc. As soon as you get on the elevator, I realize you are having a thought about me so I stop looking in the mirror and I face the door (Steps 1, 3, and 4); I also may keep an eye on you to make sure you are just trying to get to another floor on the elevator and not trying to steal my wallet (Step 2).

REFERENCE

Winner, M. (2002). *Thinking about you thinking about me.* San Jose, CA: Michelle Garcia Winner.

FURTHER INFORMATION
Winner, M. (2005). *Think social! A social thinking curriculum for school aged students.* San Jose, CA: Michelle Garcia Winner.

MICHELLE GARCIA WINNER AND JAMIE RIVETTS

FRAGILE X SYNDROME

Fragile X syndrome (fragile X) is the most common inherited form of mental retardation. A single mutated gene, which is found on the X chromosome and passed down from one generation to the next, causes fragile X. The body's building blocks are made up of proteins that perform specific jobs needed for the body's chemical functions and for the structure of organs and tissues. Fragile X occurs because a specific gene, the *FMR1* gene, is not able to make usable amounts of a specific protein. The amount of fragile X mental retardation protein (FMRP) determines how mild or severe the symptoms of fragile X are in a body. The less FMRP levels in the body, the more severe the symptoms.

The gene that causes fragile X was discovered in 1991 by scientists at the National Institute of Child Health and Human Development (NICHD). International researchers continue to study fragile X and are working to find medical and preventative treatments as well as effective therapeutic strategies for the syndrome.

The range of physical signs and symptoms varies. Often infants and children with fragile X have no discernable features from other children until they reach puberty. Some young children may have very soft skin, a broad forehead, or a bit larger head circumference than their typical counterparts. At puberty, however, more discernable features often develop. These might include a longer face or jaw, and large ears. Often individuals with fragile X do not grow as tall as might be expected based on the height of others in their family. Many males develop what is called macro-orchidism, or enlarged testicles, which does not affect sexual development and is not caused by a hormonal imbalance.

Other symptoms that might occur in fragile X are caused by loose or weak connective tissues. This can be manifested by loose or flexible joints, flat feet, and the ability to extend thumb, knee, and elbow joints further than what is considered normal. Sometimes weak connective tissues can cause a heart murmur or mitral valve prolapse. Older individuals with fragile X syndrome may develop hand tremors or have difficulty walking.

Females with fragile X are affected differently than males. Since females have two X chromosomes, they will have only one FMRP1 gene that is mutated and another that is normal. Cells randomly choose which gene on a chromosome will be used to make proteins, so if the gene that makes normal amounts of the FMRP is active, then the female, even with a full mutation, will be able to make some of the needed protein. Therefore, symptoms in females with fragile X are less severe and occur less often than symptoms in males.

One significant effect of a permutation form of the fragile X gene in females is called premature ovarian failure (POF). It is found in 16 to 19 percent of females with the permutation gene. Women with POF stop ovarian function very early, often before their forties, and sometimes as early as their twenties (the average age for menopause in normal females is 51). The possibility of early menopause can be a significant issue for women considering pregnancy, so early knowledge of the gene is a must.

Anxiety, social fears, and sensory issues are characteristic of individuals with fragile X. They may have difficulty in social situations or meeting new people, and therefore avoid situations that might make them nervous, anxious, or uncomfortable. They may be oversensitive to sounds, lights, temperatures, textures, or movement. Transitions or a change in routine can sometimes be difficult. Often the individual's reaction to overstimulation, anxiety, or sensory input can be so heightened that his behavior can potentially escalate to aggression or self-injurious behavior. The anxiety level in males with fragile X appears to last longer than in their typical peers.

There is a strong association of fragile X and autism. Children with fragile X exhibit many of the same characteristics as those with autism, but do not necessarily meet the full criteria of the ***Diagnostic and Statistical Manual of Mental Disorders*** (DSW-IV-TR; APA, 2000) definition. In recent years, researchers have found that a significant subgroup of children with fragile X also have autism. Bailey found that 25 percent of boys with fragile X met the criteria of autism using the **Childhood Autism Rating Scale** (Bailey, Hatton, Skinner, & Mesibov, 2001), and that they characteristically appeared very similar to children with autism without fragile X. Rogers, Wehner, and Hagerman (2001) found 15 to 33 percent of the children they evaluated with fragile X syndrome met the criteria for autism. Further research is needed to determine the causal genetic factors of fragile X to autism. At this time, fragile X is the most common genetically known cause of autism.

REFERENCES

American Psychiatric Association (2000). *Diagnostic and statistical manual of mental disorders* (4th ed., text rev.). Washington, DC: Author.

Bailey, D. B., Hatton, D. D., Skinner, M., & Mesibov, G. (2001). Autistic behavior, FMR1 protein, and developmental trajectories in young males with fragile X syndrome. *Journal of Autism and Developmental Disorders, 31*(2), 165–174.

National Institute of Child Health & Human Development. (2006). *What are the signs and symptoms of Fragile X syndrome?* Retrieved November 16, 2006, from www.nichd.nih.gov/publicatios/pubs/fragileX/sub8.htm.

Rogers, S. J., Wehner, E. A., & Hagerman, R. (2001). The behavioral phenotype in fragile X: Symptoms of autism in very young children with fragile X syndrome, idiopathic autism, and other developmental disorders. *Journal of Developmental & Behavioral Pediatrics, 22*(6), 409–417.

FURTHER INFORMATION

Bailey, D. B., Jr., Hatton, D. D., Mesibov, G., Ament, N., & Skinner, M. (2000). Early development, temperament and functional impairment in autism and fragile X syndrome. *Journal of Autism and Developmental Disorders, 30*(1), 49–59.

The National Fragile X Foundation. (February 3, 2006). *How do the behaviors seen in persons with Fragile X relate to those seen in autism?* Retrieved August 11, 2006, from www.fragilex.org/html/autism.htm.

ANN PILEWSKIE

FREE AND APPROPRIATE PUBLIC EDUCATION (FAPE)

As part of the **Individuals with Disabilities Education Act**, Part B, every school district must provide a free and appropriate public education (FAPE) for children with disabilities. By definition, all special education and related services should be provided to the student with a disability at no cost to his or her parents. In general, all students of school age are provided a free and appropriate public education.

The Individuals with Disabilities Education Act defines FAPE as special education and related services that (a) have been provided at public expense without charge to the parents; (b) meet the standards of the state educational agency; (c) include an appropriate preschool, elementary, or secondary school education in the state involved; and (d) are provided in conformity with the student's individualized education program (20 U.S.C.A. § 1401(8)) [2004]. IDEA defines FAPE but does not set any requirements or standards, which has troubled many school districts and parents. The definition of what is *appropriate* education has led many families to the federal court to decide what is appropriate for their student's education.

FAPE is best defined as an individualized program designed to meet the child's unique needs and from which the child receives educational benefit. The definition of FAPE first came under scrutiny with *Board of Education of the Hendrick Hudson School District v. Rowley* (1982). This case reached the U.S. Supreme Court, with the court developing a two-part test to determine if a school district provided a free and appropriate public education. The first part of the test verified that the procedural requirements of IDEA were followed during the development of the IEP. The second part determined if the IEP developed adhered to all of the law's procedural requirements and was reasonably calculated to enable the student to receive educational benefits. The Supreme Court decided that the school district did adhere to both parts of the test and that an appropriate education did not mean providing the student with a disability the best education possible (Fielder, 2000).

Many court cases followed *Rowley* regarding autism spectrum disorders and specific instructional approaches or methodologies. The courts have consistently declared that as long as an appropriate educational program is provided, the choice of approach or methodology is within the school's discretion. That being said, if the student's parents can prove that the school's methodology is not producing educational benefits, then some courts have ordered school districts to use a specific methodology. This exception only applied to cases where the methodology requested showed educational results and the school's methodology did not.

Placements of students with disabilities have also been questioned when discussing FAPE. According to IDEA, school districts must follow specific requirements in determining placement. These requirements are as follows:

- The placement must be based on the student's **Individualized Education Program** (IEP) and be designed as the most appropriate setting where the required special education and related services can be delivered (IDEA Regulations, 34 C.F.R. Sec. 300. 552(a)(2)).

The educational placement must be determined at least annually (IDEA Regulations, 34 C.F.R. Sec 300. 552(a)(1)).

- The placement must comply with the least restrictive environment requirement (IDEA Regulations, 34 C.F.R. Sec. 300. 553(a)(4)).

Any placement of a student with a disability must be made by the IEP team after the IEP is written. Disagreements regarding placement in an IEP by parents may go to mediation or due process if the school and parents cannot come to an agreement.

REFERENCES
Board of Education of the Hendrick Hudson School District v. Rowley, 458 U.S. 176 (1982).
Fiedler, C. R. (2000). Making a difference: Advocacy competencies for special education professionals. Boston: Allyn and Bacon.
Individuals with Disabilities Education Act, 20 U.S.C.A. § 1401(8) (2002).
U.S. Department of Education. (1992). IDEA Part B Regulations, 34 C.F.R. Sections 300. 500–662.

MELISSA L. TRAUTMAN

FUNCTIONAL ANALYSIS SCREENING TOOL (FAST)

The Functional Analysis Screening Tool (FAST; Iwata & DeLeon, 1996) is a behavior rating scale used to identify factors that may influence the occurrence of behavior problems. Designed to be a component of a comprehensive functional analysis, the FAST's 18 items are yes-no questions completed by a parent, therapist, teacher, or residential staff member. The "yes" items correspond with "likely maintaining variables," which include social reinforcement (attention/preferred items), social reinforcement (escape), automatic reinforcement (sensory stimulation), and automatic reinforcement (pain attenuation).

REFERENCE
Iwata, B. & DeLeon, I. G (1996). The functional analysis screening tool. Gainesville, FL: The Florida Center on Self-Injury.

JEANNE HOLVERSTOTT

FUNCTIONAL BEHAVIOR ANALYSIS

Functional behavior analysis is a technique for analyzing relationships between behavior and the environment (Pierce & Cheney, 2004). Functional behavior analysis involves manipulating **antecedents** (before) and **consequences** (after) in a highly controlled environment to determine their controlling functions (Mace, Lalli, & Lalli, 1991; Gresham, Watson, & Skinner, 2001; Pierce & Cheney, 2004). Before conducting functional behavior analysis, information needs to be gathered through observation or interview, and hypotheses should be generated. The purpose of conducting functional analysis is to (a) define problem behaviors, (b) find stimuli that extinguish problem behaviors, and (c) identify functions of problem behaviors (Foster-Johnson & Dunlap, 1993; Horner & Carr, 1997; O'Neill, Homer, Albin, Sprague, Storey, et al., 1997).

Functional behavior analysis is not generally used in school settings, and it is reserved for the most severe behaviors under the most controlled conditions since it requires intensive time and controlled conditions (Bowen, Jenson, & Clark, 2004).

REFERENCES
Bowen, J. M., Jenson, W. R., & Clark, E. (2004). School-based interventions for students with behavior problems. New York: Springer.
Foster-Johnson, L., & Dunlap, G. (1993). Using functional assessment to develop effective individualized intervention for challenging behaviors. Teaching Exceptional Children, 25, 44–50.
Gresham, F. M., Watson, T. S., & Skinner, C. H. (2001). Functional behavioral assessment: Principles, procedures, and future directions. School Psychology Review, 30, 156–172.
Horner, R. H., & Carr, E. G. (1997). Behavioral support for students with severe disabilities: Functional assessment and comprehensive intervention. Journal of Special Education, 31, 84–104.

Mace, F. C., Lalli, J. S., & Lalli, E. P. (1991). Functional analysis and treatment of aberrant behavior. *Research in Developmental Disabilities, 12*, 155–180.

O'Neill, R. E., Homer, R. H., Albin, R. W., Sprague, J. R., Storey, K., & Newton, J. S. (1997). *Functional assessment and program development for problem behavior: A practical handbook.* Belmont, CA: Wadsworth.

Pierce, W. D., & Cheney, C. D. (2004). *Behavior analysis and learning* (3rd ed.). Mahwah, NJ: Lawrence Erlbaum Associates.

HYE RAN PARK

FUNCTIONAL BEHAVIOR ASSESSMENT (FBA)

Functional behavior assessment is based on research in **applied behavior analysis**. It provides a method of examining relationships between and generating hypotheses about the **antecedents** and **consequences** that trigger or maintain behaviors (Dunlap et al., 1993; Ervin et al., 2000; Iwata, Vollmer, & Zarcone, 1990). The purpose of conducting an FBA is to determine (a) discriminative stimuli or antecedents that elicit problem behavior, and (b) the reinforcing consequences that maintain the problem behavior (Erickson, Stage, & Nelson, 2006).

The FBA consists of two stages. The first stage consists of teacher interviews, direct observation/descriptive assessment, and hypothesis development. The second stage includes functional analysis to test the conditions that are hypothesized to be maintaining the students' disruptive behaviors, and potential interventions based on the conditions that maintain appropriate behavior (Ervin et al., 2000; Kamps et al., 1995).

REFERENCES

Dunlap, G., Kern, L., dePerczel, M., Clarke, S., Wilson, D., Childs, K. E., & White, R. L. (1993). Functional analysis of classroom variables for students with emotional and behavioral disorders. *Behavioral Disorders, 18*, 275–291.

Erickson, M. J., Stage, S. A., & Nelson, J. R. (2006). Naturalistic study of the behavior of students with EBD referred for functional behavior assessment. *Journal of Emotional and Behavioral Disorders, 14*, 31–40.

Ervin, R. A., Kern, L., Clarke, S., DuPaul, G. J., Dunlap, G., & Friman, P. C. (2000). Evaluating assessment based intervention strategies for students with ADHD and comorbid disorders within natural classroom context. *Behavioral Disorder, 25*, 344–358.

Iwata, B. A., Vollmer, T. R., & Zarcone, J. R. (1990). The experimental (functional) analysis of behavior disorders: Methodology, applications, and limitations. In A. C. Repp & N. N. Singh (Eds.), *Perspectives on the use of nonaversive and aversive interventions for persons with developmental disabilities* (pp. 301–330). Sycamore, IL: Sycamore Publishing Company.

Kamps, D., Ellis, C., Mancina, C., Wyble, J., Greene, L., & Harvey, D. (1995). Case studies using functional analysis for young children with behavioral risks. *Education and Treatment of Children, 18*, 243–260.

HYE RAN PARK

FUNCTIONAL GOALS

Functional goals are based on the ultimate desired, postschool outcome for an individual. According to Cronin and Patton (1993), functional goals should be based on "events or activities typically encountered by most adults in everyday life." Essentially, the idea is to determine the most important goals for an individual to achieve optimum adult independence based on his or her needs and skills, as well as the needs of the family and major life demands. Functional goals can include those in **self-help** and **daily living skills**, as well as functional academics and **social skills**. These goals are broken down into basic steps that are taught as **functional skills**.

REFERENCE

Cronin, M. E., & Patton, J. R. (1993). *Life skills instruction for all students with special needs.* Austin, TX: Pro-Ed.

FURTHER INFORMATION

Wehman, P., & Kregel, J. (2004). *Functional curriculum for elementary, middle, and secondary age students with special needs* (2nd ed.). Austin, TX: Pro-Ed.

ANDREA M. BABKIE

FUNCTIONAL LIMITATIONS

Functional limitations refer to restrictions an individual may have in terms of development of skills or cognitive abilities and the restrictions placed on him or her in terms of opportunities to achieve. These limitations may include having difficultly mastering, maintaining, and generalizing skills taught, including those in the academic, **self-help**, **daily living**, and **social skills** areas. Limitations also include behavioral issues an individual may exhibit that interfere with successful integration into the school or community setting.

From the perspective of restrictions placed on an individual, these may include non-acceptance of differences, job or community requirements beyond an individual's skills, and the need to develop an understanding of how to work with the individual. Additionally, the term functional limitations may be used to refer to the lack of opportunities provided by the school and postschool settings to develop functional skills, especially if the focus is academically based rather than a functionally based curriculum.

ANDREA M. BABKIE

FUNCTIONALLY EQUIVALENT ALTERNATIVE BEHAVIOR

Functionally equivalent alternative behavior refers to the replacement of an undesired behavior with a new, generally more acceptable or more effective alternative behavior. This new behavior fulfills the same function as the behavior being replaced. When considering what to teach as an alternative behavior, it is important to consider what is socially appropriate, not only by parents, teachers, and other adults, but also among peers and in community settings.

KATIE BASSITY

FUNCTIONAL MAGNETIC RESONANCE IMAGING (FMRI)

Functional magnetic resonance imaging (fMRI) is a neuroimaging technique used to measure activity in structures of the brain. fMRI is different from a typical **MRI** scan in that the fMRI is taken while the patient is involved with some mental exercise or activity, thus showing which parts of the brain are being activated and used for various actions. This is crucial to understanding what areas of the brain may be different or damaged in individuals with autism and could potentially help with treatment. One area of intense fMRI study in autism has been the study of the **fusiform gyrus**.

FURTHER INFORMATION
Bremner, J. D. (2005). *Brain imaging handbook*. New York: W. W. Norton & Co.
PAUL G. LACAVA

FUNCTIONAL OUTCOMES

Functional outcomes refer to an individual achieving optimum independence in the post-school environment, based on the individual's development and on the provision of an appropriate curriculum. Functional outcomes may be focused on academic goals, and **functional goals** and skills that allow for successful integration into the adult community (whether it be socially, occupationally, and/or residentially), or a combination of both. The goal for all students with ASD is to be a participating and involved member of the community while school-aged and as an adult.

ANDREA M. BABKIE

FUNCTIONAL PROTEST TRAINING

Functional protest training involves teaching an appropriate, functional form of protest to replace nonfunctional or undesired forms of protest. For example, if a student screams when she experiences an unpleasant auditory experience, a more appropriate form of protest would be for the student to cover her ears (for a nonverbal student) or say "That hurts my ears" (for a verbal student).

KATIE BASSITY

FUNCTIONAL SKILLS

Functional skills are those skills necessary to progress successfully in school and life and can include **daily living** and **self-help skills** as well as the academic and social skills. The focus is to select and teach skills that the individual will use in immediate and future environments, and to present or teach them in such a way that the skill will be used routinely, allowing for **maintenance** and **generalization**. The decision on what is a functional skill can be thought of as a process used by teachers to answer questions such as "How, when, and where will my students use this knowledge now and in the future?" (Weaver, Landers, & Adams, 1991). Depending on the age and developmental level of the individual, as well as family desires, functional academic skills may address: (a) reading for information (basic reading such as a recipe, a newspaper article, a job application, a course, or a transportation schedule); (b) mathematical skills to allow personal independence (basic math skills, using a calculator, comparing prices, making purchases); (c) science skills (such as reading a medication chart); (d) social studies (registering to vote and **voting**, determining the appropriate bus route in the community); and (e) social skills (communication, cooperation, problem-solving, self-initiation) among others (Cronin and Patton, 1993).

See also adaptive behavior; age appropriate; developmental age.

REFERENCES
Cronin, M. E., & Patton, J. R. (1993). *Life skills instruction for all students with special needs*. Austin, TX: Pro-Ed.
Weaver, R., Landers, M. F., & Adams, S. (1991). Making curriculum functional: Special education and beyond. *Intervention in School and Clinic, 25*, 284–287.

ANDREA M. BABKIE

FUNCTIONS OF BEHAVIOR

In the field of behavior analysis, it is believed that challenging behavior serves four functions: escape/avoidance, attention, sensory, and tangible. Escape/avoidance refers to behavior that is intended to allow the child to avoid a person or escape doing a task. Behavior that seeks attention includes that which receives positive and negative attention. Sensory and tangible functions are straightforward in that they seek some type of sensory input and something tangible, respectively.

These functions may not be apparent to a caregiver in the midst of a challenging-behavior situation. In addition, a single behavior may serve more than one function. For example, through one behavior an individual may seek both to avoid an unpleasant task and to gain a preferred item (escape/avoidance and tangible). The function of a behavior can also evolve, beginning as an escape and evolving into attention seeking as the individual finds the resulting attention rewarding. It is important to note that behaviors can actually be strengthened if a consequence is put in place that does not address the correct function of a behavior. For instance, if a child originally exhibits a behavior to escape a nonpreferred activity and receives reinforcement of the behavior in the form of attention, the escape behavior is more likely to happen again because the **consequence**, attention, is even more reinforcing than escaping the activity.

KATIE BASSITY

FUNCTIONS OF COMMUNICATION

Functions of communication are the purposes for which one communicates. These functions include requesting (i.e., "I want a ball"), joint attention (shifting another's attention to an object, act, or topic), attracting attention (i.e., "Watch this!"), commenting (i.e., "I like your new shoes"), and protesting (i.e., "I don't want to eat that"). Children with autism demonstrate a restricted pattern of communicative functions, often protesting and requesting at higher frequencies than the other communicative functions (Wetherby & Prizant, 1999).

REFERENCE

Wetherby, A., & Prizant, B. (1999). Enhancing language and communication development in autism: Assessment and intervention guidelines. In D. B. Zager (Ed.), *Autism: Identification, education, and treatment* (2nd ed., pp. 141–174). Mahwah, NJ: Lawrence Earlbaum Associates.

JEANNE HOLVERSTOTT

FUSIFORM GYRUS

The fusiform gyrus (FG) is located in the temporal lobe of the cerebrum of the human brain. Imaging studies have indicated that the FG is activated when processing faces but that there is lower FG activation for those with autism. Further evidence has highlighted that the FG is involved with the processing and perception of objects or areas of expertise (such as categories, special interests, and so on). One vital area of research being explored is how the FG operates within the network of other brain regions and how this might be different and how it may affect **social cognition** for those with autism.

FURTHER INFORMATION

Gauthier, I., Tarr, M. J., Anderson, A. W., Skudlarski, P., & Gore, J. C. (1999). Activation of the middle fusiform "face area" increases with expertise in recognizing novel objects [Electronic version]. *Nature Neuroscience, 2*, 568–573.

Haxby, J. V., Hoffman, E. A., & Gobbini, M. I. (2002). Human neural systems for face recognition and social communication [Electronic version]. *Biological Psychiatry, 51*, 59–67.

Herbert, M. R. (2004). Neuroimaging in disorders of social and emotional functioning: What is the question [Electronic version]? *Journal of Child Neurology, 19*, 772–784.

Insell, T. R., & Fernald, R. D. (2004). How the brain processes social information: Searching for the social brain [Electronic version]. *Annual Review of Neuroscience, 27*, 697–722.

Pierce, K., Müller, R. A., Ambrose, J., Allen, G., & Courchesne, E. (2001). Face processing occurs outside the fusiform "face area" in autism: Evidence from functional MRI. *Brain, 124*, 2059–2073

Puce, A., Allison, T., Gore, J. C., & McCarthy, G. (1995). Face-sensitive regions in human extrastriate cortex studied by functional MRI [Electronic version]. *Journal of Neurophysiology, 74*, 1192–1199.

Sasson, N. J. (2006). The development of face processing in autism. *Journal of Autism and Developmental Disorders, 36*, 381–394.

Schultz, R. T., Grelotti, D. J., Klin, A., Kleinman, J., Van der Gaag, C., Marois, R., et al. (2003). The role of the fusiform face area in social cognition: Implications for the pathobiology of autism [Electronic version]. *Philosophical Transactions of the Royal Society, 358*, 415–27.

PAUL G. LaCAVA

G

GENERAL CASE PROGRAMMING

General case programming is a **generalization** strategy where multiple examples of a concept or behavior, and systematically varying aspects of the training or intervention, are utilized to increase the success of skill generalization to novel situations.

KATHERINE E. COOK

GENERALIZATION

Generalization occurs when a behavior can withstand many environments (settings and people) over time, and that one behavior can affect behavior change in other associated areas (Baer, Wolf, & Risley, 1968). For example, a child has generalized learning the color blue when he or she can point to any blue object in an environment at any time and label that object as blue.

REFERENCE
Baer, D. M., Wolf, M. M., & Risley, T. R. (1968). Some current dimensions of applied behavior analysis. *Journal of Applied Behavior Analysis, 1*(1), 1–7.

TARA MIHOK

GENETIC FACTORS/HEREDITY

The myth of autism being caused by inappropriate parenting or parental bonding with the infant has been shattered by scientific research over the last four decades. Although parenting abilities don't cause autism, research supports a genetic component to this disability. As with many other areas, the field of autism has been the beneficiary of genetic research over the last few decades. It has become clear that autism is a disability that is predisposed in some individuals. This genetic susceptibility has been shown in studies that have suggested that as many as 5 to 20 different genes may be associated with autism. One of the most significant findings has been the results of twin and family studies. These results have revealed that there is a much higher rate of autism between identical twins, that a family member of someone with autism has a higher probability of having an autism spectrum disorder than the typical population, and that some disorders can be linked to genetic conditions such as **fragile X syndrome**.

See also twin studies.

FURTHER INFORMATION
Pericak-Vance, M. A. (2003). Discovering the genetics of autism. *USA Today, 131,* 56–57.

PAUL G. LACAVA

GENOTYPE

Genotype refers to the internally coded, inheritable information carried by all living organisms. This stored information is used as a blueprint or set of instructions for building and maintaining a living creature. These instructions are found within almost all cells (the *internal* part), they are written in a coded language (the genetic code), they are copied at the time of cell division or reproduction, and they are passed from one generation to the next (inheritable). These instructions are intimately involved with all aspects of the life of a cell or an organism. They control everything from the formation of protein macromolecules, to the regulation of metabolism and synthesis. On-going research studies are being conducted to identify the autism genotype.

JEANNE HOLVERSTOTT

GENTLE TEACHING (GT)

Gentle teaching (GT) was originally defined as a nonaversive approach to dealing with challenging behaviors (McGee, Menolascino, Hobbs, & Menousek, 1987). It is a broad term based on a philosophical approach that emphasizes mutual bonding between caregivers and persons with behavior difficulties. As such, it is considered an alternative to any kind of aversive intervention used by parents and professionals.

The term *gentle teaching* was first introduced by McGee in 1985 (Jones, McCaughey, Connell, & Clwyd Health Authority, 1991; McGee, 1985a, b). McGee (1985b) successfully applied gentle teaching to more than 650 persons, ranging from those with severe to profound mental retardation and persistent self-injurious behaviors (Menolascino & McGee, 1983) to persons with mild to moderate mental retardation and a range of mental illnesses such as **depression** and **schizophrenia** (Menolascino & McGee, 1983) over a 5-year period. The results showed a decrease in **maladaptive behaviors**.

More recently, McGee and Menolascino (1991) redefined GT as a psychology of interdependence between caregivers and persons with behavioral difficulties. This relationship requires mutual change, starting with the need for caregivers to analyze and increase their value-centered interactions and decrease dominative ones.

To differentiate GT from behaviorism, McGee (1990) explained its basic assumptions as follows: (a) frequent and unconditional value giving is central to the interactional exchange; (b) everyone has an inherent longing for affection and warmth; (c) dominating actions, such as the use of restraint and punishment, need to be decreased and replaced with value-centered behaviors; and (d) change in both the caregiver and the person exhibiting maladaptive behaviors is critical.

According to McGee (1992), GT is distinct from **applied behavior analysis** in its unconditional valuing, its focus on mutual change, its analysis and measurement of dyadic variables, and its underlying assumptions. However, past behavioral research contributed to GT using various applied behavioral analysis techniques and the use of the following supportive techniques for enhancing relationships and decreasing challenging behaviors were recommended: (a) errorless teaching strategies, (b) task analysis, (c) environmental management, (d) precise and conservative prompting, (e) identification of precursors to target behavior, (f) reduction of verbal instructions or verbal and physical demands, (g) choice making, (h) fading assistance, and (i) integration of other caregivers and peers into the relationships (McGee et al., 1987).

Since McGee (1985a) published his first study on the effects of GT, several researchers have reported positive outcomes of this approach (Jones et al., 1991; Jordan, Singh, & Repp, 1989; Kelley & Stone, 1989; Paisey, Whitney, & Moore, 1989; Polirstok, Dana, Buono, Mongelli, & Trubia, 2003). However, several studies have reported negative effects. Some suggested that GT, while not harmful, was not effective (Cullen & Mappin, 1998). Others noted that GT might have potential risks for people who show aggression, including **self-injurious behavior** (Barrera & Teodoro, 1990; Emerson, 1990).

In addition, the original concept of GT has been criticized because the strategies used were not different from those of applied behavior analysis, and no clear definition of GT has been provided to examine the effectiveness of GT. Moreover, its research methodology was limited to conclude that GT is effective. For example McGee (1985b) did not control extraneous variables and did not have a **baseline** to be compared. Since the original reports of GT did not include quantification of behavior change or criteria for how to determine successful results, more information is needed to support an objective review of this approach (Mudford, 1995; Simpson et al., 2005).

Primarily, gentle teaching is a philosophical approach used with individuals with disabilities as an alternative to aversive intervention. To date, few empirical studies have reported **evidence-based** research on gentle teaching.

See also empirical evidence.

REFERENCES

Barrera, F. J., & Teodoro, G. M. (1990). Flash bonding or cold fusion? A case analysis of gentle teaching. In A. C. Repp & N. N. Singh (Eds.), *Current perspectives on the use of aversive and non-aversive interventions with developmentally disabled persons* (pp. 199–214). Sycamore, IL: Sycamore.

Cullen, C., & Mappin, R. (1998). An examination of the effects of gentle teaching on people with complex learning disabilities and challenging behavior. *British Journal of Clinical Psychology, 37,* 199–211.

Emerson, E. (1990). Some challenges presented by severe self-injurious behaviour. *Mental Handicap, 18,* 92–98.

Jones, R., McCaughey, R., Connell, E., & Clwyd Health Authority (1991). The philosophy and practice of gentle teaching: Implication for mental handicap services. *The Irish Journal of Psychology, 12,* 1–16.

Jordan, J., Singh, N., & Repp, A. (1989). An evaluation of gentle teaching and visual screening in the reduction of stereotypy. *Journal of Applied Behavior Analysis, 22,* 9–22.

Kelley, B., & Stone, J. (1989). Gentle teaching in the classroom. *Entourage, 4,* 15–19.

McGee, J. J. (1985a). Gentle teaching. *Mental Handicap in New Zealand*, 9(3), 13–24.

McGee, J. J. (1985b). Examples of the use of gentle teaching. *Mental Handicap in New Zealand*, 9(4), 11–20.

McGee, J. J. (1990). Gentle teaching: The basic tenet. *Metal Handicap Nursing*, 86, 68–72.

McGee, J. J. (1992). Gentle teaching's assumptions and paradigm. *Journal of Applied Behavior Analysis*, 25, 869–872.

McGee, J. J., & Menolascino, F. J. (1991). *Beyond gentle teaching: A non-aversive approach to helping those in need.* New York: Plenum Press.

McGee, J. J., Menolascino, F. J., Hobbs, D. C., & Menousek, P. E. (1987). *Gentle Teaching: A non-aversive approach to helping persons with mental retardation.* New York: Human Sciences Press.

Menolascino, F. J., & McGee, J. J. (1983). Persons with severe mental retardation and behavioral challenges: From disconnectedness to human engagement. *Journal of Psychiatric Treatment and Evaluation*, 5, 187–193.

Mudford, O. C. (1995). Review of the gentle teaching data. *American Journal of Mental Retardation*, 99, 345–355.

Paisey, T. J., Whitney, R. B., & Moore, J. (1989). Person-treatment interactions across nonaversive response-deceleration procedures for self-injury: A case study of effects and side effects. *Behavioral Residential Treatment*, 4, 69–88.

Polirstock. S. R., Dana, L., Buono, S., Mongelli, V., & Trubia, G. (2003). Improving functional communication skills in adolescents and young adults with severe autism using gentle teaching and positive approaches. *Topics in Language Disorders*, 23, 146–153.

Simpson, R. L., Boer-Ott, S. R., Griswold, D. E., Myles, B. S., Byrd, S. E., Ganz, J. B., Cook, K. T., Otten, K. L., Ben-Arieh, J., Kline, S. A., & Adams, L. G. (2005). *Autism spectrum disorders: Interventions and treatments for children and youth.* Thousand Oaks, CA: Corwin Press.

FURTHER INFORMATION

Gentle teaching: http://www.gentleteaching.nl.

Gentle teaching international: http://www.gentleteaching.com.

HYO JUNG LEE

GIFTEDNESS

Extreme giftedness, or savant skills, is rare and typically seen in individuals with some degree of mental handicap, hence the original (now unused) term of *idiot savants*, although the presence of mental handicap is not guaranteed. Around 2 to 3 percent of the general population have a mental handicap, but only around 0.06 percent of those individuals are estimated to have the exceptionally high level of ability in a certain area that goes beyond what the average individual can achieve (Hermelin, 2001). Savant skills are found more frequently in individuals with autism than in any other population, however there would still only be 1 or 2 individuals in every 200 with autism who have such abilities.

Areas of savant skill typically include the following: numbers and math, calendrical calculations, drawing and art, date memory, and musical ability. Hermelin (2001) also reports poetry skills and skills with foreign languages.

Individuals with number and math savant skills are capable of doing complex and vast mathematical calculations in their heads. Those who are calendrical calculators can tell you exactly what day a certain date will fall on any time for the past or future. Savants with drawing skills are capable of artwork such as producing phenomenal, accurate, and proportioned pictures with perspective from a very early age. A well-known autistic artist with this ability is Stephen Wiltshire. Oliver Sachs (1995) wrote an excellent essay on Wiltshire's talent and artistic ability in contrast to his autism. Savants with date memory can tell you exactly what was happening, what people were wearing, or give you the exact date for an event when asked, no matter how insignificant that event may seem to others. Those with musical savant skills often have perfect pitch and can hear every note accurately. They are able to perform such feats as sitting in front of a piano, having never learned to play, and reproducing complex pieces of classical music. Frith (2003) cites the case of Nigel, a man unable to look after himself who is nevertheless a sought-after classical pianist capable of playing any piece after having heard it only once. Those with skills in poetry or in foreign languages show an aptitude beyond their general abilities and beyond those of others around them. Smith and Tsimpli (1995), for example, discuss the case of Christopher, a multilingual savant who has learned to speak dozens of languages fluently.

There is some uncertainty about how savants possess the skills they do while at the same time often having learning disabilities. Nettlebeck (1999) suggests that general theories of intelligence cannot account for the phenomena. Many researchers suggest that it may be something to do with the tendency in autism to focus on details, on piece-meal processing, building up connecting units of information or details rather than focusing on the bigger picture (Frith, 2003; Mottron & Belleville, 1993; Heaton, Pring, & Hermelin, 1998), and some have attempted to design computer programs that can mimic the savant skills, for example of calendrical calculation (Norris, 1990). Whatever the theories, savant skills and giftedness is one area that highlights the strengths and amazing capabilities of those who are seen otherwise to be low functioning and disabled.

REFERENCES

Frith, U. (2003). *Autism: Explaining the enigma* (2nd ed.). Oxford: Blackwell Publishing.

Heaton, P., Pring, L., & Hermelin, B. (1998). Autism and pitch processing: A precursor for savant musical ability. *Music Perception, 15,* 291–305.

Hermelin, B. (2001). *Bright splinters of the mind: A personal story of research with autistic savants.* London: Jessica Kingsley Publishing.

Mottron, L., & Belleville, S. (1993). A study of perceptual analysis in a high level autistic subject with exceptional graphic abilities. *Brain and Cognition, 23,* 279–309.

Nettlebeck, T. (1999). Savant skills–rhyme without reason. In M. Anderson (Ed.), *The development of intelligence* (pp. 247–273). Hove: Psychology Press.

Norris, D. (1990). How to build a connectionist idiot (savant). *Cognition, 35,* 277–291.

Sacks, O. (1995). *An anthropologist on Mars.* London: Picador.

Smith, N., & Tsimpli, I. M. (1995). *The mind of a savant: Language learning and modularity.* Oxford: Blackwell Publishing.

FIONA J. SCOTT

GILLIAM ASPERGER DISORDER SCALE (GADS)

The Gilliam Asperger Disorder Scale (GADS; Gilliam, 2001) is an instrument used for the assessment of individuals ages 3 through 22. This tool can be used by anyone who has direct contact with the individual such as teachers, parents, and other team members. The scale consists of sections including: Restricted Pattern of Behavior, Cognitive Patterns, Pragmatic Skills, Early Development, and Key Questions. The GADS can be used to identify individuals with Asperger syndrome, assess people referred for behavior challenges, document progress in the area of behavior problems, and target goals for **Individualized Education Programs**.

See also cognitive processes; pragmatics.

REFERENCE
Gilliam, J. (2001). *Gilliam Asperger disorder scale*. Austin, TX: Pro-Ed.

BROOKE YOUNG

GILLIAM AUTISM RATING SCALE (GARS)

The Gilliam Autism Rating Scale (GARS) is a standardized, norm-referenced, behavioral checklist used to identify and measure changes in programming for individuals with autism ages 3 to 22. The checklist is divided into three subscales: stereotyped behaviors, communication, and social interaction. Items on the GARS are measurable by objective frequency of behavior; therefore, direct observation is necessary. Parents and/or professionals at school or home can complete these scales in 5 to 10 minutes.

See also norm-referenced assessment; standardization.

FURTHER INFORMATION
Gilliam, J. E. (1995). *Gilliam autism rating scale examiner's manual*. Austin, TX: Pro-Ed.

MELANIE D. HARMS

GLUTEN-FREE

Gluten is a wheat protein found in wheat, rye, and barley. A gluten-free diet excludes any food or drink that either contains gluten or could have potentially been contaminated by gluten; it is thought that most sources of oats are contaminated with gluten as well. Gluten is found in common foods such as breads, pastas, cookies, cereals, and luncheon meats. It can also be hidden in other foods with ambiguous ingredients such as natural flavoring, artificial flavorings, and caramel color. In these cases, calling the food manufacturer usually clears up questions regarding gluten in the products. Some families of children with autism spectrum disorder have decided to try a gluten-free/**casein-free** diet believing that gluten and casein may adversely affect their child's neurological processes. Some parents report that removing gluten and casein from their child's diet results in increased attention as well as reduced tantrums and aggression.

See also diet; diet therapy.

FURTHER INFORMATION
Celiac Disease and Gluten-free Diet Support Center, www.celiac.com.
Gluten Intolerance Group of North American, www.gluten.net.

MAYA ISRAEL

GOOD GRIEF!

Children with autism spectrum disorders (ASD) face myriad challenges as they encounter life's disappointments. Loss is at the center of many struggles. Sometimes, the loss experienced by a child with ASD is perceived similarly to that of a typical child, but frequently the child with ASD demonstrates responses that are similar in content but different in intensity. For example, their responses, though conventional in topic or format, may be characterized by an increased or decreased amount of emotion, endless repetition, and/or seemingly timeless duration. On other occasions, children with ASD may respond in ways that are genuinely unique!

Parents and professionals need guidelines to help them provide individuals with ASD the support they need to learn from life's unanticipated setbacks, whether it is the loss of a favorite toy (considered a day-to-day loss) or the loss of a loved one (death & dying). Over time, this translates into an effort to teach children with ASD to tie their experiences together and use the information gained when presented with future obstacles.

To help individuals with ASD turn life's losses into learning opportunities (i.e., "good grief"), parents and professionals may find the following guidelines helpful (Gray, 2003):

1. *Abandon Assumptions:* "Start from social scratch" by replacing our confidence in being able to interpret the behavior of persons with ASD with respect for their differences. This involves considering an event alongside what we know about how that child perceives the social world.
2. *Advance Notice:* Gather information before it is needed. In this matter of loss, this refers to the process of gathering background information and using activities (i.e., Social Stories or similar methods) to share what we've learned—that is, to provide the benefit of "knowing what to do" ahead of time.
3. *Accommodations and Analogies:* Teach children with ASD abstract concepts with the use of individually tailored vocabulary and examples. For children who interpret words *literally,* discussions about loss run the risk of frequent expressive and receptive misunderstanding. Carefully choosing vocabulary or using *analogies* may bridge the gap between a concept and comprehension.
4. *Affirm Feelings:* Use affirmation to acknowledge the validity and importance of the child's feelings without necessarily knowing what she is thinking or feeling. Affirmation says, "I know you and I are currently in very different emotional places, and that's okay. I am on your team and we are in this together." In instances where the source of distress is difficult to identify or the events leading up to it are hard to trace with any certainty, affirmation plays a large and helpful role.
5. *Associations:* Teach appropriate associations. Children with ASD often associate loss with negative emotion or mistakenly make a connection between two simultaneous but unrelated cues. The goal of Good Grief! is to encourage identification between accurate links of past, present, and future experiences. Use strategies that gradually, step-by-step, lead to cumulative learning and positive feelings of accomplishment.

Collectively these guidelines help children "move through" and learn from uncomfortable and/or unanticipated setbacks. In this way, losses become opportunities to gain practical skills to navigate life's unexpected twists and turns.

REFERENCE
Gray, C. (2003). Gray's guide to loss, learning, and children with ASD. *Jenison Autism Journal, 15*(3).

CAROL GRAY AND WHITNEY MITCHELL KRUSNIAK

GRADUATED GUIDANCE

Graduated guidance is the incremental adjustment of full physical prompts to assure student success in a particular task. Graduated guidance is most frequently used for tasks that are more complex or have multiple steps. However, it is not a preset system of fading and relies heavily on the instructor's judgment of student need. Prompts within graduated guidance range from: (a) full hand-over-hand, (b) light touch, and (c) shadowing. Graduated guidance can include both increasing and decreasing prompts with the focus always on providing the level of support needed for a particular task at a particular moment.

KATIE BASSITY

GRAPHIC ORGANIZER

Graphic organizers or content maps are visual strategies that display information in a concrete and organized manner (see Figure 10). They take abstract information and organize the concepts into simpler concepts, highlight important information, and display relationships. Graphic organizers can be used to structure writing projects, help in problem solving, decision making, studying, planning, and brainstorming. Graphic organizers can be used prior to reading as an advanced organizer, during reading to assist with connecting key concepts, and after reading to measure understanding.

Figure 10 Venn Diagram Supporting Common Interests

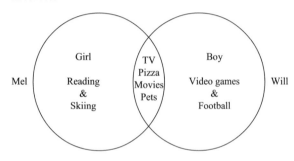

According to Myles and Southwick, graphic organizers often enhance the learning of students with autism spectrum disorders because:

1. They are visual; this modality is often a strength for students.
2. They are static; they remain consistent and constant.
3. They allow for processing time; the student can reflect on the material at his own pace.
4. They are concrete and are more easily understood than a verbal-only presentation. (p. 120, 2005)

See also cognitive learning strategies.

REFERENCE
Myles, B. S., & Southwick, J. (2005). *Asperger syndrome and difficult moments: Practical solutions for tantrums, rage, and meltdowns.* Shawnee Mission, KS: Autism Asperger Publishing Company.

FURTHER INFORMATION
Bromley, K., Irwin-DeVitis, L., & Modio, M. (1995). *Graphic organizers: Visual strategies for active learning.* New York: Scholastic.
Wiig, E. H., & Wilson, C. C. (2001). *Map it out: Visual tools for thinking, organizing, and communicating.* Eau Claire, WI: Thinking Publications.

TERRI COOPER SWANSON

GRAVITATIONAL INSECURITY

Gravitational insecurity refers to difficulty maintaining balance and coordination of movements along variable surfaces and inclines, such as stairs, a gravel walkway, or icy sidewalk. Oftentimes, gravitational insecurity is a result of an inadequately functioning **vestibular** and/or proprioceptive sensory system.

See also proprioception; sensory processing; sensory processing dysfunction.

KELLY M. PRESTIA

GROSS MOTOR DEVELOPMENTAL QUOTIENT

Gross motor development quotient is a score that refers to the results of standardized tests that measure the use of the large muscle groups and **gross motor skills**.

See also standardization.

KELLY M. PRESTIA

GROSS MOTOR SKILLS

Gross motor skills is a term used to describe any activity that requires the use and coordination of the larger muscle groups of the body, such as the legs, arms, or trunk. Examples of gross motor skills include skipping, throwing a ball, or running.

KELLY M. PRESTIA

GUIDED COMPLIANCE

Guided compliance is the use of physical guidance through a task to cause a student to comply with directions. Although similar to **hand-over-hand assistance**, guided compliance is technically not a prompt; it acts as a consequence for noncompliance. Guided compliance occurs after the student is given the opportunity to comply with direction but does not comply and/or attempts to escape. The caregiver then places her hands over the student's hands, feet, or under the student's arms (to aid in standing, moving, etc.) and physically guides the student through the task. Some research suggests that the use of guided compliance is particularly effective when noncompliance is accompanied by escape behaviors.

See also graduated guidance; prompting.

KATIE BASSITY

HABIT REHEARSAL

Habit rehearsal is the repetition of desired behaviors in order to build the behaviors to fluency. Such rehearsals are performed in as functional or as realistic settings as possible so the desired behaviors can be easily performed in natural situations. Habit rehearsal is often used for training appropriate behaviors in stressful situations, such as relaxation techniques.

KATIE BASSITY

HAIR ANALYSIS

Hair analysis measures the mineral content in hair. These types of analyses have been employed to test for the presence of **heavy metals**, such as **mercury**, in epidemiological efforts with regard to autism. According to the American Medical Association, hair analysis may not be used in the determination of medical therapies (n.d.).

See also epidemiology.

REFERENCE

American Medical Association (n.d.). *H-175.955 Hair analysis—a potential for medical abuse.* Retrieved on December 8, 2006, from www.ama-assn.org/apps/pf_new/pf_online?f_n=browse&doc=policyfiles/HnE/H-175.995.HTM.

FURTHER INFORMATION

Kirby, D. (2005). *Evidence of harm: Mercury in vaccines and the autism epidemic: A medical controversy.* New York: St. Martin's Press.

Marhon, S. (2002). *Natural medicine guide to autism.* Charlottesville, VA: Hampton Roads Publishing Co.

MYRNA J. ROCK

HALSTEAD-REITAN NEUROPSYCHOLOGICAL TEST BATTERY (HRPTB)

The *Halstead-Reitan Neuropsychological Test Battery* (HRPTB; Reitan & Wolfson, 1993) is a set of eight tests used to evaluate brain and nervous system functioning in individuals ages 15 years and older, typically for individuals with suspected brain damage, by testing concept formation and abstract reasoning. Children's versions are the *Halstead Neuropsychological Test Battery for Older Children* (ages 9 to 14) and the *Reitan*

Indiana Neuropsychological Test Battery (ages 5 to 8). The *Halstead-Reitan* evaluates a wide range of nervous system and brain functions, including: visual, auditory, and tactual input; verbal communication; spatial and sequential perception; the ability to analyze information, form mental concepts, and make judgments; motor output; and attention, concentration, and memory. The battery also provides useful information regarding the cause of damage (e.g., closed head injury, alcohol abuse, Alzheimer's disorder, stroke), which part of the brain was damaged, whether the damage occurred during childhood development, and whether the damage is getting worse, staying the same, or improving. Information regarding the severity of impairment and areas of personal strengths can be used to develop plans for rehabilitation or care.

REFERENCE

Reitan, R. M., & Wolfson, D. (1993). *The Halstead-Reitan neuropsychological test battery: Theory and clinical interpretation* (2nd ed.). South Tucson, AZ: Neuropsychology Press.

JEANNE HOLVERSTOTT

HAND-OVER-HAND ASSISTANCE (HOH)

Hand-over-hand (HOH) assistance is the practice of an adult (or peer) placing his or her hands over a student's hands and physically moving the student through a given process or task. HOH also applies to physically moving other parts of a student's body through a task. Also referred to as hand-over-hand prompting, it is the most invasive form of prompting and is generally considered best to use only when other prompts are ineffective or impractical, and should be faded as quickly as possible. Used appropriately, HOH can be an effective tool; however, there is concern that overuse of HOH assistance results in prompt dependence. In addition, some students may resist HOH assistance as a result of desired independence or control, or because of an aversion to touch. However, in some situations it may be the only way to provide assistance and may be preferred over high rates of verbal prompting.

See also graduated guidance; guided compliance; prompting.

KATIE BASSITY

HAND REGARD

Hand regard is a behavior that is repetitive or sensory generating in nature and consists of an individual looking at his fingers and/or hands. The fingers and hands can be still or moving. This behavior is common in typically developing children around four months of age but may persist for years for those with autism.

FURTHER INFORMATION

Accardo, P. J., Whitman, B. Y., Laszewski, C., Haake, C. A., & Morrow, J. D. (1996). *Dictionary of developmental disabilities terminology*. Baltimore: Brookes Publishing Co.

Oxbridge Solutions, Ltd. (2003). *Hand regard*. Retrieved May 18, 2006, from http://www.gpnote book.co.uk/homepage.cfm.

PAUL G. LACAVA

HEAD CIRCUMFERENCE

Head circumference is the measured distance of the widest part of the human skull. Typical development is measured in centimeters, and there are norms for sex and age.

Research from the 1990s into the 2000s has highlighted that some youngsters with autism have atypical head circumference due to differences in brain volume. Increased head circumference measured at birth and between 6 and 14 months was a finding in one study for 59 percent of subjects with autism spectrum disorders (Courchesne, Carper, & Akshoomoff, 2003). This head growth was significantly higher than typically developing youngsters from a reference group. This and other findings suggest that increased head growth in infancy may be either a possible symptom or a risk marker for autism.

REFERENCE
Courchesne, E., Carper, R., & Akshoomoff, N. (2003). Evidence of brain overgrowth in the first year of life of autism. *Journal of the American Medical Association, 290,* 337–344.

FURTHER INFORMATION
Courchesne, E. (2004). Brain development in autism: Early overgrowth followed by premature arrest of growth. *Mental Retardation and Developmental Disabilities Research Reviews, 10,* 106–111.

Lainhart, J. E. (2003). Increased rate of head growth during infancy in autism. *Journal of the American Medical Association, 290,* 393–394.

PAUL G. LACAVA

HEAVY METALS
Heavy metals refer to any of a number of higher atomic weight elements, which normally present as metallic substances at room temperatures. Living organisms require trace amounts of some heavy metals, including cobalt, copper, manganese, molybdenum, vanadium, strontium, and zinc, but excessive levels tend to accumulate, a process that continues as organisms age (Harte, Holdren, Schneider, & Shirley, 1991). Other heavy metals such as **mercury**, lead, and cadmium have no known vital or beneficial effect on organisms, and their accumulation over time in the bodies of mammals can exhibit toxic effects (Harte et al., 1991). Proponents of the relationship between heavy metals and autism spectrum disorders point to the toxicity to the central nervous system and multiple sources of exposure, including environmental (food, water, dust) and medical (mercury preservatives in vaccinations). **Chelation** is the predominant treatment for heavy metal toxicity. Chelation involves the use of chelation agents to bind to the metal and increase excretion.

See also vaccinations (thimerosal).

REFERENCE
Harte, J., Holdren, C., Schneider, R., & Shirley, C. (1991). *Toxics a to z: A guide to everyday pollution hazards.* Sacramento, CA: University of California Press.

JEANNE HOLVERSTOTT

HELLER'S SYNDROME. *See* Childhood Disintegrative Disorder

HIDDEN CURRICULUM
The hidden curriculum is the set of rules that everyone in the school knows, but no one has been directly taught (Bieber, 1994). Children with autism spectrum disorders do not pick up on hidden curriculum items—they must be directly taught. Knowing

the hidden curriculum is essential as it helps the student be successful in understanding: (a) teacher expectations, (b) a person's body language, (c) if a person is really their friend, and (d) how to interact or respond in social situations. It is essential to incorporate the teaching of the hidden curriculum into any social skills curriculum as well as teach them on a daily and on-going basis.

REFERENCE

Bieber, J. (Producer). (1994). *Learning disabilities and social skills—Richard Lavoie: Last one picked ... first one picked on.* Washington, DC: Public Broadcasting Service.

FURTHER INFORMATION

Myles, B. S., Trautman, M. L., & Schelvanm, R. L. (2004). *The hidden curriculum: Practical solutions for understanding unstated rules in social situations.* Shawnee Mission, KS: Autism Asperger Publishing Company.

TERRI COOPER SWANSON

HIGH-FUNCTIONING AUTISM

Although used frequently by professionals and parents, the term *high-functioning autism* is not a true diagnosis in the **Diagnostic and Statistical Manual of Mental Disorders** (DSM-IV-TR; APA, 2000). In previous generations, the term was sometimes used to refer to a person with classic autism who had vocal abilities. Today, high-functioning autism tends to be used as a short-hand term for *autistic disorder* without mental retardation (an IQ above 70). It is estimated that at least 25 to 33 percent of individuals diagnosed with autism today fall in the high-functioning category.

In order to be diagnosed with autistic disorder, an individual must have shown delays or abnormalities in social interaction, symbolic or imaginative play, or social use of language before age 3. In addition, the individual currently must show at least two symptoms of "qualitative impairment in social interaction," one symptom of "qualitative impairments in communication," and one symptom of "restricted repetitive and stereotyped patterns of behavior, interests, and activities" (APA, 2000).

There is significant disagreement today as to whether high-functioning autism and Asperger syndrome are two distinct syndromes. The only difference in the DSM-IV-TR criteria for autistic disorder and Asperger syndrome is that Asperger's requires "no clinically significant general delay in language (e.g., single words used by age 2 years, communicative phrases used by age 3 years)," and "no clinically significant delay in cognitive development or in the development of age-appropriate self-help skills, adaptive behavior (other than in social interaction), and curiosity above the environment in childhood" (APA, 2000). However, clinicians today report that people with Asperger syndrome typically *do* have significant difficulties with self-help skills and adaptive behavior (Attwood, 2006).

Some research suggests that the symptoms of high-functioning autism and Asperger's look different at an early age but are quite similar by adolescence or early adulthood. Generally, a child with high-functioning autism is diagnosed earlier and tends to show more severe and "classic" symptoms of autism. Overall, the average age for a diagnosis of autism is 3, while children with Asperger syndrome are generally diagnosed at age 7 or 8.

Children with high-functioning autism or Asperger syndrome both tend to have difficulties in several common areas. Nonverbal communication (facial expressions and body language) can be difficult for many to decipher. They often will interpret figurative speech (such as "go jump in a lake" or "drop dead") too literally. Most have trouble understanding the "hidden curriculum" (unwritten social rules, such as how far you should stand from someone, or when it's okay to interrupt). Desire for "sameness" (having difficulty with change and transitions, and deriving comfort from routines) is also common.

Often, children with high-functioning autism are described as "aloof," having little interest in interacting with other people, while children with Asperger syndrome seek out interaction, but do so in an odd or inappropriate manner.

Both groups have "restricted, repetitive" behaviors or interests, but children with high-functioning autism tend to perform more repetitive movements, especially odd hand movements, such as finger flicking or hand flapping, and are more likely to be interested in the parts of an object or in manipulating an object. These tend to be solitary interests. Children with Asperger syndrome are more likely to spend their time researching and accumulating vast amounts of information about a particular subject and often seek to share their information with other children or adults.

Children with high-functioning autism and Asperger syndrome both tend to have language difficulties, though qualitatively different ones, especially at a young age. Children with high-functioning autism may have significant speech delays or at least lag somewhat in general areas of speech such as vocabulary. They may engage in echolalia (repeating whatever is said to them). Overall, they tend to have better nonverbal abilities than verbal abilities. Conversely, many children with Asperger syndrome have extremely advanced vocabularies, particularly in their areas of special interest (hence the nickname "little professors"). Rather than repeating a word or phrase over and over, they tend more to repeat long monologues and ask repetitive questions. In fact, their superficially perfect language may play a role in delaying their diagnosis.

Medically, children with high-functioning autism and Asperger syndrome may have some differences. Children with high-functioning autism are more likely to suffer seizures than children with Asperger syndrome (although far less likely than children with autism and mental retardation). Children with Asperger syndrome, on the other hand, are more likely to have co-morbid diagnoses such as depression, ADHD, obsessive-compulsive disorder, or Tourette's disorder. Children with Asperger syndrome are also more likely to have motor difficulties or sensory integration dysfunction.

Because the DSM-IV-TR diagnostic criteria are so similar, different clinicians might give the same high-functioning child different diagnoses. For example, a clinician who believes in following the diagnostic criteria to the letter might be inclined to diagnose a 4-year-old child with autistic disorder because the child failed to speak any words until age 3. Another might diagnose Asperger syndrome based on the same child's obsessive interest in astronomy. A third might diagnose PDD-NOS, because he doesn't want to "label" the child before age 5. And yet another might diagnose autism because she knows that label will get the child more intervention services in the local school system.

Even among people diagnosed with Asperger syndrome or high-functioning autism there is tremendous variability. Their symptoms vary, their strengths vary, their behaviors vary, and their likes and dislikes vary. Ultimately, whether the diagnosis is high-functioning autism or Asperger syndrome, the most important thing is to look at each individual's strengths and weakness and to obtain appropriate intervention.

REFERENCES

American Psychiatric Association. (2000). *Diagnostic and statistical manual of mental disorders* (4th ed., text rev.). Washington, DC: Author.

Attwood, T. *Is there a difference between Asperger's syndrome and high-functioning autism?* Retrieved August 25, 2006, from http://www.tonyattwood.com.au.

FURTHER INFORMATION

Eisenmajer, R., Prior, M., Leekam, S., Wing, L., Gould, J., Welham, M., et al. (1996). Comparison of clinical symptoms in autism and Asperger's disorder. *Journal of the American Academy of Child and Adolescent Psychiatry, 35,* 1523–1531.

Freeman, B. J., Cronin, P., & Candela, P. (2002). Asperger syndrome or autistic disorder? The diagnostic dilemma. *Focus on Autism and Other Developmental Disabilities, 17,* 145–151.

Ozonoff, S., Dawson, G., & McPartland, J. (2002). *A parent's guide to Asperger syndrome and high-functioning autism.* New York: Guilford Press.

Powers, M. D. (2000). *Children with autism: A parents' guide.* Bethesda, MD: Woodbine House.

Sciutto, M. J., & Cantwell, C. Factors influencing the differential diagnosis of Asperger's disorder and high-functioning autism. *Journal of Developmental and Physical Disabilities, 17,* 345–359.

Tryon, P. A., Mayes, S. D., Rhodes, R. L., & Waldo, M. (2006). Can Asperger's disorder be differentiated from autism using DSM-IV criteria? *Focus on Autism and Other Developmental Disabilities, 21,* 2–6.

Wing, L. (2001). *The autistic spectrum.* Berkeley, CA: Ulysses Press.

LISA BARRETT MANN

HIPPOCAMPUS

Part of the **limbic system**, the hippocampus is involved in the formation of memories of experienced events and spatial orientation, or place memory and recognition. It is located deep in the temporal lobes above the **amygdala**.

BRUCE BASSITY

HIPPOTHERAPY

Hippotherapy (Greek word *hippos* for horse) is a treatment that uses the movement of the horse to improve physical mobility and cognitive functions for people with varying disabilities. It takes the client out of the clinical setting and places them in a natural environment to work on therapy goals. **Physical therapists, occupational therapists**, and **speech language pathologists** who provide this treatment have specialized training in using the movement of the horse as a therapy tool. The hippotherapy team includes the horse, rider, sidewalkers, and instructor.

Treatment strategies promote motor planning, mobility strength, and stimulation of the central nervous system. Hippotherapy is considered an effective therapy method because a horse's gait mimics the human gait and a horse takes the same number of steps per minute as a human (American Hippotherapy Association, 2005). The horse's muscle groups move forward, backward, up, down, and from side to side. The body responds to the horse's movement by trying to maintain balance, and therefore the rider develops muscle tone, stretch, and strength to the same muscle groups that are used in sitting, reaching, and walking. The rider's senses are stimulated by the warmth, smell, sight, and feel of the horse. In addition, riders connect emotionally with the horse, which makes treatment fun, and professionals report an increase in attention span and memory skills.

Hippotherapy is used to treat a variety of diagnoses that include autism, cerebral palsy, multiple sclerosis, developmental delay, traumatic brain and spinal cord injury,

Down syndrome, stroke, attention deficit disorders, learning or language disabilities, and visual or hearing impairments. People of all ages can benefit from hippotherapy; however, clients may be excluded if they weigh more that 300 lbs or more than 20 percent of the horse's weight. In addition, a client might be excluded from the treatment if they have brittle-bone osteoporosis, acute arthritis, curvature of the spine greater than 30 degrees, degenerative hip joints, or are on anticoagulant medications for heart conditions. Safety measures include sidewalkers that are ready to steady riders and help with exercises, equestrian helmets, and quick release stirrups that unhook if a rider falls. A fleece or foam pad with gripping handles strapped around the horse's belly is used instead of a saddle.

Typically, insurance does not cover hippotherapy. Sessions may last up to 1 hour, once or twice per week, and the cost may range from $50 to $120 per session. Critics believe there is not enough research to show that the benefits are different than existing forms of physical therapy. Research designs are difficult due to variables such as different kinds of horses and instructors; however, Dr. Daniel Bluestone from the University of California, San Francisco compared MRI scans of children over time and found that the repetitive movement of riding helps rework networks within the cerebellum and the motor system in the cerebrum (American Equestrian Association, 2005).

Hippotherapy should not be confused with Therapeutic Riding. The goals of hippotherapy are directed at improving balance, coordination, posture, fine motor control, articulation, and increasing cognitive skills. Therapeutic riding teaches the rider how to control the horse and stable management.

Further Information

American Equestrian Alliance. (n.d.) *What is hippotherapy?* Retrieved June 1, 2005, from http://www.americanequestrian.com/hippotherapy.htm.

American Hippotherapy Association. (n.d.) Retrieved May 31, 2005, from www.americanhippotherapyassociation.org.

CP Resource Center. Introduction to hippotherapy by Barbara Heine, PT. Reprinted from *NARHA Strides, April 1997 (Vol. 3, No. 2)*. From http://www.twinenterprises.com.

Infinitec.org. *Hippotherapy.* http://www.infinitec.org.

The Right Step therapy Services. *Hippotherapy or therapeutic riding,* http://www.rightsteptherapy.com.

Rolandelli, P. S., & Dunst, C. J. (2003). Influences of hippotherapy on the motor and social-emotional behavior of young children with disabilities. *Bridges,* http://www.evidencebasedpractices.org/bridges.

Cynthia K. Van Horn and Karla Dennis

HOLDING THERAPY. *See* Welch Method Therapy

HOMEBOUND/HOSPITAL BOUND PROGRAM

Students receive special education and related services in a hospital or homebound program when unable to attend neighborhood school for medical, behavioral, or other reasons. Less than 1 percent of all students receiving special education services receive homebound or hospital bound services. Students with multiple disabilities represent the largest category of disabilities being educated in homebound or hospital bound programs. Educational services provided in these environments can range from a few days to months depending of the needs of the students.

KATHERINE E. COOK

HORMONE REPLACEMENT

Hormone Replacement Therapy (HRT) replaces naturally occurring hormones that are deficient in the body but are needed for normal functioning and health. Common examples are thyroid hormone for underactive thyroid, insulin for diabetes, and estrogen for women who have had a hysterectomy.

BRUCE BASSITY

HOSPITAL BOUND PROGRAM. *See* Homebound/Hospital Bound Program

HUG MACHINE

Hug machine, also known as the "Squeeze Machine" or the "Hug Box," is a device developed by Temple Grandin, an individual with autism, which provides deep pressure and proprioceptive input at the control of the individual. The individual lies or squats in the center of the padded, V-shaped machine as air is pumped through cylinders that push padded sideboards together to "squeeze" the individual.

See also proprioception.

KELLY M. PRESTIA

HYPERLEXIA

Children with hyperlexia are able to read words precociously and demonstrate an intense fascination with letters or numbers at their chronological age. However, they have significant difficulty in understanding verbal language, deficits in social skills, and difficulty in socializing and interacting with people.

JOUNG MIN KIM

HYPERRESPONSIVENESS

Hyperresponsiveness is an overactive or intense response to typical sensory information. What may go unnoticed by others may be overly intense to an individual with a hyperresponsive sensory system. Examples of hyperresponsiveness may include covering the ears and screaming at the sound of a ringing telephone, or avoiding holding another's hand.

KELLY M. PRESTIA

HYPORESPONSIVENESS

Hyporesponsiveness is an underactive or slower reactive response to typical sensory information. Individuals with hyporesponsive sensory systems may require more intense, longer, or multiple sensory stimuli to get a response. Examples of hyporesponsiveness may include not looking or responding when their name is called or when tapped on the shoulder.

KELLY M. PRESTIA

I

IDIOSYNCRATIC LANGUAGE

Idiosyncratic language is frequently characterized as dialogue borrowed from a specific video, repetitive questions used with alternative meanings, or social scripts parroted in new and different contexts. Idiosyncratic language is often used to reassure the communicator.

KATHERINE E. COOK

I LAUGH MODEL OF SOCIAL COGNITION

The I LAUGH model of social cognition was developed by Winner to demonstrate how we can take an abstract concept such as social thinking and break it down into much more salient, observable parts (Winner, 2000). The I LAUGH model is an acronym to demonstrate six different skills that form the basis through which we communicate effectively with others, verbally and nonverbally (social pragmatic skills). Not coincidentally, these same skills help us engage in life skills such as personal problem solving, working as part of a group, playing, and curriculum-based skills that require social thinking such as reading comprehension, written expression, and organizational skills. Each aspect of the model has been shown through research to be relevant to address in treatment for students with social cognitive deficits.

The I LAUGH model provides parents and educators with a more specific lens through which to evaluate and understand the strengths and weaknesses of persons with social-cognitive deficits. Given that the area of social cognition is difficult to assess through formalized measures, an informal assessment that explores each of these areas of functioning can be quite revealing of a student's relative social strengths versus socially based weaknesses.

The I LAUGH model has also become a framework for understanding how better to assess students with possible social-cognitive deficits (the autism spectrum, nonverbal learning disability, ADHD, etc.). Using formal and informal tasks we can begin to understand how a child does with relationship to initiating functional communication, listening actively, abstract and inferential thinking, understanding others' perspectives, getting the big picture and humor.

The I LAUGH model is briefly reviewed here.

I=Initiation of language. Initiation of language is the ability to use one's language skills to seek assistance or information. A student's ability to talk about his own topics of interest can be in sharp contrast to how that student communicates when he needs assistance.

L=Listening with eyes and brain. Most persons with social-cognitive deficits have difficulty with auditory comprehension. Listening, however, requires more than just taking in the auditory information; it also requires the person to integrate information he sees with what he hears to understand the deeper concept of the message, or to make a smart guess about what is being said when you cannot clearly hear it.

A=Abstract and inferential language/communication. Communicative comprehension also depends on one's ability to recognize that most language/communication is not intended for literal interpretation. To interpret adequately, one must be able to be flexible enough to make smart guesses about the intended meaning of the message; at times one must pursue the analysis of language/communication to seek the intended meaning. Abstract and inferential meaning is often carried subtly through verbal and nonverbal means of communication. This skill begins to develop around kindergarten and continues through our school years as the messages we are to interpret, both socially and academically, become more abstract. Interpretation depends in part on one's ability to "make a guess"; it also depends on one's ability to take perspective of another.

U=Understanding perspective. This is the ability to understand the emotions, thoughts, beliefs, experiences, motives, and intentions of yourself as well as others. We generally acquire this skill across early development, intuitively. Most students have acquired a solid foundation in this ability between the ages of 4 and 6 years old. The ability to take perspective is key to participation in any type of group (social or academic) as well as interpreting information that requires understanding of other people's minds such as reading comprehension, history, social studies, etc. Weakness in perspective taking is a significant part of the diagnosis of social cognitive deficits.

G=Gestalt processing/getting the big picture. Information is conveyed through concepts and not just facts. When talking in a conversation, the participants intuitively should determine the underlying concept being discussed. When reading, the reader has to follow the overall meaning (concept) rather than just collect a series of facts. Conceptual processing is another key component to understanding social and academic information. Furthermore, difficulty with organizational strategies is born from problems with conceptual processing.

H=Humor and human relatedness. Most of the clients I work with actually have a very good sense of humor, but they feel anxious since they miss many of the subtle cues that help them to understand how to participate successfully with others. It is important for educators/parents to work compassionately and with humor to help minimize the anxiety the children are experiencing. At the same time, many of our clients use humor inappropriately; direct lessons about this topic should be taught often.

FURTHER INFORMATION

Fullerton, A., Stratton, J., Coyne, P., & Gray, S. (1996). *Higher functioning adolescents and young adults with autism.* Austin, TX: Pro-Ed.

Howlin, P., Baron-Cohen, S., & Hadwin, J. (1999). *Teaching children with autism to mind read: A practical guide.* New York: Wiley and Sons.

Kunce, L., & Mesibov, G. (1998). Educational approaches to high-functioning autism and Asperger syndrome. In E. Schopler, G. Mesibov, & L. Kunce (Eds.), *Asperger syndrome or high-functioning autism?* (pp. 227–263). New York: Plenum Press.

Myles, B. S., & Adreon, D. (2001). *Asperger syndrome and adolescence: Practical solutions for school success.* Shawnee Mission, KS: Autism Asperger Publishing Company.

Winner, M. (2000). *Inside out: What makes the person with social cognitive deficits tick?* San Jose, CA: Michelle Garcia Winner.

Winner, M. (2002). *Thinking about you thinking about me.* San Jose, CA: Michelle Garcia Winner.

MICHELLE GARCIA WINNER AND JAMIE RIVETTS

IMAGINATION

Delays or differences in the development of imagination are characteristic of autism spectrum disorders (APA, 2000). Difficulties in the area of imagination first manifest in a lack of pretend play appropriate to a child's developmental level. Restricted, repetitive, and stereotyped patterns of behavior, interests, and activities are further associated with problems in imagination. Imagination is the process of producing ideas or mental images in the mind of that which is not present or has not been experienced. Further, imagination involves recombining experiences to solve problems in a flexible, creative, and resourceful fashion (for reviews, see Jarrold, 2003; Leslie, 1987; Wolfberg, 1999, 2003).

REFERENCES

American Psychiatric Association. (2000). *Diagnostic and statistical manual of mental disorders* (4th ed., text rev.). Washington, DC: Author.

Jarrold, C. (2003). A review of research into pretend play in autism. *Autism: The International Journal of Research and Practice, 7*(4), 379–390.

Leslie, A. M. (1987). Pretense and representation: The origins of "theory of mind." *Psychological Review, 94,* 412–426.

Wolfberg, P. J. (1999). *Play and imagination in children with autism.* New York: Teachers College Press, Columbia University.

Wolfberg, P. J. (2003). *Peer play and the autism spectrum: The art of guiding children's socialization and imagination.* Shawnee Mission, KS: Autism Asperger Publishing Company.

PAMELA WOLFBERG

IMITATION/MODELING

From infancy, typical development includes imitation of caregivers. As those with autism spectrum disorders often have challenges with verbal and motor imitation skills, teaching these building blocks is critical. An imitation or modeling program may be developmental, behavioral, or mixed in its approach, but the programming usually includes the child's motivation and targeted objectives.

FURTHER INFORMATION

Dapretto, M., Davies, M. S., Pfeifer, J. H., Scott, A. A., Sigman, M., Bookheimer, et al. (2005). Understanding emotions in others: Mirror neuron dysfunction in children with autism spectrum disorders [Electronic version]. *Nature Neuroscience, 9,* 28–30.

Ingersoll, B., & Schreiberman, L. (2006). Teaching reciprocal imitation skills to young children with autism using a naturalistic behavioral approach: Effects on language, pretend play, and joint attention. *Journal of Autism and Developmental Disorders, 36,* 487–505.

Quill, K. A. (2000). *Do watch listen say: Social and communication intervention for children with autism.* Baltimore: Brookes Publishing Co.

Rogers, S. (1999). An examination of the imitation deficit in autism. In J. Nadel & G. Butterworth (Eds.), *Imitation in infancy* (pp. 254–279). Cambridge: Cambridge University Press.

PAUL G. LACAVA

IMMUNOGLOBULIN

Immunoglobulin is a protein produced by plasma cells that plays an essential role in defending the body from foreign substances, like bacteria.

JEANNE HOLVERSTOTT

IMMUNOLOGICAL TESTS

Immunological tests may be skin tests in which the skin is scratched and a serum of some allergen like animal dander is applied. A raised wheal or local reaction indicates an allergy. There are many other forms of immunological tests that check for antibodies or antigens indicating the presence or absence of a particular disease. ABO blood typing is a common example. Blood testing for many diseases, from rheumatoid arthritis to infectious mononucleosis to HIV, are also immunological tests.

BRUCE BASSITY

IMMUNOTHERAPY

Immunotherapy commonly refers to a type of treatment for environmental allergies where the body is desensitized to allergens by giving gradually larger doses of the allergen by injection over a period of many months to several years. It also refers to various drug treatments to stimulate or suppress the immune system. Immune stimulating drugs such as interferon and interleukin are used to treat cancers, and immune suppressive substances are used to treat autoimmune diseases such as rheumatoid arthritis and prevent rejection of transplanted organs.

See also allergy.

BRUCE BASSITY

IMPAIRMENT

Impairment refers to the reduced function or loss of any body part (i.e., hearing loss translates to a hearing impairment).

KATHERINE E. COOK

INCIDENCE

Related to **prevalence**, incidence is the number of new cases of a specific condition, disease, etc. over a period of time. Incidence levels are typically calculated for 1-year periods and are often presented as a percentage of a population (e.g., 4 percent of all school-aged children). For example, researchers could calculate all the new cases of autism in a population over a 1-year period. As with prevalence, the incidence of autism is also controversial, and much research is needed to clear up issues regarding both how many persons have autism and how many new cases of autism are occurring each year.

FURTHER INFORMATION

Fombonne, E. (2003). Epidemiological surveys of autism and other pervasive developmental disorders: An update. *Journal of Autism and Developmental Disorders, 33*, 365–382.

Rutter, M. (2005). Incidence of autism spectrum disorders: Changes over time and their meaning. *Acta Paediatrica, 94*, 2–15.

PAUL G. LaCAVA

INCIDENTAL TEACHING

Incidental teaching was designed to teach new skills within ongoing, typical activities utilizing children's interests to increase motivation for learning (McGee, Daly, & Jacobs, 1994). Table 4 shows the essential steps in implementing incidental teaching as well as an example of how each step may be implemented.

Table 4. Essential Steps in Incidental Teaching

Steps	Example
The teacher or parent chooses an educational objective.	Labeling the letters of the alphabet.
The adult arranges the environment to encourage the student motivation and to attract interest in the materials related to teaching the objective.	Eli enjoys puzzles. His teacher, Miss May, finds a puzzle with the letters of the alphabet. During center time, while Eli is working on puzzles, Miss May puts the puzzle on the table with the letters in a clear container that Eli is unable to open.
The child shows interest in the materials through verbalization or gesture, thus initiating the teaching session.	Eli points to the box and says, "letters."
The adult encourages an elaboration on the initiation. Ways to encourage elaborated responses include: Ask a question (e.g., "What color car do you want?" or, "Where is the car?") Make a gesture, sound, or word (e.g., point to the blue car) Model the desired response (e.g., "blue car") Child's response	Miss May opens the box and holds up the letter *R*, asking, "What letter do you want?"
If the child responds correctly to the prompt, the adult provides specific praise and gives the child brief access to the materials.	Eli says, "Letter *R*," so Miss May says, "That's right! It's the letter *R*!" and allows him to put the letter in the puzzle.
If the child does not respond or responds incorrectly, the adult provides up to three more prompts. Once the child responds correctly, he or she receives praise and access to the materials.	Eli repeats, "Letter," so Miss May says, "Letter *R*." Eli repeats, "Letter *R*," so Miss May says, "Right, that's *R*!" and allows him to put the letter in the puzzle.
The adult "takes a turn" with the materials and the steps begin again.	Miss May closes the box again and waits for Eli to say, "Letter," or point to the box.
The incidental teaching session should end with success, be brief, and end once the child loses interest.	

Source: McGee, Morrier, & Daly, 1999.

Incidental teaching is an efficient and positive strategy in several ways. It is likely that integrating instruction of new skills into typical, on-going activities promotes **generalization** of skills (McGee et al., 1999). Moreover, social skills, which are deficient in individuals with ASD, are integral to incidental teaching sessions. That is, interaction is required during the course of incidental teaching instruction. Additionally, incidental teaching is based in student motivation and initiation, thus encouraging student participation and decreasing the need for secondary reinforcement (e.g., rewards). Families are also able to integrate incidental teaching into typical daily routines by finding ways to encourage their children to elaborate during everyday activities (e.g., dinner time, outside play, bed time).

Support for Incidental Teaching in the Professional Literature and Research

Incidental teaching has been demonstrated to be an effective method of teaching sociocommunicative skills and to promote generalization of those skills. This strategy has been used with typically developing children (Hart & Risley, 1980) and individuals with autism spectrum disorders (ASD; McGee, Krantz, & McClannahan, 1986). Incidental teaching has been found to be more effective than clinical, teacher-directed teaching methods in decreasing dependency on prompts and cues and as or more effective then such methods in teaching new skills, such as prepositions (McGee, Krantz, & McClannahan, 1985), adjectives (Miranda-Linné & Melin, 1992), and spontaneous speech (Charlop-Christy & Carpenter, 2000). Peers have been trained to implement incidental teaching with individuals with ASD, resulting in increased speech and social interactions (Farmer-Dougan, 1994). Additionally, incidental teaching has been used with children with ASD to teach academic skills such as reading (McGee et al., 1986).

Assessment of Skills during Incidental Teaching

Evaluation should take place during teaching sessions, within other settings, with a variety of communicative partners, and with a variety of instructional materials to ensure that generalization takes place. Data should be collected frequently to make certain that the child is making progress. If the data do not show improvement, another strategy should be considered or the method of delivery should be assessed to judge if changes are necessary.

When assessing a child's skills, probe data should be used (McGee et al., 1985). Probe data collection may take place before a teaching session begins and in the setting in which prior teaching has taken place. The order of presentation of the materials should be random, so the adult can be sure that the child has not simply learned a pattern of responding. The child may receive reinforcement (e.g., praise, edibles), but it should not be connected to the correctness of his or her responses (e.g., provide praise for following directions). When collecting probe data, unlike in the middle of a teaching session during which the adult would wait for the child to initiate the session by showing interest in an item with a gesture or verbalization, the adult would initiate the data collection session by asking the child elaboration questions (e.g., "where is the juice?" might be asked to check for use of prepositions). Correct responses occur when the child uses a correct elaboration spontaneously or within approximately 5 seconds of the adult's question (McGee et al., 1985). Errors are those exchanges in

Table 5. Data Collection Sheet: Sample

Date	Environment	Materials	Question asked	Desired response (elaboration) from student	Did student respond without prompting?	If not, what prompt(s) was (were) required?
09/23	Snack time	Cookies	"What shape is this cookie?"	"Square"	No	Verbal: "say 'square'"
09/24	Snack time	Cookies	"What shape is this cookie?"	"Square"	No	Verbal: "say 'square'"
09/25	Snack time	Cookies	"What shape is this cookie?"	"Square"	Yes	

Student: *Beth*
Educational objective: *Beth will use the attribute of shape to make detailed requests.*

which the child does not respond or responds more than approximately 5 seconds after the adult's question, or the child responds incorrectly (e.g., asks for a circle cookie when the cookies are squares). In the case of an error during data collection, the adult would not prompt a correct response and the child would not receive the item. Therefore, it is important to keep the data collection sessions short to prevent frustration. A sample of a completed data collection sheet is provided in Table 5.

REFERENCES

Charlop-Christy, M. H., & Carpenter, M. H. (2000). Modified incidental teaching sessions: A procedure for parents to increase spontaneous speech in their children with autism. *Journal of Positive Behavior Interventions, 2*(2), 98–112.

Farmer-Dougan, V. (1994). Increasing requesting by adults with developmental disabilities using incidental teaching with peers. *Journal of Applied Behavior Analysis, 27*(3), 533–544.

Hart, B. M., & Risley, T. R. (1980). In vivo language intervention: Unanticipated general effects. *Journal of Applied Behavior Analysis, 13*(3), 407–432.

McGee, G. G., Daly, T., & Jacobs, H. A. (1994). The Walden Preschool. In S. L. Harris & J. S. Handleman (Eds.) *Preschool education programs for children with autism* (pp. 127–162). Austin, TX: Pro-Ed.

McGee, G. G., Krantz, P. J., & McClannahan, L. E. (1985). The facilitative effects of incidental teaching on preposition use by autistic children. *Journal of Applied Behavior Analysis, 18*(1), 17–31.

McGee, G. G., Krantz, P. J., & McClannahan, L. E. (1986). An extension of incidental teaching procedures to reading instruction for autistic children. *Journal of Applied Behavior Analysis, 19*(2), 147–157.

McGee, G. G., Morrier, M. J., & Daly, T. (1999). An incidental teaching approach to early intervention for toddlers with autism. *Journal of the Association for the Persons with Severe Handicaps, 24*(3), 133–146.

Miranda-Linné, F., & Melin, L. (1992). Acquisition, generalization, and spontaneous use of color adjectives: A comparison of incidental teaching and traditional discrete-trial procedures for children with autism. *Research in Developmental Disabilities, 13*(3), 191–210.

JENNIFER B. GANZ

INCIDENT REPORT

An incident report is a written summary that documents behavior incidents, especially situations in which someone is hurt. An incident report usually contains a description of the behavior, the antecedent, individuals involved, when and where the behavior occurred, action taken by staff, and injuries, if applicable.

THERESA L. EARLES-VOLLRATH

INCLUSION

New Zealand scholar Keith Ballard defines inclusion as:

> Inclusive education means education that is non-discriminatory in terms of disability, culture, gender or other aspects of students or staff that are assigned significance by a society. It involves all students in a community, with no exceptions and irrespective of their intellectual, physical, sensory or other difference, having equal rights to access the culturally valued curriculum of their society as full time valued members of age-appropriate mainstream classrooms. (Ballard, 1999, p. 1)

According to Meijer and his colleagues (Pijl & Meijer, 1997), inclusion is to use different instructional strategies to teach all kinds of students under the same education system. Mittler (2000), on the other hand, believes that inclusion is to see every individual as a whole and put every child together to let them learn, work, and play together. Smith and his colleagues (Smith, Polloway, Patton, & Dowdy, 1998) claim that inclusion is to put students in a regular classroom from the very beginning of their school lives, and provide individualized service as necessary. In short, the inclusion concept highlights that everyone is equal and should stand on the same position at the starting point with the others even though they have different abilities and backgrounds.

REFERENCES

Ballard, K. (1999). International voice: An introduction. In K. Ballard (Ed.), *Inclusive education: International voice on disability and justice*. London: Taylor & Francis.

Mittler, P. (2000). *Working towards inclusive education: Social context*. London: David Fulton.

Pijl, S. J., & Meijer, C. J. W. (1997). Factors in inclusion: A framework. In S. Pijl, C. J. W. Meijer, & S. Hegarty (Eds.) *Inclusive education: A global agenda* (pp. 8–13). London and New York: Routledge.

Smith, T. E., Polloway, E. A., Patton, J. R., & Dowdy, C. A. (1998). *Teaching students with special needs in inclusive settings*. Boston: Allyn & Bacon.

KAI-CHIEN TIEN

INDEPENDENT EMPLOYMENT

For those who are quite capable of self-directed activities, independent employment may prove to be a desirable option. Individuals with autism spectrum disorders (ASDs) who consider this idea must realize that even though they may not require notable accommodations at work, they may have to put effort into improving skills that help them maintain a job in a competitive situation such as taking directions, working in group situations, or knowing what individual tasks are most important to successful completion of their job. It is also advisable to choose when and where to disclose information about yourself or diagnosis in order to advocate for minor accommodations that could be the difference for successful independent employment or the need for a more supervised employment option.

Self-employment is another form of independent employment option where people capitalize on their strengths by selling their knowledge or skills to customers who need the services. Like any other self-employed person, those who choose this option must be very good at time and money management, because the availability of either one may vary with the workload. Scheduling, estimating required resources, managing cash-flow, marketing yourself, and bookkeeping are all necessary functions that do not necessarily require being completed independently to make them occur. With careful assessment and reflection of personal interests, passions, and abilities, independent or self-employment could be the key to a career or just plain paying the bills.

FURTHER INFORMATION
Shore, S., & Rastelli, L. (2006). *Understanding autism for dummies*. Indianapolis, IN: Wiley Publishing, Inc.

SHERRY MOYER

INDICATORS OF SENSORY PROCESSING DISORDER

In the Indicators of Sensory Processing Disorder (Abrash, 1996), respondents are requested to place a mark beside observed behaviors across several sensory and regulatory areas including **tactile**, **proprioception**, vision, auditory, gustatory (taste), olfactory (smell), vestibular/kinesthetic, chemical regulation, arousal and attending and social consciousness. Following completion of this checklist, a determination can be made by an **occupational therapist** or related professional as to whether or not to pursue further observation and/or assessment. Information gleaned from the checklist can also serve as a catalyst for discussion between the therapist and teacher as a way of arriving at basic interventions that can be implemented in the classroom.

REFERENCE
Abrash, A. (1996). *Clinical Connection*, 9(3), 15–17.

LISA ROBBINS

INDIVIDUALIZED EDUCATION PROGRAM (IEP)

Every student in a public school system that receives special education and/or related services must have an Individualized Education Program (IEP) as regulated by federal law. An IEP for a student must be individualized to the student's strengths and needs.

The IEP is developed by a team, which consists of the student (when appropriate according to age and ability to participate), parents or guardians, teachers, school administrators, related service providers, school psychologist, and other support personnel. Other members of the IEP team can include the school counselor, therapists outside of the school environment, and any other person directly involved with the student. Collaboration among the individuals on an IEP team directly relates to creating an effective plan for the student to succeed.

Each IEP is mandated to have certain components by the **Individuals with Disabilities Education Act** (IDEA, 2004). This law outlines the components that each IEP must have, even though school districts and states may use different forms (Drasgow, Yell, & Robinson, 2001). The components in an IEP are as follows:

- **Current performance or present levels of performance:** The present levels of performance must describe how the student is performing in school. Evaluation results from achievement testing, observations, and testing from related services providers are recorded in this section. Another required part of the present level of performance is the statement of how the student's disability affects his or her involvement and progress in the general education classroom.
- **Annual goals:** Each goal is specifically written to be accomplished by the student in one year. Goals are broken down into objectives or benchmarks that lead to the annual goal. Goals may cover academic subjects, social or behavior needs, speech needs, gross motor or occupational needs, and any other need that is required for the student to succeed in school. Goals must be written so they can be objectively measured.
- **Special education and related services:** Each IEP must reflect supplementary aids and services as well as modifications and accommodations (e.g., eating lunch in a quiet room) that the student receives. Also listed are the special education and related services received by the child.
- **Participation with peers without disabilities:** This component of the IEP states the extent (if any) to which the student will not participate with peers without disabilities.
- **Assessment:** Each IEP must outline the modifications, if any, that are needed for state and district-wide tests. If the testing is not appropriate for the student, an explanation must be provided and an alternative testing must be provided.
- **Service plan:** Every related service and special education service must record the duration (daily or weekly) and setting of services.
- **Transition service needs and services to be provided:** Upon a child's turning 14 years old, the IEP must explain the courses he or she needs to take to transition from school to the working environment.
- **Age of majority:** One year before the student reaches the age of majority, usually age 18, the rights of the student must be explained to the student. These rights are usually transferred from the parents to the student at that time.
- **Measuring progress:** Each IEP must show how the student's progress will be measured and how the parents will be informed of this progress.

Writing the IEP and Implementing the IEP

When writing the IEP, there are several factors to consider. These needs are as follows: (a) behavior that interferes with the student's learning or the learning of others, (b) a limited proficiency in English, (c) special communication needs, (d) students who are blind or visually impaired, (e) students who are deaf or hearing impaired, and (f) **assistive technology** needs for the student. To address these factors, strategies and supports must be put into place. When writing the IEP, the team must also include the student's strengths, needs, and the parent's ideas for enhancing their child's education.

After the IEP is written, a copy must be provided to the parents, and the parents must give written permission before any special education or related services are provided to their child. It is also beneficial that each member of the IEP team and any other adults that interact with the student on a daily basis have a copy of the IEP.

When implementing the IEP, it is helpful to assign a case manager, or someone who is willing to coordinate all special education services and be a contact for the family. Establishing communication between home and school is also beneficial, to aid in problem solving and generalization. Regular progress reports must also be filled out and sent home to report the progress on the student's goals and objectives.

Revising the **IEP**

According to IDEA, the IEP must be reviewed at least once a year. The parents or school may request for the IEP to be reviewed more often than once a year. Each goal must be reviewed to see if the goal has been attained or how much progress has been made toward the goal. New goals must be written if the old goals have been met.

In some cases, the parents of the student with an IEP do not agree with what the school recommends as services. In this case, if the parents and school cannot come to terms with an appropriate plan, **mediation** or **due process** can occur.

References

Drasgow, E., Yell, M. L., & Robinson, T. R. (2001). Developing legally correct and education-ally appropriate IEPs. *Remedial and Special Education, 22,* 359–373.

Individuals with Disabilities Education Improvement Act of 2004. Public Law No. 109-446, § 20 U.S.C. (2004).

Melissa L. Trautman

INDIVIDUALIZED FAMILY SERVICE PLAN (IFSP)

The Individualized Family Service Plan (IFSP) is a roadmap that a family and child use while receiving service when the child is ages birth to 3 years old. Along with a service coordinator, the family and professional personnel will develop a plan that will outline the services and locations for the child's early intervention.

Information recorded on the IFSP is child specific and requires a separate page for each child in the family. The IFSP is always developed with the family as an equal member of the team. There is only one IFSP plan per family with additional pages added per child. The following IFSP sections will be completed for each child in the family and filed in sequential order to reflect the family's plan:

Cover

The cover page must be completed in the presence of the parent. It is the part of the document where the family creates a vision for their family. Each time the service coordinator reviews the plan with the family, they will reexamine the vision statement as well. The vision statement is a fluid document and can be long- or short-term in nature. The parent(s) has the right to change the vision statement without an "official" IFSP review. The vision statement addresses the parents' hopes for the child as well as what they want their child to learn, know, and accomplish.

Parents will also receive information regarding parents' rights and procedural safeguards. This section of the document will also identify demographics and timelines. It is here that dates of reviews of the IFSP will be recorded as well as information regarding name, birth-days, household size, ethnicity, race, parents, address, communication method used, date of referral, initial IFSP date, school district, and preparation for initial transition date.

Health and Medical Information

This section of the document gathers medical information about the child from the par-ent. Consents could also be obtained in order to collect pertinent medical information from medical professionals.

Evaluations, Assessment for Program Planning, Screening

This section is to determine the child's eligibility for Part C services of the Individuals with Disabilities Education Act (IDEA, 2004). Children who are eligible for Part C services shall receive ongoing assessment in areas of delay for the purpose of gathering additional information to identify strengths and needs as well as appropriate services to meet those needs. Children who are eligible for Part C services due to a diagnosed medical condition shall have an initial and ongoing assessment in all developmental areas for the purpose of program planning.

Family Resources, Priorities, and Concerns

Here is where the family will record their concerns and immediate priorities. After completing this assessment, the family will have outlined resources, priorities, and concerns related to their family and child's development.

Everyday Routines, Activities, and Places

Collection of this information is beneficial for two reasons. First, information regarding the family's interests, routines, and activities are known, Second, these activities can be used as outcome measures on the IFSP. This information assists the service coordinator with helping the child participate in the family activities, culture, and community.

Outcome/Goal

Individual outcomes/goals related to the child and family's needs are defined here. This is not a request for service or items. This is what the parent(s) wants their child or their family to be able to accomplish and what the family needs in order to support their child's development in the next four months.

Developmental Evaluation/Assessment

Evaluations from other professionals (medical professionals, speech pathologists, physical therapists, etc.) can be added in this section.

Summary

This section summarizes the fee for service information for the parent, the outcomes, location of service, length of service, and the payment arrangements.

Justification

This is completed only if a service(s) that addresses an outcome/goal on the IFSP cannot be provided in the child and family's everyday routines, activities, and places (natural environments).

Transition Outcome/Goal

The team uses this section to assess the child's current developmental level as they prepare to transition from the early intervention setting into another program.

Transition Documentation Checklist

Documentation of the steps that are to be taken to make certain a smooth transition between early intervention and other services exists are kept here. This documentation is to promote a partnership between all agencies involved with the family.

IFSP Signatures and Consents

This section documents that the parent/guardian has participated in the IFSP development and that they agree with the plan. A section for obtaining consents from the parents is available. It also outlines the other members of the team and who needs to receive a copy of the report.

Appendices
Several appendices exist to provide information such as a glossary of terms and an early track data dictionary.

The format that a specific document takes may vary from state to state. The important thing to remember is that the IFSP places the focus on helping the child progress not only along developmental lines, but as a member of the family as well. At each level of the plan, the family's vision, needs, and desires are taken into account. The goal is to create a strong partnership with the family and all individuals serving the child.

REFERENCE

Individuals with Disabilities Education Improvement Act of 2004. Public Law No. 109-446, § 20 U.S.C. (2004).

LYNN DUDEK

INDIVIDUALIZED HEALTH CARE PLAN (IHCP)

An Individualized Health Care Plan (IHCP) is a document that outlines the diagnoses, services, and outcomes for a medically involved child while at school. Any child with a severe health care need that requires frequent nursing intervention services while at school should have an IHCP. An important part of the IHCP is the Emergency Care Plan. The Emergency Care Plan is required when a chronic condition has the potential to result in a medical emergency.

Because school nurses may be assigned to several buildings or have a large number of students, nurses must follow specific guidelines to prioritize students for an IHCP. The National Association of School Nurses (November 2003) has recommended that "the prioritization of students and their needs is essential and begins by identifying students whose health needs affect their daily functioning, that is, students who:

- Are medically fragile with multiple needs.
- Require lengthy health care or multiple health care contacts with the nurse or unlicensed assistive personnel during the school day.
- Have health needs that are addressed on a daily basis.
- Have health needs addressed as part of their IEP or 504 plan."

The school nurse is the leader of the school health team. As the leader, the nurse will assess the student's health status, collect additional information regarding health and safety, and develop a health care plan for the school. The plan will assure school staff and parents that the child is receiving the proper care.

The IHCP helps ensure that:

- communication between the school nurse and staff, students, and parents is accurate and up-to-date;
- safer processes for delegation are in place;
- the health plan can be incorporated into a 504 or IEP if necessary;

- proper safeguards are in place (i.e. Emergency Care Plan); and
- advancement of professional school nurses' practice can take place.

It is also the position of the National Association of School Nurses that the school nurse is the one who should be responsible for writing of the IHCP in collaboration with the student, family, and health care providers. In addition, the school nurse is the one responsible for seeing that the IHCP is implemented and includes periodic evaluation for evidence of desired student outcomes.

REFERENCE

National Association of School Nurses (November 2003). *Individualized Health Care Plans* (Position Statement). Silver Spring, MD: Author.

LYNN DUDEK

INDIVIDUALIZED TRANSITION PLAN

An Individualized Transition Plan (ITP) is an extension of a student's **Individual Education Plan** that looks beyond high school and plans for adulthood. The goal of the ITP is to facilitate a student's movement from school to the world of adult work, living, and community participation. The ITP takes into consideration the hopes and dreams of the student and outlines the steps that one would need to take to achieve them. According to the **Individuals with Disabilities Education Act** (IDEA 2004), the ITP must be in place by the age of 16. This is required practice; however, on a more practical level, some professionals recommend that students with autism spectrum disorders start the transition process by the age of 14, if not earlier (Swanson & Smith, in press; Holtz, Owings, & Ziegert, 2006; Schelvan, Swanson, & Smith, 2005; Myles & Adreon, 2001).

According to Holtz et al. (2006), each student's plan will be individualized to meet their postschool needs and may include information such as: (a) assessment of the child's needs, interests, and abilities; (b) a statement of preferences for education, employment, and adult living; (c) steps to be taken to support achievement of these goals; (d) specific methods and resources to meet these goals, including accommodations, services, and/or skills that are related to the transition goals; (e) instruction on academic, vocational, and living skills; (f) identification of community experiences and skills related to future goals; (g) exploration of service organizations or agencies to provide services and support; and (h) methods for evaluating success of transition activities.

To facilitate this process, each individual student will work with their ITP team to determine and design the best course of action to help the student learn or maintain the skills necessary to pursue post-high school endeavors. The ITP team must include the student, parents, or guardians, teachers, and representatives from local agencies (i.e., Vocational Rehabilitation). According to IDEA 2004, the ITP must include "appropriate measurable postsecondary goals based upon age appropriate transition assessments related to training, education, employment, and, where appropriate, independent living skills" and "the transition services (including courses of study) needed to assist the child in reaching those goals."

REFERENCES

Holtz, K. D., Owings, N. M., & Ziegert, A. K. (2006). Life journey through autism: A transition guide. Alexandria, VA: Organization for Autism Research.

Individuals with Disabilities Education Improvement Act of 2004. Public Law No. 109-446, § 20 U.S.C. (2004).

Myles, B. S., & Adreon, D. (2001). Asperger syndrome and adolescence: Practical solutions for school success. Shawnee Mission, KS: Autism Asperger Publishing Company.

Schelvan, R. L., Swanson, T. C., & Smith, S. M. (2005). Making each year successful: Issues in transition. In B. S. Myles (Ed.), Children and youth with Asperger syndrome: Strategies for success in inclusive settings. Thousand Oaks, CA: Corwin Press.

Swanson, T. C., & Smith, S. M. (in press). Transition planning for individuals with autism spectrum disorders: Building bridges to the future. In R. Simpson & B. Myles (Eds.), Educating children and youth with autism. Austin, TX: Pro-Ed.

TERRI COOPER SWANSON

INDIVIDUAL PLAN FOR EMPLOYMENT (IPE)

An Individual Plan for Employment (IPE) is similar to an **Individualized Education Plan** (IEP), but the focus is vocational. An IPE is facilitated through Vocational Rehabilitation services (VR), while an IEP is regulated by the school district. VR helps persons with varying degrees of disabilities find appropriate employment and assists them in obtaining independent skills. VR is funded by federal and state monies. Services are based on the individual's needs and limited to a short period of time. Services may be renewed or changed as necessary (deFur, 2002). VR services generally begin after high school, but they may start earlier depending on the needs of the individual (McDonald, Parker, & Goldberg, 2000).

Before an IPE is created, the individual must be determined eligible for services. To be determined eligible, an individual must have a disability that makes it difficult to find work or maintain a job. The individual must also need services provided by VR to prepare for a job, procure a job, or keep a job that fits his personal needs and abilities. Eligibility is based on job-related skills in a setting that is individualized and integrated as appropriate for the individual. Areas assessed may include: mobility, independence, independent living skills, social skills, ability to communicate, work tolerance, and work-related skills (McDonald et al., 2000).

The IPE is a plan outlining goals, objectives, and services required by an individual to meet a goal. It is a formal planning process in which goals and objectives, services and the time frame of services, and how the success of the IPE will be monitored are written into a plan (Consumer's Guide to Maine's Vocational Rehabilitation Programs, n.d.). A team of people creates the IPE and includes the individual or the individual's representative and the vocational rehabilitation counselor. Other members may include a vocational evaluator, a casework technician, and another VR counselor (possibly a supervisor of the VR counselor who handles the case), and a parent of the individual if that person requires a guardian (Hayward & Schmidt-Davis, 2003).

The Vocational Rehabilitation Act 1973 and its amendments mandate that individuals with disabilities must be actively involved in their own programs while making informed decisions about their goals and vocational services. The IPE must be developed jointly and agreed upon by the consumer and the vocational rehabilitation counselor. If the individual is unable to be actively involved, the parents, guardian, family member, or other person may make the decision. In such cases where the consumer refuses to sign or disagrees with the IPE, there is no plan. The matter should be discussed and documented, and attempts should be made to settle the concerns and redevelop the plan for employment. If the matter cannot be resolved, the consumer has a right to appeal through the Client Assistance Program (CAP). If resolution is not possible, the consumer's case will be closed. Each year the consumer or the representative must review the IPE. The employment plan may be reviewed more often as necessary. Changes to the IPE will not take effect until the consumer agrees to the changes and signs the document (New York State Office of Child and Family Services, n.d.).

Each IPE has the same set of requirements. The IPE must contain long-term goals for rehabilitation that describe the employment to be gained. The intermediate objectives should relate directly to successful completion of the long-term goal. It will also include the timeline for reaching the employment goal and the criteria to evaluate the objectives and the procedure for evaluation. Specific rehabilitation services to be provided must be included, as well as the services providers. The IPE will list the responsibilities of the state agency and those of the consumer. It will also address the conditions set forth for the services. The IPE includes a statement in the consumer's wording that describes how they were given information about alternatives such as goals, objectives, services, and service providers. A statement of the consumer's rights and responsibilities is laid out in the IPE (UT RCEP Online, n.d.). Finally, the IPE includes information about the local Client Assistance Program, assessment of the consumer's future need for postemployment services, and a listing of benefits that may help pay for the cost of services. Information regarding the need for **assistive technology**, on-the-job services, and personal assistance may be included if relevant to the individual consumer (New York State Department of Education, 1999).

If an individual receiving services under an approved IPE chooses a different vocational goal, the existing IPE will end. The consumer has 30 days to develop a new IPE. If it is not completed in 30 days, all services except those necessary to develop a new IPE will be dropped. Consumers will be notified by letter confirming the IPE is not in effect. The letter will also include the necessary steps to creating a new IPE. If the consumer appeals the end of the IPE, services will continue until a determination is made regarding the IPE (New York State Office of Children and Family Services, n.d.).

The goal of the Individual Plan for Employment is to help a consumer find success in employment that meets their personal needs and abilities. In creating a long-term goal it is helpful to consider the following items: employment availability, occupational requirements, medical concerns, and information regarding the consumer's previous jobs, interests, and strengths. The goal selection should be based on an assessment of vocational rehabilitation needs with the goal of finding placement in an integrated employment setting. Intermediate objectives are in actuality short-term goals, which build toward completion of the long-term goal. It is often helpful to assess the needs of a consumer in the areas of education, vocation, independent living skills, technology, and medical or social areas when creating long-term goals and intermediate objectives (New York State Office of Children and Family Services, n.d.). With the goal of preparing for employment, finding employment, or maintaining a job, the individual consumer and the VR counselor together create Individual Plans for Employment in a collaborative effort.

REFERENCES

Consumer's Guide to Maine's Vocational Rehabilitation Programs. Section V. (n.d.). *Individual plan for Employment*. Retrieved June 17, 2005, from http://www.caresinc.org/docs/vrguide/005.htm.

deFur, S. H. (2002). *Transition Planning. A team effort*. National Information Center for Children and Youth with Disabilities. Washington, DC.

Hayward, B. J., & Schmidt-Davis, H. (2003). *Longitudinal study of the vocational rehabilitation services program. Final report 2: VR services and outcomes*. Durham: NC: Research Triangle Institute.

McDonald, S., Parker, R., & Goldberg, P. (2000). *The road to work. An introduction to vocational rehab. A booklet for youth and adults with disabilities, family members and advocates* (2nd ed.). Minneapolis, MN: Pacer Center, Inc.

New York State Department of Education. Vocational and Educational Services for Individuals with Disabilities. (1999). *Individual plan for Employment policy*. Retrieved June 15, 2005, from http://www.vesid.nysed.gov/policies/206.htm.

New York State Office of Children and Family Services. (n.d.) *Individual plan for Employment*. Retrieved June 16, 2005, from http://www.ocfs.state.ny.us/main/cbvh/vocrehab_manual/06_IPE.htm.

UT RCEP Online. The University of Tennessee, Regional Rehabilitation Continuing Education Program. (n.d.) *Opportunity to make informed choice*. Retrieved June 19, 2005, from http://web.utk.edu/~rrcep4ut/informed/home.html.

VALERIE JANKE REXIN

INDIVIDUALS WITH DISABILITIES EDUCATION ACT (IDEA)

The Individuals with Disabilities Act (IDEA) became a federal law in 1975 and is currently the primary law governing special education in schools. IDEA ensures the right of individuals with disabilities to have free and appropriate education, as well as requiring schools and school staff to continually monitor and evaluate the individual's progress. The student's abilities, needs, and progress are monitored and measured by developing an **Individual Education Plan** (IEP). In 1997, IDEA was reauthorized, and amendments were added to further protect and benefit the education of individuals with disabilities. Some of the most significant amendments included requiring the consideration of assistive technology, educating the student in the least restrictive environment, and behavioral assessment and intervention. **Assistive technology** refers to any device that may increase, maintain, or improve the capabilities of a student with a disability. Examples of assistive technology can be as simple as using a pencil grip for a proper pencil grasp, or may be as high tech as using specific word-prediction software on a computer to promote written language. Under IDEA, the student also has the right to be educated with his peers in the **least restrictive environment**. The reauthorization of IDEA requires that the school specifically state the extent to which the student will and will not participate with nondisabled peers in academic, nonacademic, and extra-curricular settings. The amendments to IDEA also promote the use of positive behavioral supports to prevent and intervene upon inappropriate behaviors. It requires the use of a **functional behavioral assessment** to determine what the interfering behaviors are and their cause. It also requires that the school define the interfering behaviors and provide positive, supportive interventions to prevent or change inappropriate behaviors.

IDEA was reauthorized again in 2004 in an attempt to make educators more accountable for their impact on the education and functioning of students with disabilities. Under the new amendments, students with disabilities are required to take state assessments at their level of functioning. This can mean that students with disabilities take the same assessment as nondisabled peers, take a modified assessment, or take an alternate assessment. A modified assessment is essentially the same assessment the nondisabled peers take, however, the student with a disability is allowed accommodations that meet his needs, such as allowing extra time, typing rather than handwriting answers, or having questions read aloud to him. An alternate assessment generally looks very different from the state-issued assessment, and encompasses more basic, functional academic and life skills.

IDEA exists to protect individuals with disabilities from being excluded in the educational setting. Prior to the implementation of this federal law, individuals with disabilities often did not attend school, or were placed in isolated, special education programs without access to the general education curriculum or their nondisabled peers. IDEA continues to be reevaluated by legislators, educators, and individuals with disabilities in an attempt to provide better protection for individuals with disabilities and their families, as well as better guidelines for educators in providing optimal services and learning environment.

REFERENCE

Individuals with Disabilities Education Improvement Act of 2004. Public Law No. 109-446, § 20 U.S.C. (2004).

KELLY M. PRESTIA

INFANT/TODDLER SENSORY PROFILE

The Infant/Toddler Sensory Profile (Dunn, 2002) is designed for children ages 7 to 36 months to be completed by a caregiver or someone else who has daily contact with the child. Reporters are asked to respond to the frequency with which they observe the occurrence of various responses to the basic sensory systems, ranging from almost always to almost never. The responses are scored in an attempt to identify certain patterns of behavior. If areas of sensory processing difficulties are identified, the team working with the child can work to address the relationship between sensory processing and a child's performance.

REFERENCE

Dunn, W. (2002). *Infant/toddler sensory profile*. San Antonio, TX: Harcourt Assessment.

LISA ROBBINS

INFORMAL ASSESSMENT

Informal assessment measures are nonstandardized approaches for monitoring and evaluating student progress and obtaining information regarding an individual's strengths and needs. There are a variety of informal assessment measures, including curriculum-based assessments, curriculum-based measurement, criterion-referenced assessments, checklists, work samples, permanent products, observations, questionnaires, and many teacher-made tests.

FURTHER INFORMATION

Overton, T. (2003). *Assessing learners with special needs: An applied approach* (4th ed.). Upper Saddle River, NJ: Merrill/Prentice Hall.

THERESA L. EARLES-VOLLRATH

INTEGRATED EMPLOYMENT

As implied by its name, the term *integrated employment* is used to describe the type of employment available for individuals who are capable of working in a community setting. People with disabilities can engage the services of an employment agency, vocational rehabilitation agency, or private job coaches to help match their interests and skills to appropriate employers in the community. To be successful in an integrated employment setting, the individual will need to be able to work with minimal supervision, stay focused on each task required for their job, and perhaps most importantly, know when and how to ask for help. For individuals with autism spectrum disorders, this might be best achieved by utilizing their strengths or areas of special interest to help encourage a successful experience. Just a few ideas might include: guides at museums, computer repair, ticket takers at local sporting events, or dog sitters. Jobs can vary with the skill level and interest of the individual; the possibilities are endless as long as the person functions with reasonable level of independence and more ordinary types of supervision while at work.

SHERRY MOYER

INTEGRATED PLAY GROUP MODEL (IPG)

The Integrated Play Groups (IPG) model was originally developed by Wolfberg (1999, 2003) to address the unique challenges children on the autism spectrum encounter in peer relations and play. Defining features of autism spectrum disorders (ASD) include a "lack of varied and imaginative or imitative play" and a "failure to develop peer relationships appropriate to developmental level" (Charman & Baird, 2002, p. 289). These difficulties are closely connected to characteristic impairments in the development of reciprocal social interaction, communication, and imagination (APA, 2000). Guided by current theory, research, and evidence-based practices, the IPG model reflects a blending of approaches to foster development in each of these areas.

The IPG model is designed to support children of diverse ages and abilities on the autism spectrum (novice players) in mutually enjoyed play experiences with typical peers and siblings (expert players). These children regularly play together in small groups under the direction of a qualified facilitator (play guide). Through a carefully constructed system of support, play sessions are tailored to the unique interests and developmental capacities of individual children. A major effort is directed to maximizing children's developmental potential by capitalizing on each child's intrinsic motivation to socialize and play. Equal emphasis is placed on teaching the typical peers to be empathetic, responsive, and accepting of children who present differing ways of communicating, relating, and playing. Further, novice and expert players are expected to mediate their own play activities with minimal or no adult guidance.

PROGRAM AND ENVIRONMENTAL DESIGN

The IPG model was originally developed for children from preschool through elementary school age (approximately 3 to 11 years of age); however, adaptations and extensions of the model are in progress to support both younger and older children. Each IPG is customized for an individual child as a part of his or her educational or therapy program.

191

Play guides receive training and supervision to set up and carry out IPGs. They include practitioners, parents, and other care providers experienced in working with children with ASD.

Play groups include three to five children with a higher ratio of typically developing peers and/or siblings (expert players) to children with special needs (novice players). Expert players are recruited from places where children ordinarily have contact with peers (e.g., school, family friends, neighbors, community). Playmates ideally have some familiarity and attraction to one another and the potential for developing long-lasting friendships. Groups may vary with respect to children's gender, ages, developmental status, and play interaction styles.

The same group of children meets over an extended period of time (6 months or longer), two or more times per week for approximately 30 minutes to an hour. Times may vary depending upon the age and development of the children as well as the context of the intervention (i.e., school-based vs. therapy).

IPG programs take place in natural play environments within school, home, community, or therapy settings. These are primarily integrated settings where, given the opportunity, children would naturally play. Play areas are created to be safe, familiar, predictable, and highly motivating, allowing children to comfortably explore and socialize. They are designed with consideration of multiple factors such as size, density, organization, and thematic arrangements of the play area. Play materials include a wide range of sensory motor, exploratory, constructive, and socio-dramatic props with high potential for interactive and imaginative play. In addition, they vary in degree of structure and complexity to accommodate children's diverse interests, learning styles, and developmental levels.

Play sessions are structured by establishing routines and rituals that foster familiarity, predictability, and a cohesive group identity. Personalized visual calendars and schedules help children anticipate the days and times of meetings. Basic rules for fair and courteous behavior and appropriate care of materials are presented at the onset of play groups. Group membership is established by creating a "club name" and associated rituals. Play sessions begin and end with an opening and closing ritual (e.g., greeting, song, and brief discussion of plans and strategies).

Assessment

The IPG model includes a comprehensive assessment component that provides a basis for setting appropriate goals, designing effective intervention strategies, and evaluating children's progress. This includes an observation framework and corresponding assessment tools that focus on documenting children's social play styles, cognitive/symbolic and social dimensions of play, communication functions and means, play preferences, and diversity of play.

For example, within the symbolic dimension of play, manipulation, functional, and symbolic/pretend play represent acts that are directed towards objects or signify specific events. Within the social dimension of play, isolation, orientation/onlooker, proximity/parallel, common focus, and common goals represent the child's distance to and involvement with one or more peers.

How children communicate within the context of peer play activities is also examined. The functions of communication (e.g., requests for objects, peer interaction and affection, protests, declarations, and comments) may be measured through a variety of verbal and nonverbal means (including facial expressions, eye gaze, proximity, manipulating a peer's hand, face, or body, showing or giving objects, gaze shift, gestures, intonation, vocalization, nonfocused or focused echolalia, and one-word or complex speech/sign).

Documenting play preferences offers a means to identify and match children's play interests. Play preferences include a child's attraction to toys or props, mode of interacting with toys or props, choice of play themes, and attraction to particular playmates. Identifying the number and range of play interests provides a basis for measuring diversity of play.

INTERVENTION

The IPG intervention, guided participation, was inspired by the work of Vygotsky (1966, 1978). Guided participation is described as the process through which children develop while actively participating in culturally valued activity (in this case, play) with the guidance, support, and challenge of companions who vary in skill and status (Rogoff, 1990). The intervention involves methodically supporting novice and expert players to initiate and incorporate desired activity into socially coordinated play while challenging novice players to practice new and increasingly complex forms of play. Play guides apply the following key set of practices.

Monitoring Play Initiations

This practice focuses on uncovering novice players' meaningful attempts to socialize and play by recognizing, interpreting, and responding to their initiations. Play initiations may take both conventional and unconventional forms, and include acts directed to oneself, peers, and materials. Even acts that reflect unusual fascinations or obscure forms of communication are interpreted as purposeful, adaptive, and meaningful attempts to participate in play. These provide a foundation on which to build and extend each novice player's existing play repertoire, as well as for novice and expert players to establish a mutual focus and coordinate play activities.

Scaffolding Play

This practice involves building upon the child's initiations by systematically adjusting assistance to match or slightly exceed the level at which the child is independently able to engage in play with peers (i.e., within the child's "zone of proximal development"; Vygotsky, 1978). The idea is to avoid being so lax that the play falls apart, or so intrusive that it ruins the moment. The key is to find that ever-so-delicate balance for the play to unfold in genuine ways. At times, the play guide sets the stage for play by directing the event and modeling behavior. This involves arranging props, assigning roles, and scripting parts. As the children catch on to the activity, the adult gradually withdraws from the group and redirects the children to one another while extending their play. This includes posing leading questions, commenting on activities, offering suggestions, and giving subtle reminders using verbal and visual cues. Ultimately, the adult moves to and remains on the periphery of the group as a "secure base."

Social-Communication Guidance

This practice involves supporting both novice and expert players in using verbal and nonverbal social-communication cues to elicit each other's attention and sustain joint engagement in play activities. For example, experts learn how to interpret and respond to subtle or obscure forms of communication in a meaningful way so that novices may be included. Novices learn how to interpret and respond to the complex ways in which expert players communicate, as well as how to communicate in more conventional ways so that they may be more easily understood. Strategies focus on "what to do" and "what to say" to invite peers to play (including reluctant peers), join peers in play, enter peer groups, and maintain and expand interactions in play. Play guides coach the children using custom-made visual supports such as cue cards and posters.

Play Guidance

This practice encompasses a progression of strategies that support novice players in peer play experiences that are slightly beyond the child's capacity while fully immersed in the play experience. Play guidance strategies start at the level of the child and move along a continuum of development. Play guides must be well versed in a range of techniques to foster orientation, imitation-mirroring, parallel play, joint focus, joint action, role-enactment, and role-playing. Novices may participate in complex and sophisticated play scripts organized by expert players at their own level of ability, even if participation is minimal. They may carry out play activities and roles that they may not yet fully comprehend. For example, a child inclined to line up objects may incorporate this scheme into a larger play theme of pretending to be a store clerk who is responsible for arranging groceries on a shelf. The idea is to stimulate novices to explore and diversify existing play routines through repeated exposure to the experiences of peers.

EFFICACY OF THE IPG MODEL

The IPG model has been adopted by numerous schools and programs at the local, national, and international level, and has gained recognition as best practices for children with ASD (see California Department of Education, 1997; Iovannone, Dunlop, Huber, & Kincaid, 2003). This research-based model specifically incorporates elements that have been shown to be effective in enhancing social interaction, communication, play, and imagination in children with ASD. Further, the goals and methods are consistent with the recommendations of the National Research Council (2001), which has ranked the teaching of play skills with peers among the six types of interventions that should have priority in the design and delivery of effective educational programs for children with ASD.

To evaluate the efficacy of the IPG model, a series of experimental and exploratory studies have been conducted over the years (for a recent overview, see Wolfberg & Schuler, in press). This research has focused on documenting outcomes for novice and expert players, as well as perceptions of play guides and families (Gonsier-Gerdin, 1993; Lantz, Nelson, & Loftin, 2004; Mikaelian, 2003; O'Connor, 1999; Wolfberg, 1988; 1994; 1999; Wolfberg & Schuler, 1992; 1993; Yang, Wolfberg, Wu, & Hwu, 2003; Zercher, Hunt, Schuler, & Webster, 2001). More recently, several studies examined the efficacy of combining the IPG model with sensory integration therapy (Antipolo & Dichoso, 2003; Mahnken, Baiardo, Naess, Pechter, & Richardson, 2004; Schaefer & Atwood, 2003).

Although it is not feasible to determine which components of the intervention were most pertinent to the observed changes (since the IPG model is a comprehensive intervention), the cumulative findings suggest that the intervention as a whole contributed to generalized and socially valued gains. The system of support involving explicit guidance and peer mediation contributed to the children's social and symbolic development. Guided participation in intrinsically motivating play activity with more competent peers provided novice players the opportunity to refine their imitation skills and practice more advanced forms of social communication and play. Finally, the IPG model stimulated reciprocal friendships between children with ASD and typical peers through active engagement in mutually enjoyed play experiences.

REFERENCES

American Psychiatric Association. (2000). *Diagnostic and statistical manual of mental disorders* (4th ed., text rev.). Washington, DC: Author.

Antipolo, L., & Dichoso, D. (2003). *The effects of integrated play groups with sensory integration on the play and social skills of children with sensory integrative dysfunction.* Unpublished master's thesis, San Jose State University, San Jose, CA.

California Department of Education. (1997). *Best practices for designing and delivering effective programs for individuals with autistic spectrum disorders.* Produced by RiSE, Resources in Special Education, Sacramento, CA.

Charman, T., & Baird, G. (2002) Practitioner review: Diagnosis of autistic spectrum disorder in 2 and 3 year old children. *Journal of Child Psychology & Psychiatry, 43,* 289–305.

Charman, T., & Baron-Cohen, S. (1997). Brief report: Prompted pretend play in autism. *Journal of Autism and Developmental Disorders, 27,* 325–32.

Gonsier-Gerdin, J. (1993). *Elementary school children's perspectives on peers with disabilities in the context of integrated play groups.* Unpublished position paper, University of California–Berkeley.

Iovannone, R., Dunlop, G., Huber, H., & Kincaid, D. (2003). Effective educational practices for students with ASD. *Focus on Autism and Other Developmental Disabilities, 18*(3), 150–165.

Lantz, J. F., Nelson, J. M., & Loftin, R. L. (2004). Guiding children with autism in play: Applying the integrated play group model in school settings. *Exceptional Children, 37*(2), 8–14.

Mahnken, H., Baiardo, C., Naess, M., Pechter, R., & Richardson, P. (2004). *Integrated play groups and sensory integration for a child diagnosed with ASD: A case study.* Poster presented at the American Occupational Therapy Association Annual Conference, Minneapolis, MI.

Mikaelian, B. (2003). *Increasing language through sibling and peer support play.* Unpublished master's thesis, San Francisco State University, CA.

National Research Council. (2001). *Educating children with autism.* Committee on Educational Interventions for Children with Autism, Division of Behavioral and Social Sciences and Education. Washington, DC: National Academy Press.

O'Connor, T. (1999). *Teacher perspectives of facilitated play in integrated play groups.* Unpublished master's thesis, San Francisco State University, CA.

Rogoff, B. (1990). *Apprenticeship in thinking.* New York: Oxford University Press.

Schaefer, S., & Atwood, A. (2003). *The effects of sensory integration therapy paired with integrated play groups on the social and play behaviors of children with autistic spectrum disorder.* Unpublished master's thesis, San Jose State University, San Jose, CA.

Vygotsky, L. S. (1966). Play and its role in the mental development of the child (translation from 1933). *Soviet Psychology, 12,* 6–18.

Vygotsky, L. S. (1978). *Mind in society: The development of higher psychological processes* (translation from 1932). Cambridge, MA: Harvard University Press.

Wolfberg, P. J. (1988). *Integrated play groups for children with autism and related disorders.* Unpublished master's field study, San Francisco State University, CA.

Wolfberg, P. J. (1994). *Case illustrations of emerging social relations and symbolic activity in children with autism through supported peer play*. Doctoral dissertation, University of California at Berkeley with San Francisco State University. Dissertation Abstracts International, #9505068.

Wolfberg, P. J. (1999). *Play and imagination in children with autism*. New York: Teachers College Press, Columbia University.

Wolfberg, P. J. (2003). *Peer play and the autism spectrum: The art of guiding children's socialization and imagination*. Shawnee, KS: Autism Asperger Publishing Company.

Wolfberg, P. J., & Schuler, A. L. (1992). *Integrated play groups project: Final evaluation report* (Contract # HO86D90016). Washington, DC: Department of Education, OSERS.

Wolfberg, P. J., & Schuler, A. L. (1993). Integrated play groups: A model for promoting the social and cognitive dimensions of play in children with autism. *Journal of Autism and Developmental Disorders, 23*(3), 467–489.

Wolfberg, P. J., & Schuler, A. L. (in press). Promoting social reciprocity and symbolic representation in children with ASD. In T. Charman & W. Stone (Eds.), *Early social communication in autism spectrum disorders*. New York: Guildford Publications.

Yang, T., Wolfberg, P. J., Wu, S., & Hwu, P. (2003). Supporting children on the autism spectrum in peer play at home and school: Piloting the integrated play groups model in Taiwan. *Autism: The International Journal of Research and Practice, 7*(4), 437–453.

Zercher, C., Hunt, P., Schuler, A. L., & Webster, J. (2001). Increasing joint attention, play and language through peer supported play. *Autism: The International Journal of Research and Practice, 5*, 374–398.

PAMELA WOLFBERG

INTELLIGENCE TESTS

Intelligence tests assess samples of behavior to measure one's aptitude and intelligence. The result of these assessments is an Intelligence Quotient (IQ) score. Intelligence tests can be given in group or individual formats. Individually administered intelligence tests are primarily used in special education for identification, eligibility, and educational placement decisions.

FURTHER INFORMATION

Salvia, J., & Ysseldyke, J. E. (2007). *Assessment: In special and inclusive education* (10th ed.). Boston: Houghton Mifflin Company.

Taylor, R. L. (2006). *Assessment of exceptional students: Educational and psychological procedures* (7th ed.). Needham Heights, MA: Allyn and Bacon.

THERESA L. EARLES-VOLLRATH

INTERNAL REVIEW BOARD (IRB)

An Internal Review Board (IRB), also known as the Human Subjects Review Committee, is a group of individuals who are charged with the protection of human subjects used in research at universities and other institutions. An IRB reviews proposed research projects to ensure that the protocol outlined in the study complies with specified regulations and with other ethical and professional standards for use of human subjects in research. The committee also evaluates proposed projects to ensure that potential research subjects will be protected from harm and that they will be treated respectfully and fairly.

THERESA L. EARLES-VOLLRATH

INTERNATIONAL STATISTICAL CLASSIFICATION OF DISEASES AND RELATED HEALTH PROBLEMS (ICD)

International Statistical Classification of Diseases and Related Health Problems (ICD), published by the World Health Organization (WHO), is a guidebook commonly used by mental health professionals to diagnose mental disorders outside of the United States. Like the *Diagnostic and Statistical Manual of Mental Disorders* (APA, 2000), the ICD uses medical concepts and terminology, classifies disorders based on criteria into distinct categories and subcategories, and is revised periodically. The ICD is currently in its tenth edition.

REFERENCE

American Psychiatric Association. (2000). *Diagnostic and statistical manual of mental disorders* (4th ed., text rev.). Washington, DC: Author.

JEANNE HOLVERSTOTT

INTEROBSERVER AGREEMENT/RELIABILITY

Interobserver agreement or interobserver reliability refers to having two or more observers record the same data, on the same student(s), at the same time, but independent of each other. The data of all observers are then compared, and a reliability coefficient or a percent of agreement is calculated. While there is set standard for acceptable interobserver reliability, the accepted standard among some behavior analysts is a coefficient of approximately 90 (Alberto & Troutman, 1995). The higher the reliability coefficient or percent of agreement, the more accurate and reliable the data.

REFERENCE

Alberto, P. A., & Troutman, A. C. (1995). *Applied behavior analysis for teachers* (4th ed). Upper Saddle River, NJ: Prentice Hall.

THERESA L. EARLES-VOLLRATH

INTRAVERBAL

As first described by B. F. Skinner (1957), an intraverbal is the verbal response to a verbal stimulus that has no direct verbal relation to the stimulus. For example, when someone asks another, "What is your favorite food?" the person responding would say, "lasagna." The response is correct and is reinforced within the verbal exchange between two people, but the response does not directly relate word for word to the verbal stimulus. A directly related response to the question would be, "My favorite food is lasagna" (Lerman, Parten, Addison, Vorndran, & Volkert et al., 2005).

REFERENCES

Lerman, D. C., Parten, M., Addison, L. R., Vorndran, C. M., Volkert, V. M., & Kodak, T. (2005). A methodology for assessing the functions of emerging speech in children with developmental disabilities. *Journal of Applied Behavior Analysis, 38*(3), 303–316.
Skinner, B. F. (1957). *Verbal behavior*. New York: Appleton-Century-Crofts.

TARA MIHOK

IRLEN LENSES

Irlen lenses are color-tinted lenses used to reduce vision difficulties. In 1980, Olive Meares was one of the first people to note the signs and symptoms of visual distress in school-age children. Helen Irlen, the name most commonly identified with colored lenses, presented findings in 1983 that her students had less visual distortions while reading if they used a transparent colored overlay (Wilkins, 2003).

There are a variety of terms that are used in conjunction with the light-sensitivity disorder in which one needs colored overlays or colored lenses to manage perceptual distortions. Helen Irlen originally coined the phrase *scoptic sensitivity syndrome* (SSS) (1991), however the Irlen Institute now uses the phrase *Irlen syndrome* (Irlen syndrome/Scoptic syndrome, 1991). Others prefer the term Meares-Irlen syndrome to include Olive Meares, who was one of the first proponents of using color to reduce vision difficulties (Wilkins, 2003).

Irlen syndrome is not a vision problem but rather a difficulty with the visual perceptual system. It occurs in some individuals with learning or reading disorders, autism, and other developmental disorders. Individuals with SSS experience visual stress, which leads to distortions while reading or viewing the world around them. Difficulties may be expressed through problems with light brightness or types of lighting, movement of letters or words on the page, difficulty with high contrast situations, and difficulty reading groups of letters (Edleson, n.d.).

There are specific symptoms related to SSS/Irlen syndrome. Some people may experience difficulty reading for long periods of time. Others find their reading to be inefficient. Some readers are unable to skim or speed read. Strain and fatigue is often reported after reading. Phrases read aloud may sound hesitant or choppy. The reader may have poor comprehension skills and difficulty retaining information. A slow reading rate and high error rates may also be noted in readers (Irlen syndrome/Scoptic syndrome, 1991).

Deficiencies in visual skills may lead to poor academic performance. The National Institute of Health estimates that 10 million American children have difficulty reading. Eighty percent of student learning in the classroom depends on the ability of the visual system to process correctly (Stone, 2003). Basic school vision screenings only test for a few learning-related visual skills such as distance, 20/20 eyesight, using the eyes together, and muscle balance. Although states require vision screenings, most leave it to the school district to determine how the testing will be initiated. Typically, school districts do not test for other visual skill concerns. Most people are not aware of the connection between poor academics and visual skill deficiencies. Although the number of children with reading disabilities that are helped by Irlen lenses varies according to different researchers, it is possible that 460,000 to 4.6 million children could be helped by the use of color overlays or tinted lenses (Stone, 2003).

Irlen lenses are created to meet the needs of the wearer through a specific testing method. While these lenses are often used for persons with light sensitivities, disorders, and reading disabilities, individuals with autism and other developmental disorders have also worn them with success.

REFERENCES

Edleson, S. M. (n.d.). *Scotopic sensitivity syndrome and the Irlen lens system*. Retrieved June 13, 2005, from http://www.autism.org/irlen.html.

Irlen, H. (1991). *Reading by the colors*. Garden City Park, NY: Avery Publishing Group Inc.

Irlen syndrome/Scoptic syndrome. (1991). Retrieved June 12, 2005, from http://www.irlen.com/sss_main.htm.

Stone, R. (2003). *The light barrier*. New York: St. Martin's Press.

Wilkins, A. (2003). *Reading through colour*. London: John Wiley & Sons.

FURTHER INFORMATION

Ludlow, A. K., Wilkins, A. J., & Heaton, P. (2006). The effect of coloured overlays on reading ability in children with autism. *Journal of Autism and Developmental Disorders. 36,* 507–516.

Thomson, W. D., & Wilkins, A. J. (2006). Memory for the color of non-monochromatic lights. *Color Research and Application, 32,* 11–15.

VALERIE JANKE REXIN

J

JOINT ACTION ROUTINES

Joint Action Routines (JAR) is an intervention strategy used to scaffold language development for individuals with autism spectrum disorders (ASD). This instructional strategy is known also by names such as Activity Based Strategy (Bricker, 1998), and Sociodramatic Script Training (Goldstein, Wickstrom, Hoyson, Jamieson, & Odom, 1988). The term JAR was coined by Snyder-McLean, Solomonson, McLean, & Sack (1984) who developed this methodology in their work with students with various disabilities, including mental retardation, various language delays, and/or other health impairments.

JAR is a routinized series of activities and communication-based interactions between an individual and one or more communicative partners. Those interactions are purposeful and are performed repeatedly and in a certain logical order that the individual has learned. JAR treatment includes features such as a unifying theme, joint focus between one or more communicative partners, a certain number of roles (e.g., chef, waitress, customer), a logical, predetermined sequence of activities, turn-taking, repetition, and variation. These elements make JAR an intervention strategy uniquely appropriate to meet the needs of students with language and communication delays in general, and those diagnosed with autism spectrum disorders (ASD), in particular (Goldstein et al., 1988; Prizant, Wetherby, & Rydell, 2000). Professionals also consider JAR a particularly suitable treatment option for individuals with ASD because it borrows elements from both the behavioristic and the naturalistic perspectives, such as reliance on careful planning and enhancement of environmental structures designed to ensure a child's successful participation in a routine. The features of JAR that reflect a behavioristic approach include the use of repetitions and, depending on the student's developmental age, routines could also be teacher directed. JAR's characteristics associated with a naturalistic approach include limiting reinforcers only to those that are intrinsic to a routine, focusing on student-initiated activities in routines, and structuring meaningful contexts for the instruction of new communicative skills. Other strategies employed during the implementation of routines include sabotage, oversight, silly situations and time delay. *Sabotage* refers to a situation such as when a caregiver offers a child M&M's in a closed container, causing the child to ask for help to open it. An *oversight* can happen when a child is offered a bowl of soup with no spoon. A *silly situation* occurs when a parent gives a child a fork to eat soup.

Time delay is a technique in which a teacher gradually lengthens the time between a stimulus and a prompt to allow the student more time to provide the expected verbal response. Throughout this time, the teacher keeps eye contact with his student, looking at him expectantly. These procedures are designed to prevent boredom and to create a need to communicate in a child's natural environment.

Snyder-McLean et al. (1984) identified four major categories of routines: routines related to daily living skills, routines that involve preparation of a product, those that focus on a specific theme, and those that involve social games. Routines related to *daily living skills* entail instruction designed to promote communication skills related to adaptive behavior competency around topics such as bath time, getting out of bed, shopping, eating in a restaurant, using public transportation, and so forth. Routines that involve *preparation of a product* focus on instruction of language skills that involve activities such as snack preparation, creating an art project, and prevocational readiness (i.e., product assembly). JARs that focus on *a theme* foster language development around topics of interest to the students and include leisure activities (e.g., picnic, ball game, amusement park activities), or familiar stories. *Social cooperative games* provide a perfect venue for teaching turn-taking skills, and thus are especially helpful in making concrete for children with ASD the concepts that are inherent in communication, such as the "back and forth," waiting for a turn, responding based on a partner's reaction, and so forth. These activities might be of the nature of sharing a game on a computer, playing cards and other table top games, putting a puzzle together, and much more.

These routines have been developed for implementation across all age groups and levels of disability: toddlers or young children with developmental age of or below 24 months, preschool- and elementary-age students, and middle- to high school-age students. For infants or young children with a mental age below 24 months, roles may be limited to only adult and child, and might not be exchangeable between them. In addition, the adult might be the sole initiator of routines, which might also have to be simplified in their task complexity and communication requirements.

The following are basic guidelines for successfully using JAR with students with ASD:

1. Choose target behaviors that match a student's current level of performance and which are in line with the IEP objectives. Careful consideration should also be given to students' age and their familiarity with and interest in the JAR topic.
2. Establish procedures for data collection to measure students' progress.
3. Design the Joint Action Routines while considering—
   • the topic,
   • time and place of implementation,
   • the roles,
   • the props needed,
   • the order of activities, and
   • the teaching method (i.e., should the routine be taught in a backward chaining fashion, starting with the last task in the chain, or rather, should the first two to three steps be taught first, and so forth).
4. Prepare relevant props.
5. Prepare materials needed.
6. Based on the complexity of a JAR, establish a signal to indicate the beginning and ending of a routine.
7. Introduce the routine.

The following provides an example of a JAR designed to teach preschoolers with autism to follow one-step instructions, such as "get tissue," "throw away," and, "give me five."

Objective: To teach students to follow one-step instructions.
Data Collection: Data will be collected weekly on a student's correct response. A (−) will indicate a prompted response, and a (+) will indicate a correct independent response.
Time and Place: Five repetitions during mealtime (one time a day).
The Roles: Adult and child.
Props: No props needed.
Order of Activities:

- Drink or food is "accidentally" spilled.
- Teacher exclaims, "Oh, no!" points to the spill and says, "Get tissue."
- Student gets up and takes a tissue.
- After child wipes spill, he/she is then told to "throw (the tissue) away."
- Student throws tissue into a waste can.
- Teacher says, "Give me five!"
- Student "gives five."

JAR serves as a strategy for promoting communication skills in individuals with autism spectrum disorders by providing learners with a context for communication, creating a need for mutual focus and attention between and among communicative partners, encouraging students to tune into a communicative partner's perspectives, and creating a controlled environment that supports the growth and development of communication skills.

REFERENCES

Bricker, D. (with Pretti-Frontczak, K., & McComas, N.). (1998). *An activity based approach to early intervention* (2nd ed.). Baltimore: Brookes Publishing Co.

Goldstein, H., Wickstrom, S., Hoyson, M., Jamieson, B., & Odom, S. L. (1988). Effects of sociodramatic script training on social and communicative interaction. *Education and Treatment of Children, 11*, 97–117.

Prizant, B. M., Wetherby, A. M., & Rydell, P. J. (2000). Communication intervention issues for children with autism spectrum disorders. In S. F. Warren & J. Reichle (Series Eds.) & A. M. Wetherby & B. M. Prizant (Vol. Eds.), *Communication and language intervention series: Vol. 9. Autism spectrum disorders: A transactional developmental perspective* (pp. 193–224). Baltimore: Brookes Publishing Co.

Snyder-McLean, L. K., Solomonson, B., McLean, J. E., & Sack, S. (1984). Structuring joint action routines: A strategy for facilitating communication and language development in the classroom. *Seminars in Speech and Language, 5*, 213–228.

JOSEPHA BEN-ARIEH

JOINT ATTENTION

Joint Attention involves the shifting of attention from one object of desire back to another object or person. This is a developmental milestone that is typically first seen in young children as they point out objects or direct adults to look at the same object that has gained their interest. Many times infants will point to an object prior to their ability to label all aspects of the object. The use of joint attention coordinates mutual interest to a desired person, place, or thing among two or more communicative partners. For example, an infant might point to an airplane in the sky, and the adult holding the child then often labels the item, "You see a big plane."

KATHERINE E. COOK

JOURNAL

Journals are scholarly compilations of research-based articles in a peer-reviewed format. For a list of journals related to autism spectrum disorders see Appendix C.

TERRI COOPER SWANSON

KANNER, LEO

Leo Kanner (1894–1981) substantially influenced the field of child and adolescent psychiatry by providing the first description of infantile autism (Neumarker, 2003). He is recognized as the first person to formally describe and coin the term *autism* more than a half century ago (Kanner, 1943). Kanner published a description of this profile based on his case studies in a paper identifying autistic children in 1943 (Kanner, 1943, p. 227), which has become the most quoted work in the literature on autism (AMA-Autism History, n.d.).

REFERENCES

AMA-Autism History (n.d.). Retrieved July 31, 2006, from http://www.ama.org.br/autismhistory.htm.

Kanner, L. (1943). Autistic Disturbances of Affective Contact. *The Nervous Child, 2,* 217–250.

Neumarker, K. (2003). Leo Kanner—his years in Berlin, 1906–1924: The roots of autistic disorder. *History of Psychiatry, 14,* 205–218.

Sanua, V. (1990). Leo Kanner (1894–1981): The man and the scientist. *Child Psychiatry and Human Development, 21*(fall), 3–23.

FURTHER INFORMATION

Kanner, L. (1946). Irrelevant and metaphorical language in early infantile autism. *American Journal of Psychiatry, 103,* 242–246.

CAROL L. PITCHLYN

KRUG'S ASPERGER'S DISORDER INDEX

Krug's Asperger's Disorder Index (KADI) is an assessment tool used to identify individuals with Asperger's disorder. The KADI enables professionals to correctly differentiate individuals with Asperger's disorder from individuals with other forms of high-functioning autism. It can be used as a prescreening scale to immediately determine individuals who do not have Asperger's disorder. The Krug's Asperger's Disorder Index can be administered on individuals ranging from 6 years of age to 22. Information associated with the KADI can be used to help assess a student's educational needs. Administration time ranges from 15 to 20 minutes (Pierangelo & Guiliani, 2006).

REFERENCE

Pierangelo, R., & Guiliani, C. A. (2006). *Assessment in special education: A practical approach.* Boston: Allyn & Bacon.

AMY BIXLER COFFIN

L

LACTOSE INTOLERANCE

Lactose intolerance is a gastrointestinal condition in which individuals are intolerant to milk and some dairy products. It may be present from birth or acquired later in life and varies in severity. It is a deficiency of lactase, an enzyme required to absorb lactose (a form of sugar found in milk) from the intestines. Treatment varies from avoidance of dairy products to use of digestive enzyme tablets.

BRUCE BASSITY

LANDAU-KLEFFNER SYNDROME

Landau-Kleffner syndrome (otherwise known as acquired epileptic aphasia) is a rare disorder involving the loss of language skills after a period of normal development, first described by Landau and Kleffner in 1957. The onset of loss usually occurs between the ages of 3 and 9 years, and is often associated with clear-cut seizures. The loss of language skills is usually gradual, occurring over the course of months, although there are cases where the loss is more rapid. First noted loss is in receptive language skills, with the child becoming increasingly unresponsive to spoken language. Hearing tests however are normal. The loss of receptive skills is followed by loss of expressive abilities. Three different types of presentation are reported: (a) acute loss of language, sometimes in association with encephalopathic illness and/or seizures, with usually good recovery; (b) long, slow deterioration of language, which may be unresponsive to antiepileptic drugs, and moderate or poor recovery; and (c) variable onset during which there may be several episodes of language fluctuation, which, if responsive to antiepileptic drugs, may lead to a good recovery (Lees & Neville, 1996).

Types of language difficulty in addition to verbal agnosia (inability to comprehend language) include word-finding difficulties, problems with written language, a range of neologisms and paraphasias, and deficit in prosody.

Children with Landau-Kleffner do not usually present with autism spectrum disorder (ASD), although ASD might be considered in some cases due to the similarity of some of the receptive and expressive language difficulties coupled with levels of frustration, behavior difficulties, and sometimes hyperactivity in these children. The differentiating criteria include the fact that this is an aphasia with EEG abnormalities typically underlying the loss of skills, and with deficits focusing on language. There are not usually impairments in social interaction of an autistic type, but as noted frustrations, and possibly also underlying neurological deficits, may lead to some social difficulties or behavior problems (e.g., Mantovani, 2000). Tests of general mental ability or cognitive functioning can also help to clarify the selective loss of language skills seen in Landau-Kleffner syndrome versus general loss of cognitive skills in other more progressive childhood dementias (Goodman & Scott, 2005, p. 203).

In terms of outcome, Bishop (1985) reviewed the literature and reported that the younger the age of onset the poorer the prognosis for the child. A long-term follow-up by Ripley and Lea (1984) demonstrated that while low language levels were the usual outcome, most of the group had found employment and were living independently as adults. Speech and language therapy programs, antiepileptic medications, and sometimes surgery are considered as possible treatment options (Vance, 1991; Lees & Neville, 1996; Cole et al., 1988).

REFERENCES

Bishop, D. (1985). Age of onset and outcome in acquired aphasia with convulsive disorder (Landau-Kleffner syndrome). *Developmental Medicine and Child Neurology, 27*, 705–707.

Cole, A. J., Andermann, F., Taylor, L., Olivier, A., Rasmussen, T., Robitaille, Y., et al. (1988). The Landau-Kleffner syndrome of acquired epileptic aphasia: Unusual clinical outcome, surgical experience and absence of encephalitis. *Neurology, 38*, 31–37.

Goodman, R., & Scott, S. (2005). *Child psychiatry* (2nd ed.). Oxford: Blackwell Publishing.

Landau, W. M., & Kleffner, F. (1957). Syndrome of acquired aphasia and convulsive disorder in children. *Neurology, 7*, 523–530.

Lees, J. A., & Neville, B. G. R., (1996). Fit for neurosurgery? *RCSLT Bulletin* (November 1996), 535, 10–11.

Mantovani, J. F. (2000). Autistic regression and Landau-Kleffner syndrome: Progress or confusion? *Developmental Medicine and Child Neurology, 42*, 349–353.

Ripley, K., & Lea, J. (1984). *Moorhouse school: A follow up study of receptive aphasic ex-pupils.* Hurst Green, Oxted, Surrey: Moorhouse School.

Vance, M. (1991). Educational and therapeutic approaches used with a child presenting with acquired aphasia with convulsive disorder (Landau-Kleffner syndrome). *Child Learning Teaching and Therapy, 7*, 41–60.

FIONA J. SCOTT

LEAKY GUT SYNDROME

Leaky gut syndrome, also referred to as intestinal permeability, is a medial condition affecting the lining of the intestines. In leaky gut syndrome openings develop between the cells of the intestine that allow in bacteria, toxins, and food. Common symptoms of leaky gut syndrome include chronic muscle or joint pain, blurred thinking, indigestion, gas, mood swings, nervousness, skin rashes, recurrent bladder or yeast infections, constipation, and anxiety.

KATHERINE E. COOK

LEARNED HELPLESSNESS

Learned helplessness was introduced in 1965 by Martin Seligman as the result of a series of experiments with dogs (Seligman, Maier, & Geer, 1968). Based on Pavlov's classical conditioning experiments, a bell was paired with an unpleasant stimulus, rather than food. It was expected the dog would move in order to avoid the unpleasant stimulus, however it did not move. The result was an understanding that individuals may reach a frame of mind in which they do not attempt independence or exert effort toward a task. The individual comes to feel that effort would be pointless as it always ends in failure, or that they are incapable of doing something on their own. The overall mindset is that of powerlessness. Learned helplessness is relevant to people with depression and disabilities, and to people coming from at-risk backgrounds.

REFERENCE

Seligman, M. E., Maier, S. F., & Geer, J. N. (1968). Alleviation of learned helplessness in the dog. *Journal of Abnormal Psychology. 73*, 256–262.

KATIE BASSITY

LEARNING DISORDER

Learning disorder is a term that can be used in a variety of ways for a variety of conditions or disabilities. Children and adults with learning disorders tend to have challenges with academic subjects, but may in fact have normal levels of overall intelligence. The term, therefore, is rather broad and nonspecific, and can be interpreted in a variety of ways. Learning disorder is defined legally as:

> Those children who have a disorder in one or more of the basic psychological processes involved in understanding or in using language, spoken or written, which disorder may manifest itself in an imperfect ability to listen, think, speak, write, spell or do math calculations. The term includes such conditions as perceptual handicaps, brain injury, minimal brain dysfunction, dyslexia, and developmental aphasia. (IDEA, 1975)

In contrast to Public Law 94-142, which includes only individuals with normal intelligence (IQ of 70 or higher), the *Diagnostic and Statistical Manual of Mental Disorders* (DSM-IV-TR; APA, 2000) allows for individuals with IQs below 70 and with uneven cognitive profiles, but excludes those whose learning problems are due to known neurological disorders. These differences demonstrate further how opaque usage of the term can be.

Currently, learning disorders in the DSM-IV-TR (APA, 2000) are reported to include reading disorder (dyslexia), spelling disorder, mathematics disorder (dyscalculia), disorder of written expression (dysgraphia), social-emotional learning disorder, and more recently, nonverbal learning disorder.

Reading disorders, or specific reading difficulties, are perhaps the most common of the aforementioned learning disorders, affecting 3 to 10 percent of children, with research indicating they are up to three times more common in males. Reading disorders are commonly associated with spelling difficulties (Goodman & Scott, 2005).

Many learning disorders overlap with other conditions such as autism spectrum disorders (ASD). Research suggests there may be an overrepresentation of dyscalculia in individuals with Asperger syndrome; dyslexia is also commonly seen in individuals with Asperger syndrome, although there is some debate as to whether this is above what may be seen in the general population (Gillberg, 2002). Individuals with ASD are often also reported to have poor handwriting skills, although this may reflect motor difficulties rather than a specific disorder such as dysgraphia (Beversdorf et al.,

2001). Nonverbal learning disorder is often confused with Asperger syndrome, and many researchers argue there is little difference between the two, with individuals with nonverbal learning disorder often also meeting criteria for Asperger syndrome or **pervasive developmental disorder-not otherwise specified** (PDD-NOS) (Dinklage, 2001). These overlaps can often add to the confusion in interpretation and application of the term learning disorder.

REFERENCES

American Psychiatric Association. (2000). *Diagnostic and statistical manual of mental disorders* (4th ed., text rev.). Washington, DC: Author.

Beversdorf, D. Q., Anderson, J. M., Manning, S. E., Anderson, S. L., Nordgren, R. E., Felopulos, G. J., et al. (2001). Brief Report: Macrographia in high-functioning adults with autism spectrum disorder. *Journal of Autism and Developmental Disorders, 31*, 97–100.

Dinklage, D. (2001). Asperger's disorder and nonverbal learning disabilities: How are these two disorders related to each other? Retrieved July 20, 2006, from www.nldontheweb.org/Dinklage_1.htm.

Gillberg, C. (2002). *A guide to Asperger syndrome*. Cambridge: Cambridge University Press.

Goodman, R., & Scott, S. (2005). *Child psychiatry* (2nd ed.). Oxford: Blackwell.

Individuals with Disabilities Education Act, Public Law No. 94-142 (1975).

FIONA J. SCOTT

LEARNING STYLES

A learning style refers to an individual's primary learning mode, which identifies instructional techniques most likely to enhance their learning. Learning styles most commonly recognized in the classroom include visual learners (learn best when information is presented in a visual format), auditory learners (learn best when information is presented in an auditory format), and kinesthetic/tactile learners (learn best when hands-on and movement experiences are incorporated in the lesson).

KATHERINE E. COOK

LEAST RESTRICTIVE ENVIRONMENT (LRE)

Children with autism spectrum disorders (ASD) represent a heterogeneous group requiring individualized and highly unique programs. Some approaches have been found to be more beneficial than others. According to Dunlap (1999), a critical key to success is to match specific practices, supports, and services with each student's unique profile and the individual family's characteristics. That is, "Educational personnel are required, through the **Individuals with Disabilities Education Act** (IDEA) Amendments of 1997, to provide a continuum of individualized supports, services, and placements to students, ranging from inclusion in general education with varying levels of supports to extremely specific services and instruction in specialized settings" (Iovannone, Dunlap, Huber, & Kincaid, 2003, p. 153).

Planning and placement teams (IEP teams) should consider general education classroom placement as the first option for children with disabilities. Other placement considerations should occur only when supplementary aids and services implemented in the general education setting have not yielded educational benefit for the student. Many children with autism are successfully included in general education classrooms and are learning with typical peers (Wagner, 1998). In particular, peers are often able to successfully model typical behavior in addition to assist with generalization of skills taught.

The IDEA (H.R. 1350 § 612 (a) (5)(A) of IDEA '04) requires school personnel to consider the least restrictive environment (LRE) for children with disabilities. This means that students, to the maximum extent appropriate, be educated with their non-disabled peers. Special classes, separate schooling, or other removal of children with disabilities from the general education environment occur only when the nature and severity of the disability are such that education in general education classes with the use of supplementary aids and services cannot be achieved satisfactorily.

However, for some students, the general education classroom is the least restrictive environment, while for others it may not afford an appropriate education. Thus, LRE is not always the general education classroom. Considerations for determining the least restrictive environment for an individual child, based on his or her unique characteristics, learning style, and needs, should include:

1. determining appropriate supports, accommodations and modifications to support the child's access to the general education curriculum;
2. collaborating with families to establish shared preferences for goals, methods, and placement settings (Iovannone et al., 2003);
3. embedding the child's special interests and preferences in the program methods (Hurth et al., 1999, cited in Iovannone et al., 2003); and
4. clearly identifying the child's strengths and weaknesses (student profile) to determine intensity of instructional level. (National Research Council, 2001, cited in Iovannone et al., 2003)

In brief, placement decisions should not be based on the student's disability, but on where the child's needs may be appropriately addressed. That is, having a diagnosis of autism should not automatically place the student in the school's or district's "autism class or program." No one program, support, or service is likely to meet the needs of all children identified with autism. Schools should provide flexible placement and support options to meet students' individual goals (Dunlap & Fox, 2002).

It is important to note that **inclusion**, **mainstreaming**, and LRE are not synonymous. Mainstreaming, a practice that originated in the 1970s, refers to students spending portions of their school day with typical peers. This is generally based on students having achieved the expected behavior and/or academic goals necessary to participate. Inclusion refers to a belief system that drives educational practice and is not merely an issue of a student's educational placement (McGregor & Vogelsberg, 1998). More recent thinking advocates an inclusive philosophy that entails the student having a sense of belonging to the education community versus inclusion being a place or a program (i.e., the inclusion room).

The bottom line throughout the mainstreaming movement has been that the student will adapt and be ready to participate in the general education classroom, and that the general education classroom will not change. In contrast to this perspective, the current inclusion movement assumes that major changes will occur in the general education classroom, ensuring that students with disabilities will "fit into" these classes. Thus, general education classroom curriculum, instructional practices, organization, and so forth are changed to better meet the needs of the students, rather than expecting students to adapt to the classroom. (McLeskey & Waldron, 2000, p. 14)

Successful inclusion in general education settings for children with autism requires careful planning and implementation of program components to address students' social and academics needs (Kamps, Barbetta, Leonard, & Delquardi, 1994). Responsible inclusive practice refers to ensuring and maximizing student success in general education classrooms by providing teachers support to meet students' needs. Such support may involve training, materials, and time to collaborate with colleagues. Responsible inclusive practice calls for educators and parents to reflect on the following questions:

> What are the educational benefits to the student in the general education classroom, with supplementary aids and services, compared with the educational benefits of a special education classroom? [or other placement options along the continuum]
> What will be the nonacademic or personal benefits to the student in interactions with nondisabled peers?
> What will be the effect on the teacher and other students in the general education classroom?
> How will the team define and measure the success of inclusion?
> (National Research Council, 2001, p. 179)

Responsible inclusive practice does not mean providing one-to-one instruction in the back of a general education classroom without meaningful interaction with nondisabled peers. This is often referred to as a *class-within-a-class*. Instead, students need opportunities for interaction with nondisabled peers through both informal and planned activities. Children with autism should receive instruction and support to maximize successful interaction with nondisabled peers (New York State Education Department, Office of Vocational and Educational Services for Individuals with Disabilities, 2001).

References

Dunlap, G. (1999). Consensus, engagement, and family involvement for young children with autism. *The Journal of the Association for Persons with Severe Handicaps, 24*, 222–225.

Dunlap, G., & Fox, L. (2002). The *challenge of autism from a large systems perspective*. Unpublished manuscript, University of South Florida, Tampa.

Individuals with Disabilities Education Act, Public Law No. 101–476 (1990).

Individuals with Disabilities Education Act, Public Law No. 108–446 (2004).

Iovannone, R., Dunlap, G. Huber, H., & Kincaid, D. (2003). Effective educational practices for students with autism spectrum disorders. *Focus on Autism and Other Developmental Disabilities, 18*, 3, 150–165.

Kamps, D., Barbetta, P., Leonard, B., & Delquadri, J. (1994). Classwide peer tutoring: An integration strategy to improve reading skills and promote interactions among students with autism and regular education peers. *Journal of Applied Behavior Analysis, 27*, 49–60.

McGregor, G., & Vogelsberg, T. R. (1998). *Inclusive schooling practices: Pedagogical and research foundations*. Baltimore: Brookes Publishing Co.

McLeskey, J., & Waldron, N. L. (2000). *Inclusive schools in action: Making differences ordinary*. Alexandria, VA: Association for Supervision and Curriculum Development.

National Research Council. (2001). *Educating children with autism*. Committee on Educational Interventions for Children with Autism. C. Lord & J. P. McGee (Eds.), Division of Behavioral and Social Sciences and Education. Washington, DC: National Academy Press.

New York State Education Department, Office of Vocational and Educational Services for Individuals with Disabilities. (2001). *Autism program quality indicators*. Albany, NY: Author.

Wagner, S. (1998). *Inclusive programming for elementary students with autism*. Arlington, TX: Future Horizons.

DAVID R. CORMIER

LEITER INTERNATIONAL PERFORMANCE SCALE

The Leiter International Performance Scale is a cognitive assessment tool designed to measure an individual's nonverbal intelligence. The original Leiter scale was developed by Russell in 1929; the latest version is the Leiter-Revised published in 1997 (Roid & Miller).

The Leiter-R includes two batteries, the visualization and reasoning battery (VR) and the attention and memory battery (AM), each consisting of 10 subtests. The subtests in the VR battery are as follows: figure ground, design analogies, form completion, matching, sequential order, repeated patterns, picture context, classification, paper folding, and figure rotation. Subtests in the AM battery include associated pairs, immediate recognition, forward memory, attention sustained, reverse memory, visual coding, spatial memory, delayed pairs, delayed recognition, and attention divided.

REFERENCE

Roid, G. H., & Miller, L. J. (1997). *Leiter International Performance Scale–Revised*. Wood Dale, IL: Stoelting.

HYO JUNG LEE

LIFE SKILLS AND EDUCATION FOR STUDENTS WITH AUTISM AND OTHER PERVASIVE BEHAVIORAL CHALLENGES (LEAP)

LEAP stands for Lifeskills and Education for Students with Autism and other Pervasive Behavioral Challenges. Administered by the Kennedy Krieger Institute in Baltimore, Maryland (Kennedy Krieger Institute, 2005), this 12-month, intensive early intervention special education program is designed to serve students 5–21 years old who are diagnosed with autism or related disorders.

The LEAP program, developed in 1984 by Hoyson, Jamieson, and Strain, combines several learning theories with a primary focus on social development. With an emphasis on building routines that facilitate learning, the LEAP program incorporates a practical life skills curriculum, into students' **individualized education programs** (IEP), including such strategies as **applied behavior analysis** (ABA), TEACCH (Treatment and Education of Autistic and Related Communications Handicapped Children), discrete trial, incidental learning, errorless teaching, **augmentative and alternative communication, picture exchange communication systems**, sensory diets, and vocational training along with other established approaches. Instead of adhering to a fixed curriculum, teachers collect data on the IEP objectives and use data to make modifications to the teaching plans, as necessary. The main goal is to develop a treatment that fits the individual variables in each student's life. With enough data, programs can be altered to provide the most efficient use of resources and time and be altered as the students' needs change during treatment. Lessons taught at school are also practiced at home with the help of family members. This not only reinforces the lessons but allows students to see how the information applies to their everyday lives. This realization helps them to learn social skills that will help them throughout life.

LEAP RELATING TO AUTISM

The underlying focus of the LEAP program is achieved through an inclusive classroom-based program that runs 3 hours daily, year round. Developmentally appropriate

213

practice and applied behavioral analysis techniques are employed, and typically developing peers are used in modeling and encouraging appropriate behavior. A major goal is to increase students' independence and help them develop functional communication, daily living, and vocational skills. The methods used to attain this goal are one-on-one and group instruction carried out in a highly structured environment. The structure is necessary to maximize efforts and to provide cohesiveness not only to the subject matter but also to the teaching methods used. Consistency and repetition are the keys to providing an environment that is conducive to learning.

Social interaction is fostered throughout the day in the classroom and on the playground. Nondisabled peers play a major role here by teaching students social skills and getting them to interact with others. Nondisabled students receive special training so they can help achieve a constant open environment for the students to practice initiating and responding to social conditions. It is this constant reinforcement that allows the child with autism to learn to fully participate in social interaction.

LEARNING OPPORTUNITIES IN SCHOOL

For younger children, LEAP's primary teaching method involves the discrete trial approach. With some children, errorless prompting is used.

Students spend much of their day engaged in drills, learning things like colors, numbers, animals, and parts of the body. The rest of the day includes music and art therapy, and theme group activities, with therapist-led group learning about a specific topic like cooking. Since children with autism prefer to work by themselves, the goal of a group activity is to teach them social skills so they are able to sit next to peers at a group table and wait for their turn to participate.

LEARNING OPPORTUNITIES OUTSIDE THE CLASSROOM

As the children progress, teachers use the same approach in natural environments. Thus, older students practice tasks in the real world. They go to stores and look for a certain item, go to the cash register, pay for it, and then get back into the van to return to school, thus learning how to accomplish tasks necessary for everyday life.

See also augmentative and alternative communication; discrete trial training; vocational rehabilitation.

REFERENCES

Hoyson, M., Jamieson, B., & Strain, P. (1984). Individualized group instruction of normally developing and autistic-like children: The LEAP curriculum model. *Journal of the Division for Early Childhood, 8,* 157–172.

Kennedy Krieger Institute. (2005). LEAP program (Lifeskills and Education for Students with Autism and other Pervasive Behavioral Challenges). Retrieved August 22, 2006, from http://www.kennedykrieger.org/kki_school.jsp?pid=1422&bl=1.

FURTHER INFORMATION

Dawson, G., & Osterling, J. (1997). Early intervention in autism. In M. J. Guralnick (Ed.), *The effectiveness of early intervention* (pp. 307–326). Baltimore: Brookes Publishing Co.

Educating Children with Autism. (2001). *Front matter executive summary* (pp. 168–169). Retrieved August 22, 2006, from http://newton.nap.edu/books/0309072697/html/168.html.

Erba, H. W. (2000). Early intervention programs for children with autism: Conceptual frameworks for implementation. *American Journal of Orthopsychiatry, 70*(1), 82–94.

The PDA Center at the University of Colorado at Denver (1998). (The Professional Development in Autism Center). Retrieved August 22, 2006, from http://depts.washington.edu/pdacent/sites/ucd.html.

Psychosocial Paediatrics Committee. Canadian Paediatric Society (CPS). (2004). Early intervention for children with autism. *Pediatrics & Child Health*, 9(4), 267–270. Retrieved August 22, 2006, from http://www.cps.ca/english/statements/PP/pp04-02.htm#Committee#Committee.

Schopler, E., Reichler, R. J., DeVellis, R. F., & Daly, K. (1988). *The Childhood Autism Rating Scale* (CARS). Los Angeles: Western Psychological Services.

Shaw, G. (2005). Autism in the classroom: What works. *Neurology Now*, 1(3), 32–33. Retrieved August 22, 2006), from http://www.neurologynow.com.

Strain, P. S. (1987). Comprehensive evaluation of young autistic children. *Topics in Early Children Special Education*, 7, 97–110.

Strain, P. S., & Hoyson, M. (2000). On the need for longitudinal, intensive social skill intervention: LEAP follow-up outcomes for children with autism as a case-in-point. *Topics in Early Children Special Education*, 20, 116–122.

JOUNG MIN KIM

LIFE SKILLS SUPPORT

Life skills support refers to an educational or vocational support program or setting targeting the **psychosocial** and interpersonal skills that assist individuals in the process of making informed decisions, communicating effectively, and developing coping and self-management skills. Life skills supports often provide instruction in personal hygiene, functional academics, culinary skills, and social competence in order to help individuals lead a healthy and productive life.

JEANNE HOLVERSTOTT

LIMBIC SYSTEM

The limbic system is a set of brain structures (the list varies with the source consulted), which includes the **amygdala**, **hippocampus**, hypothalamus, and several other nearby structures. The limbic system is mainly involved in emotions and formation of memories. It also influences the autonomic nervous system (involuntary body functions) and endocrine system (hormone secretion).

BRUCE BASSITY

LINDAMOOD-BELL

The Lindamood-Bell learning process was cofounded by Pat Lindamood and Nanci Bell. It is headquartered in San Luis Obispo, California and has 39 learning centers in the United States and one in London.

Lindamood-Bell conducts diagnostic evaluations on students, designs lessons, schedules instruction, and sets up learning environments (Lindamood & Bell, 2005). Based on the students' needs, they use an interactive, balanced approach entailing Socratic questioning and clinical teaching, and provide follow-up services to continue processing and development in everyday life.

Lindamood-Bell School Services provides workshops for teachers, onsite consulting, and professional support in the areas of sensory cognitive programs, professional development, learning environments, leadership, and accountability.

REFERENCE

Lindamood, P., & Bell, N. (2005). Lindamood-Bell learning process. Online Resource: http://www.lblp.com.

JOUNG MIN KIM

LOCAL EDUCATION AGENCY

A Local Education Agency (LEA) ensures that school personnel are trained and qualified to provide educational services for students with special needs at the local public school district level.

KATHERINE E. COOK

LOCOMOTION

Locomotion refers to the ability to walk or move in a forward motion.

KELLY M. PRESTIA

LOSS AND LEARNING THEORY. *See* Good Grief!

LOW/POOR REGISTRATION

Low registration is a neurological characteristic of individuals who have a high sensory threshold, or tolerance, that must be met for typical stimuli to produce a response. Individuals with low registration often appear lethargic and inattentive and may require intense sensory stimulation to gain their attention or engage them in activities.

See also sensory stimuli.

KELLY M. PRESTIA

MAGNETIC RESONANCE IMAGING (MRI)

Magnetic resonance imaging (MRI) is a technology used to create detailed images of the insides of humans or other organisms. MRI use is extremely expensive but is generally a noninvasive procedure with few known side effects. An MRI can take 2-D images or 3-D models, and the outcome is of high quality. In the field of autism, MRI has been used extensively over the last decade to make images of the brain. This includes pictures of the brain to chart seizure damage, brain structure and anatomy, brain volume, amount of gray and white matter, and other structures.

FURTHER INFORMATION
Bremner, J. D. (2005). *Brain imaging handbook*. New York: W. W. Norton & Co.
Radiological Society of North America, Inc. (2006). *MR Imaging (MRI Body*. Retrieved June 5, 2006, from http://www.radiologyinfo.org/content/mr_of_the_body.htm.

PAUL G. LaCAVA

MAINSTREAMING

Mainstreaming is a term that is used when considering placement of a student with an autism spectrum disorder (ASD) in a general education classroom (Zionts, 1997). It has been used interchangeably with the term **inclusion**; however, mainstreaming and inclusion are two different approaches to serving students with disabilities. Usually, when an IEP team considers mainstreaming, it is assumed that the student is able to show progress with the nondisabled peers in the regular educational setting. These students have the appropriate skills to progress using the same curriculum, usually with some adaptations or modifications.

The term mainstreaming was used in the late 1970s and early 1980s after the **Individuals with Disabilities Education Act** (IDEA) was passed into law. During this time, mainstreaming was implemented by including students with disabilities in nonacademic portions of the curriculum, such as music, art, and physical education, while continuing academic instruction in self-contained classrooms, limiting the time with nondisabled peers.

Educators and parents did not approve of the act of mainstreaming, creating the Regular Education Initiative (REI). REI had three major goals, which included sharing responsibility of students with special needs, including students with special needs into regular education classrooms full time, and increasing the achievement of students with mild disabilities (Fuchs & Fuchs, 1994). This debate between special educators and general education leaders resulted in a new term, inclusion. Inclusion became the model for serving students with disabilities in school settings.

Now, mainstreaming is considered as placing a student with a disability in a classroom with the expectation that the student is able to keep pace or make progress in the general education classroom. Mainstreaming has definite benefits. The student with an ASD would benefit from being around appropriate social and behavioral role models. It is important to evaluate if being mainstreamed in the regular education classroom is the **least restrictive environment** (LRE) for the student. If a student with ASD is mainstreamed in the regular education classroom, it is important for the regular classroom teacher and special education teacher to consult regularly on how to help create the most successful environment possible. Mainstreaming does not have to be the entire school day; the IEP can be selective and choose times that the student is able to participate and show progress the same as other nondisabled peers. This may be during different academic times of the day, physical education, music, or any other time of the day.

REFERENCES

Fuchs, D., & Fuchs, L. S. (1994). Inclusive school movement and the radicalization of special education reform. *Exceptional Children, 60*(4), 294–305.

Zionts, Paul. (Ed.). (1997). *Inclusion strategies for students with learning and behavioral problems: Perspectives, experiences, and best practices.* Austin, TX: Pro-Ed.

MELISSA L. TRAUTMAN

MAINTENANCE

Maintenance, also known as generalization across time, refers to an individual's ability to use a skill at an acceptable rate for a specific amount of time following the termination of part or all of a systematic instructional procedure or intervention. For a skill to be maintained, it should be durable and resistant to extinction. For example, if a student learned to write numbers 1–10, staff should intermittently perform maintenance checks to assess the skill and to ensure that the student can perform the skill at the same proficiency.

FURTHER INFORMATION

Alberto, P. A., & Troutman, A. C. (2006). *Applied behavior analysis for teachers* (7th ed). Upper Saddle River, NJ: Prentice Hall.

Cooper, J. O., Heron, T. E., & Heward, W. L. (1987). *Applied behavior analysis.* Upper Saddle River, NJ: Prentice Hall.

Heflin, J. L., & Alaimo, D. F. (2007). *Students with autism spectrum disorders: Effective instructional practices.* Upper Saddle River, NJ: Prentice Hall.

Scheuermann, B., & Webber, J. (2002). *Autism: Teaching does make a difference.* Belmont, CA: Wadsworth/Thomson Learning.

Westling, D. L., & Fox, L. (2004). *Teaching students with severe disabilities* (3rd ed.). Upper Saddle River, NJ: Prentice Hall.

THERESA L. EARLES-VOLLRATH

MALADAPTIVE BEHAVIOR

Maladaptive behavior refers to undesirable, deviant, or negative behaviors displayed over a period of time to meet a want or need in place of a more socially appropriate behavior.

KATHERINE E. COOK

MAND

A mand is a request. The term mand was created and introduced by B. F. Skinner in his 1957 book, *Verbal Behavior*. In it Skinner defines a mand as something that names its **reinforcer** and is brought about by deprivation or aversion. For example, when a child wants juice he says "juice" and is given juice. "Juice" is a mand. As long as manding is reinforced, the response is giving the child what he asks for; manding tends to increase over time, therefore increasing language. As may be anticipated, manding is typically the first step in the development of functional language.

REFERENCE

Skinner, B. F. 1957. *Verbal behavior*. New York: Appleton-Century-Crofts.

KATIE BASSITY

MASSED PRACTICE

Also referred to as mass trials in some forms of discrete trial programming, massed practice is repeated trials of one task or skill. In massed practice, a student is required to demonstrate a particular skill for many consecutive repetitions. Massed practice is generally one of the first steps in learning a new task or skill within more structured forms of applied behavior analysis, such as **discrete trial training** instruction.

KATIE BASSITY

MASTURBATION

Like their neurotypical counterparts, most people with autism spectrum disorders (ASD) develop an interest in intimacy, relationships, and sexuality (Lawson, 2005; Shore, 2003). One natural means for satisfying some of this interest could be masturbation or exploration of our own bodies for sexual gratification (Realmuto & Ruble, 1999). Masturbation is reported in several studies to be a common occurrence among children, adolescents, and adults with ASDs (Koller, 2000; Haracopos & Pederson, 1999; Realmuto & Ruble, 1999; and Reichle & Palmer, 1997).

While there is little written material specifically addressing the subject of sexuality issues and ASDs, most experts agree that teaching necessary information in a proactive and factual manner is the most responsible route for parents, caregivers, or professionals to assume (Shore & Rastelli, 2006). Blum and Blum (1981) cited in Hinsburger (1995) suggest the following learning objectives when teaching the topic of masturbation:

- Masturbation is NORMAL and HEALTHY. Myths about the effects of masturbation can be very destructive (Grandma's story about going blind is nonsense!). Feelings of shame, guilt, immorality, and fear can interfere with masturbation in such a way that leads to obsessions, anxiety, and inappropriate public behaviors.
- There are appropriate times and places to engage in masturbation. Discussion about private versus public behavior becomes very important at this point because public masturbation

is illegal in most places and one of the most frequently noted inappropriate behaviors in the autistic population (Helleman and Deboutte, 2002). Since nonverbal communication, perspective taking, and sensory deficits are all well-documented challenges for individuals with ASD, comprehensive educational programming should include very clear and open discussion of ways to help compensate for these challenges that lead to successful social or sexual experiences.

- Learning what kind of stimulation leads to pleasure goes back to the sensual nature of sexual stimulation. Because many individuals with autism have sensory processing deficits, programming should include awareness of the physiological nature of sensory issues and compensatory strategies for whatever tactile sensitivities may exist.

With some effort, parents and professionals can find books and curricula that will help them initiate and support appropriate education regarding sexuality issues for individuals with ASD, just like they would for any other person. It is not unreasonable to suggest that the person providing the instruction should allow themselves the opportunity to examine their own social bias and values prior to taking on such a responsibility in order to avoid the potential for inadvertent subjective or judgmental messages during instruction. There is no denying that sexuality along with drug or alcohol abuse and many other culturally defined issues can make for very awkward conversations that promote myths and misinformation. As with any other population, a genuine understanding of the issues that influence social success can provide caregivers and professionals with some of the best tools for supporting healthy development.

REFERENCES

Haracopos, D., & Pederson, L. (1999). *The Danish report*. Kettering: Autism Independent UK.

Helleman, H., & Deboutte, D. (2002). *Autism spectrum disorders and sexuality*. Paper presented at the Melbourne World Autism Congress.

Hinsburger, D. (1995). *Hand made love: A guide for teaching male masturbation through understanding and video*. New Market: Diverse City Press.

Koller, R. (2000). Sexuality and adolescents with autism. *Sexuality and Disability, 18*(2), 125–135.

Lawson, W. (2005). *Sex, sexuality and the autism spectrum*. London: Jessica Kingsley Publishers.

Realmuto, G. M., & Ruble, L. A. (1999). Sexual behaviors in autism: Problems of definition and management. *Journal of Autism and Other Developmental Disabilities, 29*(2), 121–127.

Reichle, N. C., & Palmer, A. (1997). Sexual behavior in adults with autism. *Journal of Autism and Other Developmental Disabilities, 27*(2) 113–125.

Shore, S. (2003). *Beyond the wall: Personal perspectives with autism and Asperger syndrome*. Shawnee Mission, KS: Autism Asperger Publishing Company.

Shore, S., & Rastelli, L. (2006). *Understanding autism for dummies*. Indianapolis, IN: Wiley Publishing, Inc.

FURTHER INFORMATION

Henault, I. (2006). *Asperger's syndrome and sexuality*. London: Jessica Kingsley Publishers.

Kempton, W. (1993). *Socialization and sexuality: A comprehensive guide*. Santa Barbara, CA: James Stanfield Company.

Diverse City Press at www.diverse-city.com.

SHERRY MOYER

MEAN LENGTH OF UTTERANCE

Mean Length of Utterance (MLU) is one tool used to calculate the linguistic activity or proficiency of young children's spoken language. To calculate the mean length of utterance of a child, you add up the total number of words spoken by the child and divided by the number of morphemes within the spoken words. A *morpheme* is defined as the smallest unit of meaning within a word. For example, "I see plane" would have a MLU of (3).

KATHERINE E. COOK

MEDIATION

Mediation is a process that helps resolve disputes between two parties. According to the **Individuals with Disabilities Education Act** (2004), all school districts are required to make special education mediation available to parents of children with disabilities. Special education mediation is designed to be a cooperative discussion where both parties can reach an agreement. A mediator is used to facilitate this process; once an agreement is met, the written agreement is binding.

REFERENCE

Individuals with Disabilities Education Improvement Act of 2004. Public Law No. 109-446, § 20 U.S.C. et seq.

FURTHER INFORMATION

Vocational and Education Services for Individuals with Disabilities. (n.d.). *Special education mediation*. Retrieved December 13, 2006, from www.vesid.nysed.gov/specialed/mediation.htm.

TERRI COOPER SWANSON

MENTAL AGE

Mental age (MA) is the level of intellectual development as measured by intelligence tests. MA is expressed as the age at which that level of development is typically attained. For example, when a child is described as having a MA of 12, he is able to solve the same test problems as average 12-year-old children.

THERESA L. EARLES-VOLLRATH

MENTAL HEALTH COUNSELOR

A mental health counselor is a licensed counselor that helps individuals, couples, and families discuss their problems for the purpose of resolving interpersonal and intrapersonal conflicts. Mental health counselors often counsel parents and siblings of autistic children and typically work closely with other professionals such as **psychologists** and **psychiatrists**.

STEVE CHAMBERLAIN

MENTAL RETARDATION

Mental retardation is a broad term used to describe someone who has limits in their cognitive or thinking skills as well as difficulties with adaptive skills such as communication, self-help, social skills, and academics. This disability originates before the age of 18 (American Association on Mental Retardation, 2002). In order to receive a diagnosis of mental retardation, an individual must score significantly below average on an intelligence test, as well as exhibit limited functioning in the previously listed areas. The average score on an **intelligence test** (IQ test) is 100. People scoring below a 70 are said to have mental retardation.

The **Individuals with Disabilities Education Act** of 2004 (IDEA) defines mental retardation as "significantly subaverage general intellectual functioning, existing concurrently with deficits in adaptive behavior and manifested during the developmental period, that adversely affects a child's educational performance" (Federal Register, 1999).

Individuals with mental retardation develop and learn but at a much slower rate than typically developing peers. The degree to which mental retardation affects a person ranges from profound, severe, or moderate, to mild.

Mental retardation is the most common developmental disorder. The Centers for Disease Control and Prevention (CDC) found in 1993 that 1.5 million children and adults in the United States had mental retardation (Mental Retardation, 2005). The highest rate of mental retardation was found in West Virginia, while the lowest rate was found in Alaska.

The causes of mental retardation are extremely varied. The condition can be caused by disease, injury, or neurological abnormality. Some of the most common causes are Down syndrome, fetal alcohol syndrome (FAS), and **fragile X syndrome**. Diseases such as cytomegalovirus and measles may also cause mental illness. In addition, lead exposure and lack of prenatal care may lead to mental retardation. Additional causes may involve asphyxia, head injury, stroke, metabolic conditions (phenylketonuria), or hydrocephalus.

Most diseases or events that cause mental retardation cannot be prevented. However, some, such as fetal alcohol syndrome, can be prevented if no alcohol is ingested while a mother is pregnant. Additionally, prompt treatment for jaundice can prevent a specific type of brain damage that can occur if the bilirubin is allowed to reach too high of a level. Metabolic conditions may be able to be identified after birth through blood tests. Once identified, these babies are treated with medications and/or special diets.

Several organizations exist to support families and individuals with mental retardation. Some of the bigger ones are The Arc of the United States, The American Association on Mental Retardation, and the Division on Developmental Disabilities.

See also adaptive behavior.

REFERENCES

American Association on Mental Retardation. (2002). *Mental retardation: Definition, classification, and systems of supports* (10th ed.). Washington, DC: Author.

Federal Register Department of Education Assistance to States for the Education of Children with Disabilities and the Early Intervention Program for Infants and Toddlers with Disabilities; Final Regulations. 34 CFR Parts 300 and 303. Vol. 64, No. 48. Friday, March 12, 1999.

Mental Retardation (October 29, 2005). Developmental Disabilities. Retrieved October 30, 2006, from http://www.cdc.gov/ncbddd/dd/mr3.htm.

LYNN DUDEK

MERCURY

Mercury is an element that has been historically used in a number of ways including in chemical production, thermometers, dental fillings, and electronics. Mercury and its many forms can become very toxic to humans and other animals. Research has lead to the phasing out of mercury thermometers as well as increased emphasis on environmental safety. From the 1990s to the publication of this volume, increased research was conducted to explore the effects of ethyl mercury contained in the vaccine preservative thimerosal for a possible connection to an increase in the prevalence of autism. At this writing, although no conclusive evidence has been revealed that shows causality between thimerosal and increased autism rates, the controversy has not been settled.

See also vaccinations (thimerosal).

FURTHER INFORMATION

Centers for Disease Control and Prevention. (2004). *FAQs about MMR vaccine and autism.* Retrieved March 30, 2005, from http://www.cdc.gov/nip/vacsafe/ concerns/autism/autism-mmr. htm.

Kirby, D. (2005). *Evidence of harm: Mercury in vaccines and the autism epidemic: A medical controversy.* New York: St. Martin's Press.

National Broadcasting Company. (Executive Producer). (February 23, 2005). *The Today Show* [Television Broadcast]. New York: National Broadcasting Company.

PAUL G. LaCAVA

METALLOTHIONEIN

Metallothioneins (MTs) are proteins that participate in the uptake, transport, and regulation of zinc in a biological system. By binding and releasing zinc, metallothioneins regulate its level within the body. Metallothionein also carries zinc ions (as signals) from one part of the cell to another. When zinc enters a cell, it can be picked up by thionein (becoming *metallothionein*) and carried to another part of the cell where it is released to another organelle or protein. This system is particularly important in the brain, where zinc signaling is prominent both between and within nerve cells. In a 2001 presentation to the American Psychiatric Association, Dr. William J. Walsh of the Pfeiffer Treatment Center suggested a potential link between metallothionein disorders and autism. He concluded that "Many classic symptoms of autism may be explained by a MT defect in infancy including [gastrointestinal] tract problems, heightened sensitivity to toxic metals, and abnormal behaviors. These data suggest that an inborn error of MT functioning may be a fundamental cause of autism" (Walsh and Tarpey, 2001).

REFERENCE

Walsh, W. J., & Tarpey, J. (May 2001). *Disordered metal metabolism in a large autism population.* Presented at the American Psychiatric Association annual meeting, New Orleans.

JEANNE HOLVERSTOTT

MILIEU TEACHING

Milieu teaching is a naturalistic approach to teaching language in a child's environment (Goldstein, 2002). Many studies have shown that milieu teaching is the effective way to teach language, especially for children with autism spectrum disorders (Goldstein, 2002; Hancock & Kaiser, 2002; Koegel, Koegel, & Surratt, 1992; Koegel, O'Dell, & Dunlap, 1988). According to Paul and Sutherland (2005), milieu teaching includes the following components: (a) teaching and training occur in the child's everyday environment rather than in a "therapy room"; (b) activities take place as part of the daily routine rather than only at "therapy time"; (c) preferred toys and activities are included in the environment so that participation in activities is self-reinforcing; (d) adults encourage spontaneous communication by refraining from prompting and using "expectant waiting" such as facial expression or eye gaze; (e) the child initiates the teaching situation by gesturing or indicating interest in a desired object or activity; (f) teachers provide prompts and cues for expanding the child's initiation; and (g) expanded child responses are rewarded with access to a desired object or activity.

Incidental teaching is one of the most common types of milieu teaching. Teachers can plan expected learning for children based on their interests or desires. For instance, if the child always wants to have a specific toy in the playroom, the teacher can place the toy in sight but out of reach in the playroom. The teacher then waits for the child to initiate his need to have the toy. The teacher may gaze at the child or use facial expressions to prompt the child's initiation to get the toy. If the child does not initiate, the teacher may ask the child what he or she wants. If the child produces the target initiation, the teacher meets the child's need. By carefully arranging the environment, teachers can promote child engagement with activities and communication (Ostrosky & Kaiser, 1991). Teachers and parents can use "teachable moments" in the daily routine as well as in planned situations.

The **mand** model also uses natural situations based on the child's desire. For example, when the teacher observes the child's interest, the teacher utters a request such as "What is this?" or "Do you want this?" If the child shows the target response, the teacher gives him the preferred object and allows him to play with it for a certain time.

Time delay or prompt-free approaches are also examples of milieu teaching methods (Goldstein, 2002; Paul & Sutherland, 2005). Using time delay, adults wait for a certain length of time for the child to respond appropriately. With a prompt-free approach, if the child reaches or touches the provided pictures or objects without being prompted, she gets the target object.

Even though milieu teaching is generally used to teach requesting, because of the high motivation inherent in requesting desired items that presumably function as **reinforcers** (Goldstein, 2002), it can also be a helpful way to maintain and generalize new behaviors in the child's natural environment.

REFERENCES

Goldstein, H. (2002). Communication intervention for children with autism: A review of treatment efficacy. *Journal of Autism and Developmental Disorders, 32*, 373–396.

Hancock, T., & Kaiser, A. P. (2002). The effects of trainer-implemented enhanced milieu teaching on the social communication of children with autism. *Topics in Early Childhood Special Education, 22*, 39–54.

Koegel, R. L., Koegel, L. K., & Surratt, A. (1992). Language intervention and disruptive behavior in preschool children with autism. *Journal of Autism and Developmental Disorders, 22*, 141–153.

Koegel, R. L., O'Dell, M. C., & Dunlap, G. (1988). Producing speech use in nonverbal autistic children by reinforcing attempts. *Journal of Autism and Developmental Disorders, 18*, 525–538.

Ostrosky, M. M., & Kaiser, A. P. (1991). Preschool classroom environments that promote communication. *Teaching Exceptional Children, 23*, 6–10.

Paul, R., & Sutherland, D. (2005). Enhancing early language in children with autism spectrum disorders. In F. R. Volkmar, R. Paul, A. Klin, & D. Cohen (Eds.), *Handbook of autism and pervasive developmental disorders* (pp. 946–976). Hoboken, NJ: John Wiley & Sons, Inc.

HYO JUNG LEE

MINDBLINDNESS

Mindblindness refers to an inability to read or be aware of others' minds. Baron-Cohen developed the term in order to describe a major characteristic of autism (1990). Understanding others' minds is one of the key factors in social interaction because most people use nonverbal information such as gestures, facial expression, or voice tone to understand social situations. Mindblindness is a common characteristic of individuals with autism spectrum disorders.

REFERENCE

Baron-Cohen, S. (1990). Autism: A specific cognitive disorder of "mind-blindness." *International Review of Psychiatry, 2,* 79–88.

HYO JUNG LEE

MODIFIED CHECKLIST FOR AUTISM IN TODDLERS (M-CHAT)

The M-CHAT (Robins, Fein, Barton, & Green, 2001) is an American modified version of the original UK CHAT. The M-CHAT is a 23-item parent-report checklist (yes/no responses) designed to screen children ages 16 to 30 months old for possible autism. Research identified six critical items, and children failing any three total items or any two of the six critical items are recommended to undergo further investigation. Sensitivity of the M-CHAT is reported to be good, based on children being diagnosed after age 2 years with autism who had failed the M-CHAT screen. Researchers suggest that rescreening after the initial M-CHAT with a second M-CHAT can help rule out those who have developed skills after the original screen.

REFERENCE

Robins, D. L., Fein, D., Barton, M. L., & Green, J. A. (2001). The Modified Checklist for Autism in Toddlers: An initial study investigating the early detection of autism and pervasive developmental disorders. *Journal of Autism and Developmental Disorders, 31,* 131–144.

FIONA J. SCOTT

MOOD DISORDERS

Every year 44 million people are afflicted with mental illness (United States Department of Health and Human Services–Substance Abuse and Mental Health Administration [USDHH-SAMHA], 2006). Mood disorders are common mental illnesses, and according to the **Diagnostic and Statistical Manual of Mental Disorders** (DSM-IV-TR; APA, 2000), they are divided into four categories: (a) depressive disorders, (b) bipolar disorders, (c) mood disorders due to a general medical condition, and (d) substance-induced mood disorders (APA, 2000). Depressive disorders and bipolar disorders are the most common types of **mood disorders** (USDHH-SAMHA, 2006).

According to the APA (2000), there are three types of depressive disorders: (a) major depressive disorder, (b) dysthymic disorder, and (c) depressive disorder not otherwise specified. The four types of bipolar disorders include: (a) bipolar I disorder, (b) bipolar II disorder, (c) cyclothymic disorder, and (d) bipolar disorder not otherwise specified (APA, 2000). Mood disorders due to a general medical condition are characterized challenges with depression due to physiological difficulties due to a general medical condition. Substance-induced mood disorders are characterized by drug abuse or exposure to a toxin.

Mood disorders can be treated, and individuals affected by them can lead productive lives. Types of treatment may include medication and psychotherapies. Treatment may be short- or long-term depending upon the type of mood disorder and the length of time it has occurred.

For additional information on the specific diagnostic features of mood disorders, see the *Diagnostic and Statistical Manual of Mental Disorders* (APA, 2000).

REFERENCES

American Psychiatric Association. (2000). *Diagnostic and statistical manual of mental disorders* (4th ed., text rev.). Washington, DC: Author.

United States Department of Health and Human Services–Substance Abuse and Mental Health Administration. (2006). *Mood disorders*. Retrieved December 1, 2006, from http://mental-health.samhsa.gov/publications/allpubs/ken98-0049/default.asp.

TERRI COOPER SWANSON

MOOD STABILIZING MEDICATIONS

Mood stabilizing medications are used to control extreme behaviors, mood swings, depression, and mania, which cause disruption in functioning. Various types of medications are used such as antidepressants, some antipsychotics, and anticonvulsants such as valproic acid (Depakote), carbamazepine (Tegretol), and lithium.

See also antidepressant medications; antipsychotic medications.

BRUCE BASSITY

MOTIVATION ASSESSMENT SCALE

The Motivation Assessment Scale (MAS; Durand & Crimmins, 1988) is an indirect assessment designed to assess the function of a challenging behavior. Family members, teachers, case managers, or others with knowledge of the challenging behavior answer the 16 questions on the MAS by assessing frequency from 0 (never) to 6 (always) and are directly correlated to one of four behavioral functions: self-stimulation, escape/avoidance, attention, and tangible. The MAS should be used with other tools to determine the function of and a replacement behavior(s) for a challenging behavior.

REFERENCE

Durand, V. M., & Crimmins, D. B. (1988). Identifying the variables maintaining self-injurious behavior. *Journal of Autism and Developmental Disorders, 18*, 99–117.

JEANNE HOLVERSTOTT

MOTOR IMITATION

Motor imitation is the ability to replicate a motor movement or group of movements from a model or demonstration.

KELLY M. PRESTIA

MULTIDIMENSIONAL ANXIETY SCALE FOR CHILDREN (MASC)

The Multidimensional Anxiety Scale for Children (MASC; Pierangelo & Giuliani, 2006) is a diagnostic tool, which assesses the key features of anxiety problems in children and adolescents, ages 8 to 19. It consists of 39 items disseminated across four basic scales: Physical Symptoms, Harm Avoidance, Social Anxiety, and Separation/Panic. Subscales include Somatic Symptoms and Tense Symptoms, Perfectionism and Anxious Coping, and Humiliation Fears and Performance Fears. The MASC is commonly used in schools, outpatient clinics, residential treatment centers, juvenile detention centers, child protective services, and private practices.

REFERENCE

Pierangelo, R., & Giuliani, G. (2006). *The special educator's comprehensive guide to 301 diagnostic tests*. New York: Wiley.

AMY BIXLER COFFIN

MULTIDISCIPLINARY EVALUATION (MDE)

A multidisciplinary evaluation (MDE) is a comprehensive evaluation conducted by a **multidisciplinary team** (MDT) consisting of professionals from various disciplines such as special education, speech-language pathology, **occupational therapy, physical therapy**, and school health services. The purpose of the MDE is to determine eligibility for special education, establish current levels of performance, and assist in developing appropriate programming.

See also speech-language pathologist.

THERESA L. EARLES-VOLLRATH

MULTIDISCIPLINARY TEAM

When providing services to students with disabilities, professionals from different disciplines (i.e., **occupational therapy, speech therapy**, special education, general education) that generally work independently of each other work together during assessment, program planning, and implementation.

KATHERINE E. COOK

MUSIC THERAPY

The American Music Therapy Association (AMTA) defines music therapy as "the clinical and evidence-based use of music interventions to accomplish individualized goals within a therapeutic relationship by a credentialed professional who has completed an approved music therapy program" (2006). Music therapy may take place in a variety of settings including homes, community programs, or schools, and is considered a related service under the **Individuals with Disabilities Education Act** (2004).

The nonthreatening environment afforded by the music therapy session often enables individuals and often results in improved outcomes. Academic skills can be addressed through structured music drills for math facts, letter identification, and more. Reading comprehension can be addressed over time with musically assisted attention development and the expansion necessary for making inferences in reading, writing, and day-to-day living.

When designing interventions, music therapists consult with other professionals to determine and construct a treatment plan that will serve the individual's needs in a proactive manner. For example, is a school setting they will be part of the child's **Individualized Education Program** (IEP) team, and that team will determine and construct the treatment plan together.

When working with individuals with autism, a *music therapist* may do some of the following activities.

Communication

When working to increase and build communication, a music therapist may use familiar songs or repetitive melodies with original lyrics. Utilizing intermittent breaks in the lyrics while keeping the rhythm steady provides opportunities for the individual to predict and often produce a response. The music therapist extends these activities to expand vocabulary for use in receptive and expressive language, as well as developing language use in a social context.

Socialization

When working to develop, increase, and/or improve socialization, a music therapist may utilize rhythm to provide structure and melody to organize information by setting Social Stories or social scripts to music. The music may be original or familiar depending on the individual's needs. The music therapist may construct peer groups to practice socialization in a true social context while using instrument play. Structured and unstructured instrument play allows the music therapist to embed opportunities for turn taking, verbal and nonverbal communication of needs and wants, attention, awareness of others and self, as well as an opportunity to be successful.

Behaviors

When working to address specific behaviors, the music therapist will begin by working with the individual's team to identify the function of the behavior. In the event that the function is communication, necessary vocabulary and concepts can be taught through the use of repetitive melodies and lyrics paired with visuals if necessary and rehearsal and reinforcement across contexts. An example of this might be a student's inability to understand the concept of "wait" or "don't interrupt." The music therapist can compose a simple and repetitive song paired with actions that aid the individual to learn the basic behaviors of "waiting" that function across settings such as keeping hands in lap and/or lips together with the voice turned off. In this example we also introduce the concept of time over space. Music exists naturally over time and space and serves as an excellent medium for experiencing and teaching such an abstract concept as "wait."

Other behaviors are the function of situational problem solving. Musically adapted Social Stories and social scripts are one way to address preparing individuals for transitions, changes in schedule, asking for help, and asking a peer to play. Playing instruments that require two or more pieces to produce a sound are also used to rehearse problem solving skills.

Sensory Needs

Sensory needs can also be addressed through music therapy. Music therapists may provide a variety of interventions suited to the individual that may range from psychoacoustical therapies (special training required) to scheduled music listening times.

The music therapist is held to national Standards of Practice (AMTA, 2006) for assessment, treatment planning, documentation, evaluation, and termination. No standardized music therapy assessment currently exists for individuals with autism. Models of treatment and documentation vary based on the professional training of the music therapist, the setting the music therapist is working in, and the individual needs of the client.

References

American Music Therapy Association (2006). *Autism spectrum disorders: Music therapy research and evidence based practice support.* Retrieved November 20, 2006, from www.musictherapy. org/factsheets/MT%20Autism%202006.pdf.

Individuals with Disabilities Education Improvement Act of 2004. Public Law No. 109-446, § 20 U.S.C. (2004).

FURTHER INFORMATION

American Music Therapy Association: www.musictherapy.org.

Kaplan, R. S., & Steele, A. L. (2005). An analysis of music therapy program goals and outcomes for clients with diagnoses on the autism spectrum. *Journal of Music Therapy, 42*(1), 2–19.

Kielinen, M., Linna, S. L., & Moilanen, I. (2002). Some aspects of treatment and habilitation of children and adolescents with autistic disorder in Northern-Finland. *International Journal of Circumpolar Health, 61*(Suppl. 2), 69–79.

Thaut, M. H. (2005). *Rhythm, music, and the brain: Scientific foundations and clinical applications.* New York: Taylor and Francis Group, LLC.

Whipple, J. (2004). Music in intervention for children and adolescents with autism: A meta-analysis. *Journal of Music Therapy, 41*(2), 90–106.

MELANIE D. HARMS

MUTUALLY ACCEPTABLE WRITTEN AGREEMENT

A mutually acceptable written agreement is a binding document that is the result of **mediation**.

FURTHER INFORMATION

Vocational and Education Services for Individuals with Disabilities. (n.d.). *Special education mediation.* Retrieved December 13, 2006, from www.vesid.nysed.gov/specialed/mediation.htm.

TERRI COOPER SWANSON

N

NATURAL LANGUAGE PARADIGM

The natural language paradigm (NLP) is an intervention procedure that approximates the manner in which typically developing children acquire language (Koegel, O'Dell, & Koegel, 1987). NLP is built upon arranging the environment to increase a child's opportunities to use language. Children are encouraged to initiate the interaction as stimulus items are chosen by the child, varied every few trials, age appropriate, and found in the child's natural environment. Both teacher and child play with the stimulus item (the item is functional within the interaction). A loose-shaping contingency is used to reinforce attempts to respond verbally, except for self-stimulation (Koegel, Koegel, & Parks, 1995). NLP represented a shift from pull-out procedures using drill procedures and imitation to more naturalistic procedures for language intervention. **Pivotal response training** has emerged from NLP (Koegel & Koegel, 2006).

REFERENCES

Koegel, R. L., & Koegel, L. K. (2006). *Pivotal response treatments for autism*. Baltimore: Brookes Publishing Co.

Koegel, R. L., Koegel, L. K., & Parks, D. R. (1995). "Teach the individual" model of generalization: Autonomy through self-management. In R. L. Koegel & L. K. Koegel (Eds.), *Teaching children with autism: Strategies for initiating positive interactions and improving learning opportunities* (pp. 67–77). Baltimore: Brookes Publishing Co.

Koegel, R. L., O'Dell, M. C., & Koegel, L. K. (1987). A natural language paradigm for teaching nonverbal autistic children. *Journal of Autism and Developmental Disorders, 17,* 187–199.

JEANNE HOLVERSTOTT

NEUROFEEDBACK

Neurofeedback, also referred to as EEG biofeedback, is a form of **biofeedback**. It uses the principles of biofeedback to create a learning opportunity through operant conditioning. Like traditional biofeedback, neurofeedback increases awareness of a bodily state and increases control over that state. In the case of neurofeedback, the individual learns to impact his or her states of arousal through operant conditioning through feedback of brainwave activity.

Operant conditioning waits for a behavior to occur and then consequates the behavior. The purpose of the training is to increase awareness and allow the brain to practice shifting states of arousal. Arousal is the state of awareness from internally focused to our own thoughts and feelings to external focus within the environment. When we are very internally focused we emit brain waves that are large in amplitude and slow in frequency. The lower brain waves are called *delta waves*. During sleep the majority of the brain is emitting delta waves. Delta waves range from 0.5 to 3 cycles per second (cps). At a resting or daydreaming state, the majority of the brain is emitting brainwaves with the frequency range of 8 to 11 cps, and these are called *alpha waves*. The sensorimotor rhythm (SMR) is a state of calm that is often associated with external awareness yet quietly alert. And finally, the so-called thinker waves or *beta* are characterized as focused, analytic, often externally oriented and intense thinking, and are measured at 16 to 20 cps.

The function states of arousal are to tune ourselves into internal and external demands within our environment. A healthy nervous system will effortlessly shift from internal states such as sleep (0.05–3 cps) to meet task demands of a learning task within a classroom; for example, they could range from 8 to 20 cps. An example of alpha wave activity is when you have been driving for some time and look up and realize you have been daydreaming and do not remember passing through some traffic. The theory is that some neurological-based disorders are impacted arousal states that are predominant or do not meet the internal or external environmental task demand.

Through this "brain workout" the individual learns to better attend to the internal and external environment. The benefits of the training are largely individual and can impact several neurological symptoms. The hypothesized reason that there are such varied results is the nature of the brain functioning.

The materials necessary for neurofeedback are an EEG and a specially designed computer program. A typical session includes the following steps. First, the individual is clinically assessed and a training program is established. A trained, certified clinical professional will design an individual training program depending on their neurological profile. The individual will have electrodes placed on their scalp with a sticky paste. Then the individual will watch a video game. This game is actually a visual and auditory feedback system of their own brainwave activity. When they bring their brain waves within a set cycle per second, then they are reinforced and the game progresses. In many of the games, when they produce brainwave activity outside the set parameters the game stops or does not progress. Through this game the individual's brain undergoes a "mental workout." This requirement to shift their focus from either more internal to external or vice versa is the exercise. This, in turn, produces a brain that adapts to the environmental task demands.

FURTHER INFORMATION

Bitsika, V., & Sharpley, C. (2000). Development and testing of the effects of supports on the well-being of parents of children with autism—II: Specific stress management techniques. *Journal of Applied Health Behaviour, 2*(1), 8–15.

EEG Spectrum International. (2001). Retrieved June 1, 2005, from http://www.eegspectrum.com.

Evans, J. R., & Abarbanel, A. (1999). *Introduction to quantitative EEG and neurofeedback.* San Diego: Academic Press.

Jarusiewicz, B. (2002). Efficacy of neurofeedback for children in the autistic spectrum: A pilot study. *Journal of Neurotherapy, 6*(4), 39–49.

Robbins, J. (2000). *A symphony in the brain.* New York: Atlantic Monthly Press.

Schwarts, M., & Androasik, F. (2003). *Biofeedback: A practitioner's guide*. New York: Guilford Press.

Sichel, A. G., Fehmel, L. G., & Goldstein, D. M. (1995). Positive outcome with neurofeedback treatment in a case of mild autism. *Journal of Neurotherapy, 1*(1), 60–64.

STEPHANIE NICKELSON

NEUROIMAGING

Neuroimaging is the use of **MRI**, PET, SPECT, and **CAT scans** to evaluate and monitor development and/or alterations in brain anatomy and function. This is an expanding and experimental area with much current research into developmental and degenerative disorders. More is being learned about structural differences in the brains of persons with what had previously been considered "behavioral" disorders.

BRUCE BASSITY

NEUROLOGIST

A neurologist is a medical doctor who treats patients with neurological disorders, which are disorders that affect the central, peripheral, and autonomic nervous systems. Such disorders include epilepsy, cerebral palsy, migraine headaches, tic disorders, sleep disorders, multiple sclerosis, traumatic brain injuries, and spinal cord disorders.

STEVE CHAMBERLAIN

NEUROLOGY

Neurology is the branch of medicine that deals with disorders of the nervous system. Neurologists are specialized physicians trained to diagnose and treat these disorders, and are mostly trained to work with adults. Pediatric neurology is a subspecialty of pediatric medicine.

BRUCE BASSITY

NEUROMOTOR

Neuromotor is a term relating to the connection between nerves and muscles, generally an impulse transmitted from the nervous system to the musculoskeletal system.

BRUCE BASSITY

NEUROPSYCHOLOGY

A combination of neurology and psychology, this discipline seeks to understand the relationship between the structure and function of the brain on psychological processes and behavior. As in neurology, these specialists may work in research, clinical diagnosis and treatment, or teaching.

BRUCE BASSITY

NEUROTOXIC

Neurotoxic is a term referring to toxicity or harm against the nervous system. Many chemicals that were previously thought harmless, such as lead (in paint, plumbing), are now known to cause damage to the brain and nervous system.

BRUCE BASSITY

233

NEUROTRANSMITTER

A neurotransmitter is a substance (such as acetylcholine, **dopamine**, **serotonin**, norepinephrine) that is released from the axon terminal (outgoing end) of a neuron or nerve cell, travels across the gap to the receptor end of anther nerve cell to either inhibit or excite that next cell. Dysfunction of brain neurotransmitters, which are sometimes referred to as chemical messengers, can be related to various psychiatric and cognitive disorders.

BRUCE BASSITY

NEWSLETTER

Newsletters discuss general information related to autism spectrum disorders in a user-friendly format. Newsletters provide information relevant to a specific geographic region. For a list of newsletters, please see Appendix A.

JEANNE HOLVERSTOTT

NO CHILD LEFT BEHIND ACT 2001 (PL 107-110)

President George W. Bush proposed a framework based on bipartisan education reform that became the No Child Left Behind (NCLB) Act of 2001. The NCLB Act aims to increase accountability; give more choices to parents and students; offer greater flexibility for states, school districts, and schools; make reading a priority; and offer other program changes that best suit state and school needs.

REFERENCE

U.S. Department of Education. (n.d.). No Child Left Behind. Retrieved November 30, 2006, from www.ed.gov/nclb/landing.jhtml.

MELANIE D. HARMS

NO-NO PROMPT PROCEDURES

A no-no prompt procedure is a form of **error correction**. The procedure is as follows. A directive or discriminative stimulus (Sd) is given. If the student responds incorrectly, the instructor says, "No." The same directive is given a second time. If the student responds incorrectly, the instructor again simply responds, "No." The third trial is then prompted, meaning immediately after giving the directive the instructor prompts the student so that he responds correctly. This form of error correction is used after an initial teaching period during which other forms of prompting may and should be used. Once a designated level of acquisition is achieved, the instructor may then shift to a no-no-prompt schedule of prompting whenever the task is presented in the future.

KATIE BASSITY

NONVERBAL LEARNING DISABILITY

A nonverbal learning disability (NLD) is a neurological syndrome that includes both specific strengths and precise deficits. Strengths include: (a) early speech and vocabulary development; (b) exceptional rote memory skills; (c) attention to detail; (d) early reading skills; (e) excellent spelling skills; (f) strong auditory retention; and (g) articulate verbal skills. Deficits include: (a) motor delays such as poor coordination, balance, and handwriting skills; (b) visual-spatial-organizational weaknesses; (c) social difficulties such as nonverbal communication, transitions, social judgments; and (d) sensory issues such as disorders or dysfunctions in any of the sensory modes.

Specific causes of nonverbal learning disorders are not known. A genetic or familial link has yet to be identified as has been in language-based learning disorders (i.e., dyslexia). Brain scans of individuals with NLD have revealed mild abnormalities of the right cerebral hemisphere. Developmental histories revealed several children suffering from NLD have had one of the following: (a) moderate to severe head injury, (b) repeated radiation treatments on or near their heads for an extended amount of time, (c) congenital absence of a corpus callosum, (d) hydrocephalus, or (e) brain tissue removed from the right hemisphere (Thompson, 1996).

At this time, nonverbal learning disability has not been recognized by the American Psychiatric Association. Diagnosis is made using a neurological profile that has been defined in the literature. Johnson and Myklebust (1967) were the first to describe a definition of nonverbal learning disorder in which children have specific difficulties with social awareness. Rourke (1995) further defined nonverbal learning disorders as having primary, secondary, and tertiary deficits that result in socioemotional or adaptational deficits.

Children with Asperger syndrome and nonverbal learning disability may present similarly in several areas of strength and deficit. The children with nonverbal learning disorders appear to not exhibit the restricted interests or special skills that would meet the criteria for a diagnosis of Asperger syndrome.

REFERENCES

Johnson, D., & Myklebust, H. (1967). *Learning disabilities: Educational principles and practices.* New York: Grune & Stratton.

Rourke, B. (Ed.). (1995). *Syndrome of nonverbal learning disabilities: Neurodevelopmental manifestations.* New York: The Guilford Press.

Thompson, S. (1996). Nonverbal learning disorders. *NLDline.* Retrieved October 30, 2006, from http://www.nldline.com/.

LYNN DUDEK

NORMALIZATION

The concept of normalization was first introduced by Nirjie in the 1960s and popularized by Wolfensberger in the 1970s. Normalization involves the acceptance of individuals with disabilities, offering them the same living and learning experiences as those available to individuals without disabilities. According to Wolfensberger (1972), the concept of normalization does not refer to making individuals "normal," or to making them behave in a certain manner, or forcing them to conform to societal norms. Rather, normalization aims to ensure that individuals with disabilities have the opportunities to live a normal rhythm of life. Inclusion is based on the concept of normalization.

REFERENCES

Nirje, B. (1969). The normalization principle and its human management implications. In R. Kugel & W. Wolfensberger (Eds.), *Changing patterns in residential services for the mentally retarded* (pp. 179–195). Washington, DC: President's Committee on Mental Retardation.

Wolfensberger, W. (1972). *Normalization: The principle of normalization in human services.* Toronto: National Institute on Mental Retardation.

FURTHER INFORMATION
Westling, D. L., & Fox, L. (2004). *Teaching students with severe disabilities* (3rd ed.). Upper Saddle River, NJ: Prentice Hall.

THERESA L. EARLES-VOLLRATH

NORM-REFERENCED ASSESSMENT

A norm-referenced assessment compares an individual student's performance to persons of the same age and/or grade level (norming group). This assessment measures how much one knows in comparison to others. The comparison can occur at the classroom, local, or national level.

FURTHER INFORMATION
Salvia, J., & Ysseldyke, J. E. (2007). *Assessment: In special and inclusive education* (10th ed.). Boston: Houghton Mifflin Company.
Taylor, R. L. (2006). *Assessment of exceptional students: Educational and psychological procedures* (7th ed.). Needham Heights, MA: Allyn and Bacon.

THERESA L. EARLES-VOLLRATH

NOTICE OF RECOMMENDED EDUCATIONAL PLACEMENT (NOREP)

Notice of Recommended Educational Placement is a procedural notice provided to all **Individualized Education Program** (IEP) members that identifies the multiple placements considered and the chosen educational placement. The notice of recommended educational placement must provide a written statement why placement was chosen and why alternative educational placements were not appropriate for the individual student.

KATHERINE E. COOK

NUTRITIONAL SUPPLEMENTS

Nutritional supplements are intended to supply nutrients that are missing or not consumed in sufficient quantity in a person's diet. Varied amounts of research have been done on supplements for persons with autism spectrum disorders. The largest, most promising body of evidence comes from studies focusing on B vitamins, especially B6, given in combination with magnesium. For other nutrients, the data are not robust. Appropriate dosing presents a key problem with regard to the empirical study of supplements. Nutritional supplementation should be undertaken only with the assistance and supervision of a physician with a strong background in autism, nutritional analysis, and nutritional treatments. Nutritional supplements as treatment options for autism include, but are not limited to, vitamin A (retinol) and beta carotene, vitamins B1 (thiamin), B2 (riboflavin), B3 (niacin), B5 (pantothentic acid), B6 (pyridoxine), and folic acid, vitamin C (ascorbic acid or sodium ascorbate), vitamin E (alpha tocopherol), coenzyme Q10 (antioxidant), magnesium, selenium, and zinc (minerals), and dimethylglycine (DMG).

FURTHER INFORMATION
Hamilton, L. M. (2000). *Facing autism*. Colorado Springs, CO: Waterbook Press.
Marhon, S. (2002). *Natural medicine guide to autism*. Charlottesville, VA: Hampton Roads Publishing Co.
Shaw, W. (2002). *Biological treatments for autism and PDD*. Lenexa, KS: Sunflower Publishing.

MYRNA J. ROCK

O

OBJECT INTEGRATION TEST

An object integration test involves sets of line drawings depicting objects and people intended to be either visually integrated to make the most coherent scene or compared for similarities. Individuals with autism exhibit impairments in their ability to integrate objects, not in their ability to look for similarities. This test provides support for Frith's (1989) central coherence hypothesis. Central coherence has been defined as the natural built-in propensity to process incoming stimuli globally and in context, pulling information together to acquire higher-level meaning.

REFERENCE

Frith, U. (1989). *Autism: Explaining the enigma*. Oxford, UK: Blackwell.

JEANNE HOLVERSTOTT

OBJECTIVE

An objective is a stated and desired outcome of intervention based on a derived set of educational goals and individual needs. Objectives are written in observable and measurable terms to ensure consistency among staff and to provide for precise evaluation of progress.

THERESA L. EARLES-VOLLRATH

OBJECT SORTING TEST

An object sorting test is a test of cognitive functioning designed to assess abilities at category development. As the name implies, the test consists of sorting objects by specified categories.

JEANNE HOLVERSTOTT

OCCUPATIONAL THERAPIST

An occupational therapist (OT) is a health professional with a bachelor's or master's degree from an accredited university who has passed the national **occupational therapy** certification exam. The word *occupation* in occupational therapy refers to the activities, roles, and goal-oriented behaviors of individuals from birth to old age in their daily lives. An OT may work in a school, hospital, skilled nursing facility, community mental health center, or other related organizations in which individuals require the assistance of a skilled professional to remediate, adapt, or prevent a disability from interfering in their daily lives. An OT may complete a task analysis of the activity or situation in which the child with an autism spectrum disorder is having difficulty to determine a step-by-step intervention to improve a skill, such as using a fork. For example, an OT may use clay for finger and hand strengthening, finger painting on a window for eye-hand coordination, and tossing and catching weighted beanbags for body awareness, all of which are necessary components of using a fork appropriately.

KELLY M. PRESTIA

OCCUPATIONAL THERAPY

Occupational therapy (OT) is a health profession that provides purposeful activities and interventions to individuals of all ages who need to regain the skills necessary to participate fully in their life roles. For individuals with autism spectrum disorders (ASD), those life roles may include going to school, playing, socializing with peers, being an active member of their family and community, engaging in sports and other extra-curricular activities, and taking care of their own personal needs.

OT services for a child with ASD may take place in a hospital or private practice, in the child's own home, in the community, or in the school. In a hospital, community, or in-home setting, occupational therapy services may not be provided without a written order from the child's physician. In a school setting, occupational therapy is provided as a related service to other special education services, and may not be provided as the only service for the child. **Occupational therapists** have a background in neurology, child development, psychology, and sensory processing. OT services can be provided in two ways: (a) as a direct service, or (b) as a consultation service. When providing direct service, the OT works directly with the child with ASD to remediate, improve, or maintain a specific skill. Prior to working with the child, the OT analyzes the skill to be worked on, as well as the student's strengths and needs, to develop a step-by-step program for that particular skill development. For example, for a student who is unable to button his own shirt, the OT must first determine why he is unable to perform this skill. It may be due to poor strength, hand-eye coordination, or vision. The OT may use formal, standardized testing, and/or informal screenings and observations to determine the cause of the child's difficulty. An OT assessment may include an evaluation of a child's fine and gross motor skills, daily-living skills, sensory processing, or visual perception. Based upon the analysis, interventions are individually tailored to address the skill deficit.

Consultation OT service is appropriate when the child is able to maintain learned skills and apply them to everyday situations. The purpose of consultation is to monitor the child's performance on a regular basis to determine if changes (e.g., in daily routine, the environment) need to be made to continue his success or improve his overall independence. Consultation involves observation, planning, and contact with the child, his family, and any staff that may work with the child on a regular basis to determine if adjustments in his program must be made. For example, a child with ASD might receive OT consultation services to monitor his computer and keyboarding skills in the classroom as an alternative to handwriting his work. The OT may check in weekly with the student, parents, and teacher to ensure that he is completing necessary work, is independent in using the computer, and is able to stay on task. Modifications may be necessary to address specific problems. For instance, if the student is distracted and not able to stay on task while on the computer, the OT may provide headphones and a study carrel to minimize distractions.

Occupational therapy can provide valuable services and resources to students and their families to help the individual with ASD perform at his or her optimal level. By understanding the student's strengths and needs, making necessary modifications, or directly intervening to gain or improve a skill, an OT can help the individual with ASD experience success in a variety of situations and environments.

FURTHER INFORMATION
Christiansen, C., & Baum, C. (1991). *Occupational therapy: Overcoming human performance deficits*. Thorofare, NJ: SLACK Inc.

KELLY M. PRESTIA

OPERANT CONDITIONING

Operant conditioning is a behavioral paradigm that states that the consequences of a behavior affect the future occurrences of that behavior. Operant conditioning relies upon a behavioral framework that includes an antecedent stimulus that precedes a behavior, a behavior, and a consequence contingent upon the behavior. The probability of a behavior occurring again is increased if it is reinforced or rewarded. The behavior is less likely to occur again if the consequence is unpleasant or aversive. When the rate of the behavior is changed due to the consequences, then the behavior is considered to be an operant (Cooper, Heron, & Heward, 1987). The principles of operant conditioning have been used to increase or decrease existing behaviors or teach new behaviors through the manipulation of consequences.

REFERENCE
Cooper, J. O., Heron, T. E., & Heward, W. L. (1987). *Applied behavior analysis*. Upper Saddle River, NJ: Prentice Hall.

ANDREA HOPF AND TARA MIHOK

OPTIONS (SON-RISE PROGRAM)

The Son-Rise Program, developed by Barry Neil Kaufman and Samahria Lyle Kaufman for their son Raun, is a specific and comprehensive program based on joining in a child's behavior to discover his or her own motivation (Autism Treatment Center of America, n.d.a). Raun Kaufman was diagnosed as being severely autistic. Instead of institutionalizing their son, the Kaufmans created a treatment program that used the home environment as the place to nurture the growth of their son in a caring and respectful way.

The Kaufmans believe that autism is a relational and interactive neurological disorder. When a child displays self-regulatory or so-called "stimming" behaviors, or ritualistic or perseverative behaviors, the Son-Rise Program intervenes in enthusiastic, play-based interventions to build rapport and connect with the child. The idea is that by participating in the child's activity or behaviors rather than teaching through drills or repetition, eye contact and other socialization skills will increase.

Although the Kaufmans have worked with many skilled and caring professionals, they believe that parents hold the key as the most powerful and committed teachers to develop a specific program to meet the unique needs of their own children. Their program involves empowering parents with tools to create the attitudinal changes needed to teach a child with autistic spectrum and other developmental disorders.

The Son-Rise Program is based at the Option Institute in Sheffield, Massachusetts. The staff at the Option Institute must complete "a rigorous and comprehensive educational curriculum ..., which includes extensive work with children of varying ages and diagnoses, classroom education, group instruction, comprehensive ideological and attitudinal training, and continual observation and feedback by experienced Son-Rise Program Teachers" (Autism Treatment Center of America, n.d.b).

The staff at the Option Institute has worked many years with hundreds of families. Staff members come from a multitude of disciplines and experiences, and hold degrees in special education, psychology, sociology, and physical therapy, among others. The Autism Treatment Center of America at the Option Institute is the only learning and treatment center that offers professional training for the Son-Rise Program. At the Option Institute, all child facilitators and teachers are certified by the Son-Rise Program professional certification programs.

The Son-Rise Program is designed to be a one-on-one, home-based program that helps in the development of socialization, communication, self-help, and other learning skills. The Son-Rise Program is based on the following principles:

1. Joining in a child's repetitive and ritualistic behaviors supplies the key to unlocking the mystery of these behaviors and facilitates eye contact, social development, and the inclusion of others in play.
2. Utilizing a child's own motivation advances learning and builds the foundation for education and skill acquisition.
3. Teaching through interactive play results in effective and meaningful socialization and communication.
4. Using energy, excitement, and enthusiasm engages the child and inspires a continuous love of learning and interaction.
5. Employing a nonjudgmental and optimistic attitude maximizes the child's enjoyment, attention, and desire throughout their Son-Rise Program.
6. Placing the parent as the child's most important and lasting resource provides a consistent and compelling focus for training, education, and inspiration.
7. Creating a safe, distraction-free work/play area facilitates the optimal environment for learning and growth. (Autism Training Center of America, n.d.c)

The Son-Rise Program can be used in conjunction with other therapies, treatments, and interventions such as diet and vitamin therapies, sensory integration, and biological interventions.

REFERENCES

Autism Treatment Center of America. (n.d.a). History of the Son-Rise Program? Retrieved November 13, 2006, from http://www.autismtreatmentcenter.org/contents/about_son-rise/history_of_the_son-rise_program.php.

Autism Treatment Center of America. (n.d.b). Frequently Asked Questions About the Son-Rise Program. Retrieved November 13, 2006, from http://www.autismtreatmentcenter.org/contents/about_son-rise/faq.php.

Autism Treatment Center of America. (n.d.c). "What Is the Son-Rise Program?" Retrieved November 13, 2006, from www.autismtreatmentcenter.org/contents/about_son-rise/what_is_the_son-rise_program.php.

FURTHER INFORMATION
The Option Institute: www.option.org.

ANN PILEWSKIE

ORAL-MOTOR SKILLS

Oral-motor skills refer to any activity that requires the use and coordination of the muscles in and around the mouth and tongue. Examples of oral-motor skills are chewing, licking, and puckering the lips.

KELLY M. PRESTIA

ORAL SENSITIVITY

Oral sensitivity is an observable response to an overactive gustatory (taste) system. Observable responses of oral sensitivity are the dislike of or refusal to brush one's teeth or eat certain textures or temperatures of foods.

KELLY M. PRESTIA

OVERCORRECTION

Overcorrection is a form of **punishment** that requires the individual to engage in a repetitive behavior intended to decrease the reoccurrence of an undesired behavior. There are two types of overcorrection techniques: restitution and positive practice. Restitution requires the individual to not only correct what he did wrong, but to do something else in addition. A commonly used example is an individual who creates a mess while throwing a tantrum. In restitution, that individual is required to clean up the mess he made, as well as any mess that already existed in the room before the tantrum. Positive practice involves the student repeatedly engaging in the alternate, positive behavior—the desired behavior in the given situation. For example, for the student who runs to get in line first, having him repeatedly walk to the line and walk back to his seat is positive practice. In addition, negative practice is sometimes associated with overcorrection, although in fact it is the opposite of overcorrection. Negative practice requires the student to engage in the negative behavior numerous times, under the teacher's or adult's control. There are ethical and practical concerns regarding the use of negative practice.

KATIE BASSITY

OVERSELECTIVITY/OVERFOCUSED ATTENTION

Overselectivity/overfocused attention, also referred to as tunnel vision, describes when an individual intently focuses upon an object, person, or activity, disregarding all other stimuli or environmental cues. Overselectivity may result from an individual's difficulty screening out or discriminating irrelevant stimuli to determine what is most important. For example, an individual with an autism spectrum disorder may fixate on the blinking light on a computer across the room.

KELLY M. PRESTIA